D1590157

Executor
& Trustee
SURVIVAL GUIDE

How to settle an estate and manage a trust

∼

What executors and trustees are required to do

∼

A blueprint for managing the process

∼

Includes illustrations, forms and checklists

Douglas D. Wilson, CFP, CTFA

Executor & Trustee Survival Guide

© 2001 by Douglas D. Wilson

ISBN 0-9704890-0-5
Library of Congress Card Number pfs20607

Publisher's Note: This book contains general information only and is not intended to be a substitute for professional or legal advice. If legal or other professional assistance is needed, a qualified attorney or other professional should be consulted.

For information, address Fiduciary Publishing, P.O. Box 351, Honolulu, HI 96809
Email: fiduciarypub@aol.com

CONTENTS

Managing Trusts

Getting Help

PREFACE

My passion for writing this book came from a desire to help newly appointed, or about-to-be-named, executors and trustees who are bewildered by the complexities of managing an estate or trust. Most people feel honored when a parent, aunt, uncle or grandparent has named them the executor or trustee of their estate. Sooner or later they discover that they haven't a clue what to do. Perhaps the real eye opener for them is the realization that they may be liable for what they do or don't do. This book is intended to describe some of the basics of estate and trust administration and hopefully alleviate some of their anxiety.

Estate planning is an important life step. Whether an individual is wealthy or of modest means, everyone needs to have an estate plan. Estate planning is a process of building wealth during one's lifetime and protecting and managing those assets in the event of incapacity and for the next generation. The plan may involve a simple Will or a more complex arrangement that includes a trust. Under a Will a personal representative (executor/executrix) is designated to manage the financial affairs of the decedent during the period of estate administration, which may last one to two years. The personal representative has the responsibility to ascertain and collect the decedent's property, pay all expenses, including taxes, and distribute the remaining assets to those designated to receive the property under the decedent's Will. If there is no Will then the property is distributed to the decedent's heirs at law. Once the distribution of the decedents' assets has been completed the personal representative's job is done.

If a trust is involved in the estate plan, the trust agreement will designate a trustee to carry out the purposes of the trust as outlined in the trust agreement. Unlike the administration of an estate, a trustee's responsibilities can continue for many years beyond the decedent's death including the lifetime of an entire generation. Trustees are responsible for administering the trust during the period of its existence and deciding how much, when and under what circumstances payments are made to beneficiaries. Other responsibilities include maintaining accurate records, filing tax returns and making tax elections.

Personal representatives and trustees are fiduciaries and their activities, while managing estates and trusts, are subject to specific laws and standards of conduct that govern those who serve in this capacity. The job can be simple and straightforward or very complex. This book by no means covers everything a personal representative or trustee needs to know. However, my hope is that it will give the reader a general understanding of the duties and responsibilities imposed on fiduciaries and the basic issues involved in administering an estate or trust. Understanding the basics is important for efficient administration, limiting personal liability and managing the estate or trust in the best interests of the beneficiaries.

Acknowledgements

Completion of this project would have been far more difficult without the help and encouragement of many friends. I very much appreciate all of their support.

My heartfelt thanks to attorney David Larsen, Certified Financial Planner Roberta Lee-Driscoll, Wendell Wong, CPA, Melanie King, CPA, and Gloria Ursal Munson, Ph.D., who took the time to read my manuscript and provide me with their valuable input. Their feedback helped me improve the final version of the book.

I am truly indebted to my editor, Barbara Hastings. Her insight and expertise was invaluable to this very novice writer. She was able to decipher my poor attempt at describing some very complex concepts and make some sense out of it. Her patience was admirable. She is truly a gifted professional and I am grateful that she took me on as a client.

Thanks to Kathy Campbell, Kurt Gorham and the rest of the Gorham Printing crew for doing the cover, layout and final printing of the book. Their expertise in this area is obvious and I appreciate, in particular, Kathy Campbell's patience and artistic touch.

Very special thanks to Linda Quarberg who helped format, edit and type several versions of the manuscript. She spent untold hours on this project and without her dedication and ability to handle the computer this book would have taken a lot longer to complete. I am very grateful for her tireless contribution.

Thank you all for the parts you played in delivering this book.

TO SERVE
OR
NOT TO SERVE

CHAPTER 1

Serving As a Personal Representative and/or Trustee

Someone Must Be Appointed to Handle a Decedent's Affairs After Death

KEY POINTS

- Settling an estate requires appointing someone to take charge of the process.

- Being a personal representative (executor) or trustee of an estate can require a significant time commitment.

- Managing an estate requires adherence to established standards of conduct.

- Serving as a personal representative or trustee is manageable if you understand the basic responsibilities and get help where you need it.

Surely, everyone is familiar with the two certainties of life … death and taxes. Once we are gone, most of us will leave things that need to be attended to whether or not we plan properly during our lifetime. To handle these matters, a personal representative (executor) of the decedent's estate must be appointed. The personal representative accepts nomination under a Will or is appointed by the probate court. A trustee may also be involved and is nominated under the decedent's trust.

Before the settlement process begins, there is usually a lot of anxiety among the decedent's heirs. As the grieving process is running its course, family members often perceive a financial crisis. How are we going to pay the bills? How much will the taxes be? When will they have to be paid? Will there be anything left? Who will be in charge? Concerns such as these commonly surround someone's death and usually with a great deal of emotion. A decedent's representative (personal representative or trustee) is responsible for addressing these concerns and managing the decedent's estate. A representative will likely and quickly face family members' overreaction to the settlement process. The family typically wants matters settled in an unrealistically short time. The representative should understand that settling the estate or managing the trust must be done methodically; great care must be given to managing the process and avoiding mistakes that could be detrimental to the heirs.

Personal representatives and trustees generally feel honored to have been chosen, but seldom ask themselves if they are up to the task. Settling an estate has many time-sensitive steps; missing a deadline can be costly. Estate settlement also requires significant time. Managing a trust requires even greater time commitment and can extend over a very long period. Before deciding whether to accept the assignment, a nominated personal representative or trustee should understand what responsibilities are involved. Serving as a personal representative or trustee can be a perplexing and often daunting responsibility, but it does not have to be. If one takes the time to understand the basics of the process and seeks professional assistance when needed, the responsibility is manageable for most people.

What is a Fiduciary?

KEY POINTS

- **A fiduciary relationship is one of trust. A fiduciary oversees, protects and manages property for the benefit of others.**

- **Fiduciaries, by law, must act solely in the interests of the beneficiaries they serve and no one else.**

- **A fiduciary has a duty to be honest and faithful to beneficiaries.**

For those who have never been in a *fiduciary relationship* the term *fiduciary* is probably mysterious. Most people associate it with something legal. Defined in its simplest terms, a fiduciary relationship is a relationship of trust. It is the act of managing property for, and representing the interests of, others. Examples of fiduciary relationships include the relationship between members of the board of directors of a company and its stockholders, an attorney and his/her client, a guardian and a protected person, a personal representative (executor) and the estate's beneficiaries and creditors, and a trustee and the beneficiaries of the trust.

In a trust, the fiduciary relationship requires the trustee to hold property, or an interest in property, and use that property for the benefit of the beneficiaries. A personal representative must protect the interests of the creditors of a decedent's estate as well as the beneficiaries of the estate. Personal representatives and trustees are usually given full authority to manage assets and distribute those assets to the decedent's beneficiaries. Under common law, the duty of loyalty is an important part of this relationship. Fiduciaries are expected to act solely in the interest of beneficiaries and, by law, are held to a high standard of ethical and moral conduct.

This standard of conduct is different than the ethics associated with ordinary business relationships, where a transaction between parties at "arms length" is acceptable behavior. The fact that a personal representative or trustee has total control over the management and disposition of assets in an estate or trust requires that the fiduciary show more than ordinary candor in dealing with beneficiaries and their interests in the estate or trust. The standards of conduct that apply to personal representatives and trustees are intended to assure that a decedent's wishes with regard to the disposition and management of his estate are carried out as he or she intended.

Personal Representative (Executor)

KEY POINTS

- A personal representative is in charge of settling a decedent's probate estate.

- The job can be relatively simple or very complex.

- A personal representative is not obligated to accept a nomination.

- Before accepting the nomination, the personal representative must consider the responsibilities of the position.

- Settling a decedent's estate may require a considerable time commitment.

- A personal representative is responsible to assemble the decedent's assets, pay the debts and manage the estate until it is distributed to the heirs.

- A personal representative is permitted to hire professionals to assist in the administration of the estate.

When someone dies, the appointed representative takes charge of the property that was titled in the decedent's own name and oversees the legal transfer of that property to the decedent's legal heirs. This process is called probate. The representative is also responsible for paying the decedent's obligations and distributing what is left to those heirs. This person (or institution, such as a bank or trust company) commonly called an *executor* (or *executrix* if a female) is usually named by an individual in his or her Will. If no reference is made in the Will, or if the individual dies without a Will, a court that has jurisdiction over the decedent's estate appoints an executor (in some states the court appoints an *administrator*.) Under the Unified Probate Code, which most states have adopted, executors are now referred to as *personal representatives.*

Frankly, it can be a pain in the neck to be a personal representative. The job carries many responsibilities, can require a sizable time commitment, and could potentially subject an individual to personal liability. It might be akin to taking over a business without knowing much about the enterprise. The personal representative must determine what assets the decedent accumulated over an entire lifetime, what he owed, and manage the assets and liabilities on behalf of the decedent's creditors and heirs until the estate has been closed. The responsibilities parallel those a chief executive officer has to his stockholders.

To Serve or not to Serve? The job of a personal representative can be straightforward; it might involve no more than collecting a few items belonging to the decedent, paying a few bills and distributing what remains to the heirs. Managing an estate can also be very complex. The personal representative might be required to deal with legal issues left behind by the decedent and make decisions involving tax elections under the Internal Revenue Code that may have a material affect on the interests of the beneficiaries. The personal representative might have to run a business, negotiate leases, buy and sell assets, and other involved and time-consuming tasks.

What are your options if Uncle Harry names you as his personal representative? Well, for one thing you have no legal obligation to serve. That is, no one can hold you legally accountable if you choose not to be Uncle Harry's personal representative. What about a moral obligation? That depends on the situation. You may feel morally obligated if Uncle Harry had asked you to handle his affairs prior to his death. Or you may even feel that you owe it to him because he has left you something under his Will. Some feel that the decedent has honored them because only a trusted family member or friend would be named to such an important position. Whatever the situation, you must decide soon after the decedent's death whether or not you will accept the responsibility. The settlement of the estate must be completed as expeditiously as possible and the sooner the personal representative accepts the appointment and gets started the better.

What should you consider before accepting the nomination as personal representative? First you should look at the complexity of the estate. No two are alike. Some are relatively simple, requiring little time and minimal expertise. Others can require as much time and effort as a full time job and involve a period of administration that may extend over several years. To properly manage a complex estate you may also require the expertise of accountants, attorneys, and other professionals. Because the personal representative is ultimately responsible for proper administration of the estate you must monitor the activities of these professionals continuously until the estate is closed.

Time commitment is obviously another principal consideration. For several reasons, the duties of settling an estate cannot be performed at the convenience of the personal representative. For one thing the heirs expect their inheritance the day after Uncle Harry died. Your explanation of the technical reasons delaying it is not what they want to hear. They do have a right, however, to expect that the estate will be settled efficiently and that distribution of their inheritance will be made in a timely manner. Even if the heirs are not pressuring the personal representative, states' laws require distribution of the estate's assets within a reasonable period. The personal representative is also faced with many deadlines, including court filings and appearances, publishing a public notice to creditors, filing tax returns, and other requirements promulgated by state and federal laws.

A personal representative can consult with an attorney to get an estimate of the time required to settle the estate. Accountants familiar with settling estates, or a trust company or bank are good sources of information as well. The clerk of the probate court with jurisdiction over the estate can tell you any specific requirements of the court and how long the average estate takes to make its way through the system. This will give you an indication of the time it takes to settle an estate in your area. If the time commitment is more than you can devote, you should consider declining the nomination. To do otherwise would be unfair to the beneficiaries, and might also expose you to unnecessary liability.

If you decide to serve, you should spend time understanding the basic responsibilities of a personal representative, the complexity of the particular estate, your relationship with the beneficiaries, the requirements of local law and the need for professional advisors. Also consider that it will be disruptive to the efficient settlement of the estate if you accept, and later decide to resign.

Can You Handle the Job? In most situations the answer is clearly yes. Almost anyone can manage an estate if they simply hire a professional, such as a bank or trust company to handle the day-to-day administration. Of course this may not be what you have in mind. You might feel obligated to minimize the costs of settling Uncle Harry's estate by doing everything yourself. Minimizing estate settlement costs is the right thing to do; it is also a basic responsibility of the personal representative. However, personal representatives (as well as other fiduciaries) are permitted to incur reasonable expenses for administration. A personal representative is allowed to hire professionals to assist with estate administration. If you do not have the time or expertise, you should hire professionals. By law, any administration costs that personal representatives incur for these services are properly chargeable to the estate.

Whether you handle the estate through professionals or manage it yourself, ultimately you are responsible for protection of the interests of the decedent's creditors and heirs. You are also responsible for timely distribution of the estate assets to the heirs. If you pay attention to the job, get things done when they need to be, and hire professional expertise when you need it, you should not have any problems carrying out these responsibilities. The role of a personal representative is time limited, usually from eighteen months to two years. Remember, the personal representative is responsible for marshaling the decedent's assets, paying the decedent's debts and taxes and distributing what's left to the decedent's heirs. This process will take some time to complete.

Trusts and Trustees

KEY POINTS

- **Trust arrangements are often misunderstood.**

- **Trusts are created to avoid probate, minimize taxes, protect the creator of the trust in the event of incapacity and provide for heirs.**

- **Anyone who is of legal age and is competent can be a trustee.**

Most people are not familiar with trusts. Misconceptions abound particularly among people who have had a bad experience as a beneficiary of a trust. The typical trust is set up to minimize estate taxes, avoid probate and, in some cases, provide protection for family members. Many beneficiaries do not understand why someone else (the trustee) decides what he or she can have and is convinced that this "is not what my wife, husband, father, mother, grandfather, aunt, Uncle Joe, had in mind." The reality is that the trustee has explicit instructions under the terms of the trust to do what the creator of the trust intended. Nevertheless beneficiaries often are not convinced.

What is a trust? A trust is created when an individual transfers property to someone called a *trustee* who manages the property for the benefit of someone else (the *beneficiary*) according to the written terms of a trust document or instrument. A trust is used to deal with a variety of estate planning, tax and asset management issues. A trust can address the full spectrum of estate planning including estate tax savings, avoiding probate, protecting family members and handling how and when to distribute assets to named beneficiaries. There are two general types of trusts, the revocable trust and the irrevocable trust. The revocable trust can be altered or terminated by its creator (the *settlor*). The irrevocable trust, generally, cannot be altered or terminated except by court order. Normally, the court will not order a trust revoked or altered unless there is fraud, proof that there was undue influence when the trust was established, or a technical change needs to be made that does not adversely affect the interests of the beneficiaries or the purposes of the trust.

The Revocable Living Trust

One of the most popular and widely used estate-planning tools is the *Revocable Living Trust.* This arrangement is designed to address several estate planning concerns:

Avoiding Probate

Property held in a revocable living trust avoids having to go through the court-supervised probate process at the death of the creator of the trust. The title to the property is registered in the name of the trust, not in the name of the decedent. Only property that is owned individually by a decedent is subject to probate.

Minimize or Avoid Federal Estate Tax

Federal estate tax is by far the largest expense associated with death. A revocable living living trust can reduce, or even eliminate altogether in some cases, the federal estate tax. A properly drafted living trust assures that the personal exemption available to both husband and wife is fully utilized to maximize the amount of property that can pass free of estate tax to children, grandchildren and other beneficiaries. *Chapter 10 Funding The Marital, Credit Shelter And Generation-Skipping Trusts* contains an explanation of how this works.

Protection Upon Incapacity

When someone becomes physically or mentally incapacitated and cannot handle his or her financial affairs, someone else must manage them. This can be handled with a durable power of attorney or a trust. If the incapacitated person has not given power of attorney to anyone or does not have a trust, the court appoints a guardian. In some states this person is called a *conservator.* This is expensive and inflexible. In addition, because the court supervises this proceeding, the incapacitated person's affairs are a matter of public record. The court's permission is required for certain payments to be made on behalf of the incapacitated person. Even a durable power of attorney has limitations. Some financial institutions will accept them only under certain conditions. Others may not accept them at all. All of these issues can be avoided through a living trust. The trust simply gives the trustee the authority to handle the affairs of the incapacitated settlor. This authority lapses upon the settlor's recovery.

Bequests to Heirs

Most people think of their Will as the primary means of passing property to their heirs. A trust can do anything a

Will can do and more. Since the living trust usually has the title to most, if not all, of an individual's property, it becomes the principle means for distributing the decedent's property. Beneficiaries are named in the trust document to receive the trust's property. A trust, in addition to passing property at death, can delay distribution until a beneficiary reaches a certain age or can continue for the lifetime of a beneficiary. A Will typically transfers property at death.

Protection of Minors and Other Heirs
No one knows when they are going to die and whether or not they will leave minor children. If a decedent is survived by a minor, and provisions have not been made, a guardianship proceeding may be required to manage the minor's property until he or she attains legal age. As mentioned, this is an expensive and inflexible arrangement. A trust can provide for the needs of a minor and avoid interference by the court. A trust can also be used to protect a beneficiary who has disabilities. A properly drafted trust can also protect a beneficiary from creditors and divorce.

The settlor (creator) of the revocable living trust can also be the trustee of the trust. This type of arrangement is known as a *self-trusteed trust*. The settlor signs checks, stock powers, deeds and other legal documents as trustee instead of signing in his or her individual name. Other than this technical difference, the self-trusteed trust, as a practical matter, is no different than owning property in one's individual name.

Someone other than the settlor can also be the trustee. A spouse, child, friend, relative, attorney, CPA, trust company, bank or any combination of these can be appointed the trustee while the settlor is alive and after death. Anyone of legal age who is competent can serve as a trustee. The difference between the self-trusteed trust and this arrangement is that the trustee must conduct the affairs of the trust at the direction of the settlor, who is also the beneficiary of the trust and, in the absence of any direction, solely for his or her benefit. A settlor will appoint a trustee other than himself or herself because he or she does not want to be bothered with the nuances of managing his or her own affairs, wants to take advantage of the expertise of a particular trustee or wants the assurance of continuity in the management of his or her affairs in the event of incapacity or death.

The settlor can also appoint himself or herself and someone else as co-trustee. In this case the responsibility for managing the trust property is shared, although as long as the settlor is competent the co-trustee must act in accordance with the settlor's instructions. If two or more trustees, other than the settlor, are appointed they must act in concert in dealing with the trust property. Co-trustees are often used in situations that require the special knowledge or expertise of more than one person.

Revocable Living Trusts That Terminate at Death

KEY POINTS

- **The responsibilities of administering a trust that terminates at the death of the settlor is similar to the administration of a probate estate. The difference is that there is no necessity for probate with a trust.**

- **The trustee's duties are carried out over a relatively short period and end with the distribution of the assets to the beneficiaries.**

Many people establish a revocable living trust simply to avoid probate and to protect themselves against guardianship in the event of incapacity. These types of trusts often terminate at death. In terms of disposition of estate assets they serve a similar purpose as a Will. That is, once all of the decedent's expenses and taxes have been paid, the property in the trust is distributed to the beneficiaries named in the trust. The responsibilities of the trustee under a revocable living trust that terminates at death are similar to that of a personal representative under a Will. The trust property must be collected, final expenses paid, tax returns filed, and the remaining property distributed to the trust beneficiaries.

The major advantage of handling someone's estate this way is the fact that probate is avoided and the trustee does not have to deal with the court. No hearings or court filings are necessary and the decedent's estate can often be settled quickly. However, the time to settle an estate depends on whether or not estate taxes are payable, how long it takes to appraise assets, whether or not there are matters being litigated and how long it takes to liquidate assets to pay expenses and satisfy bequests.

Like the personal representative under a Will, the trustee distributes the remaining property to the beneficiaries and closes the trust once the expenses, taxes and other obligations of the trust have been satisfied. Unlike the personal representative, the trustee does not usually need to seek a discharge and release of responsibility from the court. Instead, the trustee's duties terminate at the final distribution of the assets and closing of the trust.

Trusts That Continue After Death

KEY POINTS

- **Continuing trusts are designed to minimize taxes and protect beneficiaries beyond the life of the settlor (creator of the trust.)**

- **A trustee's responsibilities in a continuing trust are considerably more complex and require a greater commitment over an extended period.**

A trust that continues after death can either be a *revocable living trust*, created during one's lifetime, or a *testamentary trust* created under a decedent's Will. Continuing trusts fall into two general categories. One is designed to manage property and protect a beneficiary from himself or herself and his or her creditors. These trusts are typically set up for a beneficiary until he or she reaches a certain age or until the beneficiary's death. They are designed to have a trustee pick up where the decedent left off in terms of protecting and providing for the beneficiary. For example, a decedent may have been survived by a minor child or a child with a life-long disability.

The other category of continuing trust is the more common in estate planning. In addition to providing financial protection and management for family members, its primary purpose is to minimize or, in some cases, avoid estate taxes. The key feature under this type is the *credit shelter trust,* commonly referred to as the *family trust, by-pass trust, residuary trust* or *"B" trust.* The credit shelter trust is a separate trust created at death under a revocable living trust. It is funded with an amount equal to the decedent's personal exemption from the federal estate tax (i.e., Unified Credit Exemption Equivalent) determined at the decedent's death. The assets that are *not* transferred to the credit shelter trust are either distributed outright to the surviving spouse or retained in another trust called the *marital trust.*

Continuing trusts can extend for a fixed period after death, for the life of a surviving spouse or beyond an entire generation. The trustee is responsible for managing the trust until it finally terminates. The trustee is responsible for managing all administration during the term of the trust, including funding of the marital and credit shelter trusts, making tax elections, maintaining fiduciary accounting records, exercising discretion with regard to payments to beneficiaries and investing trust assets. This will be discussed further in later chapters.

Irrevocable Trusts

KEY POINTS

- **Irrevocable trusts are created primarily for tax purposes.**

- **The trustee has the same basic fiduciary responsibilities as for any other trust. The trustee of an irrevocable trust may have specific administrative functions that are unique to the type of trust.**

Irrevocable trusts can be used for a wide range of purposes, but usually are designed to minimize estate and income taxes. They have one thing in common. Property transferred to the trust is no longer owned by the individual who transferred the property. The property is owned by the trust and controlled by the trustee, the terms of the trust, and applicable state and federal laws. As the name implies, the trust cannot be revoked and usually cannot be altered. Once property has been transferred into an irrevocable trust the transferor has, in effect, given the property away.

Unlike a revocable living trust, the trustee under an irrevocable trust must act independently and is precluded from taking direction from the settlor in managing the affairs of the trust. Each type of irrevocable trust has its own unique characteristics. Although the basic fiduciary responsibilities are the same, the trustee's administrative duties will differ from one trust to another depending on the terms of the trust and the laws that apply to the particular type of trust. There are several common types of irrevocable trusts.

Children's Gift Trust

Many people want to make gifts to their children before they become adults. A Children's Gift Trust allows parents to qualify for the annual gift tax exclusion (i.e., $10,000 per individual each year; husband and wife can give up to $20,000) and gets the property out of their estates to avoid its taxation upon death. The children's trust described under Section 2503(c) of the Internal Revenue Code allows a parent or anyone to make gifts to a trust with the requirement that the funds be paid out when they are needed by the beneficiary for education, medical expenses, etc.

The trust must provide that:

1) **the property and the income from it be available for expenditure, usually at the discretion of the trustee, by or for the child prior to attaining the age of twenty-one,**

2) **the property and unexpended income will pass to the child when the child attains the age of twenty-one and**

3) **if the child dies prior to reaching the age of twenty-one the assets must pass to the child's estate.**

A variation of the 2503(c) trust is the 2503(b) trust. Under this arrangement, the beneficiaries *must* receive all of the income during the term of the trust rather than receiving the income at the discretion of the trustee.

The trustee's responsibility is to manage the trust assets and make expenditures, when appropriate, to or for the benefit of the child until he or she reaches age twenty-one. When the beneficiary is twenty-one the trustee must allow the beneficiary to have direct access to the funds or deliver the assets and any undistributed income to the beneficiary and terminate the trust.

Irrevocable Life Insurance Trust

This is an estate tax savings device that shelters life insurance proceeds from federal estate taxes. The trustee purchases a life insurance policy on the life of the settlor or the settlor transfers the ownership of an existing policy to the trust. Since the policy is legally owned by the trust the proceeds are not included in the estate of the insured settlor upon death. The trustee's duties are to pay the premium(s) on the policy and inform the beneficiaries of their interest and rights under the trust.

These trusts typically contain *"crummey powers"* that allow the money contributed to the trust to pay the premium to qualify for the annual gift tax exclusion. The "crummey powers" give the beneficiaries the right to withdraw a portion of the contributions made to the trust. The trustee has the responsibility to give proper notification of this right to the beneficiaries in order to qualify the contribution for the annual gift tax exclusion. Upon the death of the settlor the trustee collects the proceeds under the policy and either distributes it outright to the beneficiaries named in the trust (terminating trust) or manages the funds according to the terms of the trust (continuing trust) until it terminates.

GRITs, GRATs and GRUTs

The grantor retained income trust (GRIT), grantor retained annuity trust (GRAT) and grantor retained unitrust (GRUT) are irrevocable trusts designed to avoid federal estate tax and accumulate the future appreciation of the trust property for the named beneficiaries. While the advantages of these *"estate freezing"* trusts have been significantly curtailed by Congress, under certain circumstances their objectives can still be achieved.

As the name implies, a grantor retained income trust is a trust whose income is retained by the grantor (i.e., settlor) for a fixed term or until the grantor dies if that occurs first. Once the fixed term of years expires, the trust property passes to the named beneficiaries even though the grantor is still alive. If the grantor dies while receiving the income from the trust, all of the trust assets are subject to federal estate tax.

A grantor retained annuity trust and a grantor retained unitrust closely resemble the GRIT. The GRAT requires that a fixed dollar amount be paid out to the beneficiary at least annually from the trust. The GRUT pays out a fixed percentage of the fair market value of the trust's assets valued each year. Under these types of trusts, a trustee's primary responsibility is to make certain that the assets are managed appropriately to meet the payout requirement and protect the assets for the beneficiaries who will inherit the trust property upon termination of the trust.

Qualified Personal Residence Trust (QPRT)

The qualified personal residence trust ultimately transfers a personal residence to children at a discounted value thereby reducing the transfer tax (i.e., estate and gift tax). Only property used by the grantor as his or her personal residence may be in the trust. Any funds received by the trust must be distributed within two months of receipt. If the property is sold the proceeds must be rolled over to another residence within two years or paid back to the grantor. The trustee's responsibility is to abide by the tax rules that apply to the administration of the trust so the tax savings goal is achieved.

Charitable Remainder Trusts

A charitable remainder trust allows the settlor (i.e., donor) as beneficiary, and other beneficiaries named by the settlor, to retain the right to receive income from the trust for life. Upon the death of those entitled to receive income, the trust assets are paid to a charity(ies). There are several advantages to a charitable remainder trust.

- **The settlor can take an income tax deduction for the year in which a contribution was made to the trust.**

- **The assets transferred to the charity are not subject to estate taxes.**

- **When highly appreciated assets, such as securities and real estate, are transferred into the trust and subsequently sold, no capital gains tax is paid. The assets are technically owned by the named charity, which is a tax-exempt entity.**

There are two types of charitable remainder trusts, a charitable remainder annuity trust (CRAT) and the charitable remainder unitrust (CRUT). The charitable remainder annuity trust pays out a fixed dollar amount each year regardless of how much income is produced by the trust or any change in the trust's value. In other words if the income from the trust assets goes down, the amount paid to the settlor remains the same. The pay out does not change even in the case where the income produced by the trust increases beyond the amount required to be paid out. No additional gifts can be made to this type of trust once it has been established.

The charitable remainder unitrust pays out a percentage of the value of the trust assets. The amount of the payout is determined by valuing the trust assets at the beginning of each year. The income paid out can go up or down each year depending on the value of the assets. Unlike the charitable remainder annuity trust, additional assets can be added to a unitrust to increase the earning power of the trust or add to the charitable bequest.

The trustee of a charitable remainder trust has the responsibility of meeting the payout requirements of the trust as well as protecting the trust assets for the charitable remainder beneficiary. The trustee must also manage the trust in accordance with the rules prescribed by the Internal Revenue Code to assure that the tax-exempt status of the trust is preserved.

CHAPTER 2

Fiduciary Standards and Limiting Liability

The power and authority personal representatives and trustees (fiduciaries) have come from several sources. Fiduciaries should know where they get their authority to act. Fiduciaries should also understand that they will be held to certain standards of conduct while carrying out their responsibilities. Most people select a personal representative or trustee based on who they feel they can trust to settle their affairs. The key word is "trust." The laws that govern estate and trust administration are designed to assure that this trust is not breached. A fundamental understanding of what these laws and standards of conduct mean can substantially reduce the risks of being a fiduciary. At the very least it should relieve some of the anxiety.

Power to Act

KEY POINTS

- **A fiduciary's principal authority comes from the Will or trust document under which he or she serves.**

- **If the Will or trust is silent with regard to a particular power or authority, a fiduciary must look to local law and ultimately to the courts for guidance.**

The powers that a fiduciary needs to carry out the administration of an estate or trust are normally in the Will or trust agreement. These powers are fairly standard and most Wills and trust agreements contain *"boiler plate"* provisions to give the fiduciary sufficient power to conduct the business of the estate or trust. The common boiler plate provisions found in Wills and trusts are the power to:

- Retain assets.

- Receive assets.

- Sell or exchange property.

- Invest and reinvest assets (trusts).

- Lease, manage, repair, improve, subdivide, develop, and dedicate for public use, real estate.

- Employ attorneys, accountants, and other agents.

- Borrow funds with or without security.

- Allocate items of income and expense between the income and principal accounts.

- Satisfy and settle claims.

- Negotiate, prosecute, or defend claims.

- Pay taxes, assessments, and other administration expenses.

- Make distributions to beneficiaries in cash or kind.

- Continue any business or venture.

- Vote stocks and other securities in person or by proxy.

- Insure assets against damage, loss, or liability.

Some Wills and trust documents may limit or broaden the fiduciary's authority. For example, the creator of the Will or trust may prohibit the sale of a particular stock, though that stock may be a logical security to liquidate because of current market conditions. He or she could also direct that the personal representative or trustee liquidate a business in a prescribed manner even though it would be logical, from a business point of view, to carry on the enterprise.

All estates and estate plans are unique. It is imperative that a fiduciary thoroughly examines the Will or trust to determine what powers have been specifically authorized and whether any restrictions have been imposed. Beyond the powers provided by the governing document, a fiduciary can exercise those powers provided by law to carry out the administration of the estate or trust—as long as they are not prohibited by the terms of the Will or trust.

There are three very important rules that every personal representative and trustee should follow—1) *read the document!*; 2) *read the document!*; and 3) *read the document!*

Statutory Law

In the administration of estates and trusts common state laws include:

The Uniform Probate Code
The rules and regulations governing the administration of probate estates are covered under the Uniform Probate Code, which has been adopted in one form or another by most states. In addition to defining the requirements for probating a decedent's estate, the Code also provides the necessary powers for the personal representative to carry out his or her responsibilities. The code may also contain provisions that affect some aspects of trust administration.

The Revised Uniform Principal and Income Act
One of the most difficult tasks of estate and trust administration

is preparing and maintaining accounting records. Fiduciary accounting is unique; it involves keeping separate records for income and principal transactions. The Revised Uniform Principal and Income Act describes how fiduciaries account for receipts and expenditures during the administration of an estate or trust. A Will or trust document may not always give sufficient guidance. The following states have adopted the Revised Uniform Principal and Income Act:

Alaska	Idaho
Arizona	Illinois
Arkansas	Indiana
California	Kansas
Connecticut	Kentucky
Florida	Maryland
Georgia	Michigan
Hawaii	Minnesota
Mississippi	Ohio
Montana	Oregon
Nebraska	South Carolina
Nevada	South Dakota
New Jersey	Texas
New Mexico	Utah
New York	Washington
North Carolina	Wisconsin
North Dakota	Wyoming

Case Law

Many of the general rules that govern fiduciaries have evolved from case law. That is, a legal action or suit is looked to or cited as a precedent for handling a particular administration matter. The laws that govern the administration of estates and trusts are largely statutory. However, decisions in new court cases continue to clarify how fiduciaries should deal with particular estate and trust issues. If a fiduciary finds that a transaction is not covered by the terms of a Will or trust or by statutory law, an attorney should be consulted to see if there is case law on the subject, which can give guidance to the fiduciary.

Court Authority

The express powers articulated in a Will or trust or under statutory law are what the personal representative or trustee should rely on. There may be a circumstance, though, where the language in the document is ambiguous or where a deviation from the terms of the trust would be in the best interest of the beneficiaries. In these circumstances, a fiduciary can and should seek court clarification or authority to modify the terms of the trust. This should be done sparingly and only in those situations where to do nothing would bring harm to the beneficiaries.

Standards of Conduct

KEY POINTS

- **Fiduciaries are held to certain standards of conduct under the law. They include the:**

  Duty of loyalty

  Duty of impartiality

  Duty to make property productive

  Duty of care

  Duty to preserve and protect property

  Duty to segregate assets

  Duty to keep accounts

  Duty not to delegate

  Duty to pay or apply income

  Duty to defend actions and enforce claims

- **Understanding of and adherence to these standards is essential in carrying out the responsibilities of a fiduciary.**

If you think settling an estate or managing a trust is a simple and straightforward responsibility, try obtaining liability insurance. Insurance companies, often, will not underwrite personal fiduciary liability coverage for an individual personal representative or trustee. Why, do you suppose? Simple. It is too risky. Considerable liability can be associated with being a personal representative or a trustee because it is easy to make a mistake. In addition to understanding specific tasks associated with estate and trust administration, personal representatives and trustees must also know how the law expects them to conduct themselves. The law, again, focuses on protecting the interests of beneficiaries and following the instructions of the decedent with respect to the disposition of his or her property.

Now you may be ready to resign and let someone else put life's fortunes at risk. "Hang in there." It is not as bad as it sounds if you follow the rules—basic standards of conduct that all fiduciaries are expected to follow. Established by common law, case law, tradition, and common sense, these principals of conduct are used to determine whether or not a fiduciary is doing the right thing. These are the rules that fiduciaries are expected to live by. Those who understand and adhere to their tenets will avoid any difficulties in carrying out their responsibilities under the law.

DUTY OF LOYALTY
A trustee shall administer the trust solely in the interest of the beneficiaries, and in the case of a personal representative for the benefit of the creditors first and then the beneficiaries.

The duty of loyalty is perhaps the most important rule for personal representatives and trustees. It mandates that the fiduciary cannot be in a position where self-interest will influence the performance of his or her duties. In other words, a fiduciary may not profit at the expense of a beneficiary or creditor.

For example, a fiduciary with the power to sell trust property may not buy it, or otherwise acquire any interest in the asset, though it might be purchased at a fair price and at "arm's length." Even if the fiduciary does not conduct the transaction himself, he violates the duty of loyalty in spite of purchasing the property at a foreclosure sale. To permit a fiduciary to purchase the property in this way would be in conflict with his duty to sell the property at the highest possible price. In other words, he should be exclusively on the selling side of the transaction—seeking a buyer who will pay the best price. Obviously, if the fiduciary were permitted to be the only bidder it would be to his or her advantage to limit the number of bidders as well as the bid price. The point is that it is next to impossible for someone to act impartially in a situation in which he or she can benefit.

The duty of loyalty also applies to transactions involving the sale of property by the fiduciary to the estate or trust. For example, the sale of an investment owned by a fiduciary to an estate or trust he or she manages is improper even though the investment is a proper one for the estate or trust and he or she acted in good faith. It is also a violation of the duty of loyalty for the fiduciary to enter into any transaction with an entity (i.e., corporation, partnership, proprietorship) in which he has a substantial ownership interest. Any activities that may give the fiduciary an advantage he or she otherwise would not have will almost invariably be in violation of the duty of loyalty.

DUTY OF IMPARTIALITY
The fiduciary shall deal impartially with all beneficiaries.

A personal representative or trustee may not favor one beneficiary over the other. In the case of a trust, the trustee must balance the competing interests between the current and future beneficiaries. Income beneficiaries are concerned with one thing and one thing only—how much income can they get. The future beneficiaries (i.e., remaindermen) are interested in how much the assets will grow and what the value of their future inheritance will be. The trustee cannot bend to the pressure from the income beneficiaries to maximize the current yield from the portfolio. To the extent potential growth is adversely affected by weighting the portfolio toward high income producing assets the trustee is violating his or her duty of impartiality by favoring the income takers. The trustee must balance the portfolio to meet the needs of the income beneficiaries and protect the value of the assets for the remaindermen.

The duty of impartiality also applies to the general administration of the trust with regard to the charging of expenses. Expenses charged against income obviously affect the current income beneficiaries. Charges against principal affect the amount that will be inherited by the remaindermen upon the termination of the trust.

Distributions of income and/or principal among current beneficiaries must be made with impartiality. One beneficiary cannot receive favored treatment over another with regard to discretionary payments from the trust. However, the trust document may alter the trustee's duties by directing the trustee to favor one beneficiary over another under certain circumstances. If as a trustee, you use reasonable care in carrying out these provisions, you are usually protected from liability.

DUTY TO MAKE PROPERTY PRODUCTIVE
A trustee shall use reasonable care and skill to make trust property productive.

A trustee is duty bound to manage trust property so that it produces income to meet the needs of the income beneficiaries and growth of principal for the remainder beneficiaries who will receive the trust assets upon termination. This entails balancing the interests of two sets of beneficiaries.

Making trust assets productive means different things to different people. The duty of impartiality does not allow the trustee to invest all of the trust property into assets with a high current yield. Neither can the trustee invest exclusively in property that will appreciate in value, but produce no income. Making the trust productive means that the trust assets must produce reasonable income and growth of principal. Assets cannot be void of both income and capital growth. A trustee who leaves money uninvested for a long period of time may be liable for the return that the funds would have earned if properly invested.

DUTY OF CARE
A fiduciary shall exercise the same skill and care as an individual would exercise in dealing with his or her own property.

The prudent investor rule requires a fiduciary to invest trust assets with a high degree of care. One obvious example of exercising proper care is being thoroughly familiar with the provisions of the Will or trust and what specifically is required. As a fiduciary you must be careful to preserve the estate that has been entrusted to you, a caution that is greater than dealing with your own property. Care and skill must be used in every aspect of managing a trust or probate estate. When a beneficiary questions a transaction involving his or her interest, the test will be whether or not the fiduciary exercised reasonable care to protect those interests.

DUTY TO PRESERVE AND PROTECT PROPERTY
A fiduciary shall ensure that all assets are protected and not lost or destroyed.

In addition to safekeeping cash and securities, a fiduciary has the duty to protect assets by making repairs to buildings, see that property tax and mortgage payments are made, store valuables such as jewelry and artifacts in a secure place and maintain adequate insurance coverage. The duty to preserve and protect property requires that the fiduciary insure that assets will not be subject to any loss of value. All property that can be insured against loss must be covered by an appropriate amount of insurance. Should a loss occur, a fiduciary could be held personally liable for inadequate insurance coverage.

Protecting property is most critical in the early stages of a probate estate. One of the first things a personal representative must do is gather all of the decedent's property, including tangible personal property such as jewelry, silverware, paintings, artifacts, etc. When someone dies, these things sometimes have a way of disappearing. Family members will distribute these items to themselves and others because "that is what Uncle Harry wanted." Uncle Harry may have instructed otherwise in his Will and the personal representative could be held responsible if these items end up in the wrong hands. The personal representative must protect the items until they are distributed to the heirs who are legally entitled to them.

Protection and preservation of property also includes depositing securities in a safe place and monitoring the portfolio. This includes not letting stock options and warrants expire if they can be exercised to the advantage of the beneficiaries. For securities held in a brokerage account, proper legal documentation must be provided to the broker to give the fiduciary control over the account.

DUTY TO SEGREGATE ASSETS
The fiduciary shall keep all trust and estate property separate from his or her own property.

It is improper for a personal representative or trustee to deposit trust or estate assets in his or her personal account, whether it is a bank or brokerage account. Trying to separate what is owned by the estate or trust from what is individually owned by the fiduciary in a personal account can be difficult. And, there is always the possibility that the fiduciary could inadvertently access the funds for his or her own use. The practical reason for not commingling funds is the accounting nightmare it causes. Take for example the interest earned on a savings or checking account. The portion of the account that belongs to the estate or trust must receive its share of the interest. The amount of interest to be allocated to the estate or trust will change every time a payment is made and every time funds are deposited. If transactions are put through the account daily or even weekly, interest accounting alone could be costly in terms of the time spent. It may be very expensive to hire an accountant to unscramble the mess.

Earmarking assets and accounts that belong to an estate or trust is obviously very important. Assets, such as checking accounts, brokerage accounts, etc., should be registered in the name of the estate or trust, or in the name of the fiduciary as personal representative or trustee.

DUTY TO KEEP ACCOUNTS
The fiduciary shall keep up-to-date and accurate records of the activities of the estate or trust.

A record of the financial activities of the estate or trust must be maintained for the courts and beneficiaries. This requires the fiduciary to maintain current accountings of all transactions in the estate or trust. Keeping good records is not as easy as it sounds, as will become clearer in later chapters. The fiduciary personally can maintain accounting records and other documentation or can hire an accountant. In either case the records must be current. A fiduciary should update these records frequently because the volume of transactions makes it difficult to catch up once he or she falls behind.

In some states accountings for both estates and trusts must be filed with the probate court. In other states the fiduciary is only obligated to provide accountings to the beneficiaries. However, a beneficiary can ask the court to compel the fiduciary to render an accounting if the beneficiary suspects that the fiduciary is not managing the estate or trust properly. Take the case of a trustee who decides that it is none of the beneficiary's business to know how the trust is being managed. The fiduciary might feel he or she is in charge and "knows what is in their best interest." After unsuccessful attempts to get an accounting and other information from the trustee, you guessed it, the beneficiary is likely to seek the services of an attorney. A petition is usually filed in court to order the trustee to provide an accounting to the beneficiary. The court will so order and may also order the removal of the trustee.

DUTY NOT TO DELEGATE
A fiduciary shall not delegate to others those duties that he or she can reasonably perform.

A fiduciary is obligated to perform the duties of a trustee or personal representative and cannot transfer these responsibilities to another person or institution unless authorized to do so under the terms of the trust document, Will or court order. However, the fiduciary can delegate those acts that would be unreasonable to expect him or her to perform. Factors that are important to consider in determining whether a proposed delegation is reasonable or not include:

1) **The amount of discretion involved in performing the delegated act.**

2) **The value and character of the asset affected by the delegated act.**

3) **Will the performance of the delegated act directly or indirectly affect the assets of the estate or trust or its beneficiaries?**

4) **Will the delegated act affect the principal or income of the estate or trust to the detriment of the beneficiaries?**

5) **Does the delegated act call for certain skills which the trustee or executor does not possess and cannot reasonably be expected to acquire?**

It is important to distinguish between the delegation of a duty and the hiring of an agent to assist the fiduciary in discharging his or her responsibilities. For example, a trustee may hire an independent investment advisor or investment management firm to handle the trust's portfolio, even with complete discretion. The ultimate responsibility still rests with the trustee though the actual management of the investments is performed by the agent. The fiduciary must closely supervise any agent that is retained.

A fiduciary may be permitted to delegate certain administrative duties to agents, co-trustees, or other individuals under the terms of the Will or trust document. However, the fiduciary still has an obligation to the beneficiary(ies) to oversee the activities of the person to whom the duty has been delegated.

DUTY TO PAY OR APPLY INCOME
The trustee shall pay income to the beneficiary in the manner prescribed by the terms of the trust.

A trustee has a duty to pay the net income of the property at reasonable intervals to a current income beneficiary if directed by the terms of the trust. If the trust does not specify the frequency of income distributions, they can be made annually, semi-annually, or quarterly depending on local law. A reasonable amount of income can be withheld to meet current and future expenses that are properly chargeable against income. If a beneficiary is a minor or under a legal disability, the trustee also has a duty to apply the income for the benefit of that beneficiary. The duty to pay income can be modified by the terms of the trust document in the following ways:

1) **If the trust document directs the trustee to accumulate income, then the trustee is under no obligation to distribute income to the beneficiary.**

2) **If the trust document gives the trustee the discretion to distribute income, he or she has no obligation to pay out income unless in the trustee's judgment a distribution is necessary and appropriate.**

3) If the trustee is directed to pay the income for a beneficiary's support, he or she is not required to distribute the income directly to that beneficiary.

The terms of the trust document may allow accumulation of income that is not needed currently for the beneficiary's support. The trust document may also allow accumulated income to be transferred to and become a part of the principal of the trust. The trustee must always look to the trust document for guidance before making decisions concerning the payment, or nonpayment, of income from the trust.

DUTY TO DEFEND ACTIONS AND ENFORCE CLAIMS
Fiduciaries shall defend claims of third parties against the estate or trust and enforce claims held by the estate or trust.

The estate or trust must be defended against any claims that would result in a loss if they were successful. In this regard, the personal representative or trustee has a duty to the beneficiaries to act reasonably in preventing the dilution or destruction of estate or trust assets.

The personal representative or trustee must also take all reasonable steps in enforcing claims. If someone fails to pay a debt owed to the estate or trust, the personal representative or trustee has a duty to bring an action to enforce payment. If a claim is not enforced, the personal representative or trustee could be surcharged for any uncollected sums. The personal representative or trustee must act reasonably, however, in enforcing a claim. If there is a high probability that the expenses of litigating a claim might exceed the amount that could ultimately be collected, the claim should not be pursued.

Conflicts of Interest

KEY POINTS

- **Fiduciaries should not commingle estate or trust accounts with their own.**

- **Fiduciaries should not conduct financial transactions between themselves and the estate or trust they manage.**

Whatever the rationale, dealing directly with an estate or trust where there is a possibility of personal gain or advantage is a conflict of interest. Even if the deal is fair and equitable, the mere appearance of a conflict of interest may raise questions about the integrity of the personal representative or trustee. If others might think that a conflict exists, the fiduciary should consider finding another way of handling the transaction.

Avoiding conflict is relatively easy. Fiduciaries should understand and abide by the standards of conduct discussed earlier and stay away from transactions involving the estate or trust and the fiduciary personally. The following simple rules should be followed. A fiduciary should not:

1) **purchase property from an estate or trust. Even if the purchase price and terms are fair, the fiduciary puts himself/herself in a position of not getting the best price and terms possible for the estate or trust by not offering the same opportunity to others;**

2) **sell property to an estate or trust. Whether or not the estate received fair value in the transaction will always be open to question;**

3) **enter into any transaction where the fiduciary is**

both the seller and buyer, i.e., trust selling property to another trust where the fiduciary is trustee of both trusts. One cannot be loyal to two groups of beneficiaries whose interests are independent of one another;

4) employ himself or herself to perform special services for the estate or trust. The fiduciary has the potential of self enrichment at the expense of the estate or trust;

5) borrow funds from an estate or trust. Again the potential for gaining advantage at the expense of the estate or trust exists; or,

6) accept gifts from someone who does business with an estate or trust. The fiduciary has the opportunity in this situation of providing an advantage to a friend or colleague in exchange for personal gain.

"And please protect me from the appearance of wrongdoing."

Keeping the Beneficiaries Informed

One of the most important things a fiduciary must do is keep the beneficiaries informed. These are the people who are going to sue you if something goes wrong. People tend to be forgiving when a mistake is made if they know what is going on and have a good relationship with the personal representative or trustee. They are much less inclined to let you off the hook if you are secretive and keep things from them.

Whom do you keep informed? Typically it is the beneficiaries of the estate and, in the case of a trust, the current beneficiaries. That is, those beneficiaries of a trust who are entitled to receive income and/or principal during the term of the trust. However, some state statutes require that a trustee provide information about a trust to remainder beneficiaries upon request. What kinds of information are you obligated to provide? The trust or estate accounting that is provided to the beneficiaries usually is sufficient to inform them of the routine transactions affecting the administration of the estate or trust. However, the fiduciary is obliged to inform the beneficiaries of a non-routine transaction before it is consummated if the transaction will have a significant effect on their interest in the estate or trust. The sale of a business, the leasing or sale of a parcel of real estate, for example, would be transactions that fall into this category. A beneficiary may want to acquire the asset or may have some information that is pertinent to the transaction and should be given the opportunity for input.

Serving As a Successor or Co-Fiduciary

KEY POINTS

- A successor personal representative or trustee may have responsibility for the action of his or her predecessor.

- Co-fiduciaries must agree. If there is disagreement, the court must ultimately resolve any disputes.

- Wills and trusts sometimes contain language that protects the fiduciary from liability in taking a particular action or actions.

The law is fairly clear about what is expected of a successor personal representative or successor trustee regarding the actions that were taken or not taken by the predecessor. A fiduciary must take the steps necessary to collect all of the estate or trust property. A successor personal representative or trustee must not allow a known wrongdoing committed by a predecessor to continue. A fiduciary must take action against the predecessor personal representative or trustee for any breach unless there is language in the Will or trust document absolving the successor of this responsibility. A trust may contain protective language similar to the following:

"No successor Trustee shall have any duty to investigate or review any action of a predecessor Trustee and may accept the accounting records of such Trustee showing assets on hand without further investigation and without incurring any liability to any person claiming or having an interest in this trust."

Similar language might be found in a Will with respect to a successor personal representative or contained in a court order appointing the successor personal representative.

Serving as a co-personal representative or co-trustee adds another level of responsibility. A fiduciary is liable for the actions of his/her co-fiduciary and has an obligation to monitor the activities of the co-fiduciary. In general the following rules apply if you serve as a personal representative or trustee with someone else:

- **Co-fiduciaries must agree to all actions taken in the administration of an estate or trust unless the governing document permits delegation to one or more co-fiduciaries.**

- **A fiduciary is liable if he or she participates in a breach of trust with a co-fiduciary.**

- **A fiduciary is liable if he or she allows a breach by a co-fiduciary to continue.**

- **A fiduciary is liable for not taking proper action to have a co-fiduciary pay for any damages caused by a breach.**

- **A fiduciary may be liable for improperly delegating a duty or responsibility to a co-fiduciary who has breached his/her duties.**

- **Disputes between co-fiduciaries must ultimately be settled by the courts.**

Many states allow discretionary authority to be exercised by a majority when there are three or more trustees. Under these statutes, a dissenting trustee usually will not be held liable for the actions taken by the other trustees if the objection is given in writing to any of the co-trustees.

A Will or trust can also contain protective language:

"No Co-Trustee (Co-Personal Representative) shall be liable for any act, omission, or default of any other Co-Trustee (Co-Personal Representative), provided the Co-Trustee (Co- Personal

Representative) shall have had no knowledge of any facts that may reasonably be expected to have put the Co-Trustee (Co-Personal Representative) on notice in sufficient time to have prevented the act, omission or default."

Obtaining a release and indemnification from a beneficiary may offer some protection from liability. However, it may not be effective if the beneficiary did not have knowledge of all the facts and circumstances related to the transaction or action taken.

Limiting Your Liability

The duty of loyalty is the basic underpinning of the laws that govern the activities of fiduciaries. This should be obvious if you consider the level of trust that is expected with regard to the disposition of one's property after death. Entrusting someone to carry out the wishes of a decedent is to require that he or she act solely in the best interests of the decedent's heirs. The do's and don'ts listed below are logical expectations of how personal representatives and trustees should conduct themselves:

DOS

- **Keep clear and accurate records.**

- **Inform beneficiaries of the nature and amount of their interest in the estate or trust.**

- **Take possession and keep control of all estate and trust property.**

- **Segregate estate and trust property from all other property and earmark all deposit accounts (i.e., bank accounts, brokerage accounts, etc.) as estate or trust property.**

- **Exercise reasonable care and skill to make trust property productive.**

- **Supervise the activities of all agents.**

DON'TS

- **In administering the estate or trust do not allow yourself to be guided by the interests of third parties.**

- **Do not use estate or trust property for your own benefit.**

- **Do not allow an agent to do something that is not in the best interest of the estate or trust.**

- **Do not delegate to others those duties that you can reasonably perform yourself.**

- **Do not purchase property for yourself if that property is owned or has close connection to the estate or trust.**

- **Do not disclose confidential information to third parties.**

- **Do not accept commissions from third persons for work done in connection with the administration of the estate or trust.**

Checklist for Limiting Your Liability

✓ Read the trust document; read the trust document; read the trust document.

✓ If the terms of a Will or trust are misleading or ambiguous, seek clarification from an attorney or instructions from the court.

✓ Review the Standards of Conduct that apply to Personal Representatives and Trustees.

✓ Retain professionals to assist you with those administration tasks that you do not have time for or for which you lack expertise.

✓ Communicate with beneficiaries about the administration of the estate or trust on a regular basis.

✓ Keep accurate and current records.

✓ Take possession of and protect all assets of the estate or trust.

✓ Review and monitor the activities of all professional agents that you hire.

✓ Do not commingle estate or trust assets with your own.

✓ Do not purchase from or sell assets to an estate or trust if you are the personal representative or trustee.

✓ Do not employ yourself to perform special tasks, such as appraisals, accounting services, property management, etc., for a separate fee.

✓ Do not borrow money from the estate or trust.

✓ Do not accept gifts or commissions from someone who does business with the estate or trust.

✓ Do not share confidential information with individuals who do not have an interest in the estate or trust.

SETTLING AN ESTATE

CHAPTER 3

How Property Passes At Death

KEY POINTS

- Individually owned property is subject to probate procedures, which may require court supervision.

- Joint property is not part of the probate administration process.

- Contract property, such as life insurance policies, 401(k) plans, IRAs, revocable living trusts, etc., are also not subject to probate.

When someone dies a personal representative (executor) is appointed to settle the decedent's affairs. As discussed in *Chapter 1 Serving As A Personal Representative and/or Trustee*, a personal representative has the responsibility of taking charge of the decedent's estate, which involves: marshaling the decedent's assets; paying his or her debts and taxes, and distributing what is left to the decedent's legal heirs. If the decedent held all of his or her property in a revocable living trust, the trustee usually has the responsibility for settling the affairs of the decedent. The role of the personal representative is of limited duration, usually lasting anywhere from eighteen months to two years. In smaller estates, the period of administration may be shorter.

Before beginning the administration of an estate, the personal representative needs to be familiar with how property passes at death. This is important because it identifies the assets the personal representative is legally responsible for and those that are not subject to probate administration. Property ownership has several different forms and, upon death, passes under laws that are unique to each form of ownership. The three common ways of owning property are individual ownership, joint ownership and ownership that is subject to the terms of a contract.

Individually Owned Property

Property, such as real estate, stocks and bonds, mutual funds, bank accounts, automobiles, etc., that are titled in an individual's own name, is subject to the probate laws, or laws of descent, in the decedent's state of domicile (i.e., his or her permanent home, not necessarily where he or she lived.) Tangible personal property, such as jewelry, furniture, books, stamp collections, paintings, artifacts, etc., owned by the decedent are also subject to probate. These assets are referred to as probate property. The probate laws may or may not require a formal probate court proceeding for distribution of this property. Each state has its own rules on how this type of property is handled at death. Probate property passes to the beneficiaries named in a Will or, if the decedent did not have a Will, to the decedent's *heirs at law* described under the laws of intestacy in the decedent's state of domicile.

Jointly Owned Property

If the decedent owned any property jointly with others, it is important to know what kind of ownership it is. Property that is registered as *joint tenants* or *tenants by the entirety* pass to the surviving tenant(s) by operation of law and is not subject to probate. Ownership as *tenants in common*, however, does not pass to the surviving owner(s) by operation of law. This form of ownership represents an undivided interest in property that is considered individually owned. Tenancy in common property is subject to probate and passes by Will or the laws of intestacy.

Contract Property

Property that is subject to the terms of a written contract such as a life insurance policy, an interest in a profit sharing, 401(k) plan or IRA, revocable living trust, pay on death (POD) account etc., pass to the beneficiary named in the contract. This property is also not subject to probate unless the decedent's estate has been designated as the beneficiary.

HOW PROPERTY PASSES AT DEATH

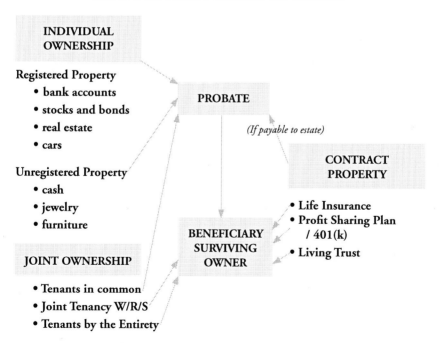

Passing Property by Will

A Will is a legally enforceable declaration by an individual with regard to the disposition of his or her assets. It may also address other matters that the Will creator wants handled at death, such as burial and who will care for minor children. A Will only controls the property that is owned by the decedent individually, or as a tenant in common, and is subject to probate. If a decedent also has a revocable living trust, typically the trust is named as the residual beneficiary under the Will. After the payment of specific bequests, administration expenses, creditors' claims, and taxes, the Will distributes to the trust whatever assets remain. This is called a *"pour over"* Will.

Intestacy

If someone dies without a Will and owns property in his/her individual name, or as tenants in common, the *laws of intestacy* of the state in which the decedent was domiciled will determine who will inherit the property. Only a surviving spouse and lineal (blood) descendants are eligible to inherit the decedent's property if there is no will. The person(s) and the amount each will inherit differ from state to state. As with a Will, only the property owned by the decedent individually, or as a tenant in common, will be subject to probate and the laws of intestacy.

Passing Property under A Trust

A Will is usually designed to distribute property outright at death and may be subject to a probate court proceeding. A trust can also be used to pass property outright at death (i.e., *terminating trust.*) However, when used in this way, the assets owned by the trust avoid probate because they are not registered in the decedent's own name. After payment of estate expenses and taxes, the property owned by the trust is distributed to the beneficiaries named to receive it. A trust can also provide control and management of assets for a specified period beyond death (i.e., *continuing trust.*) The purpose of this type of trust is to protect beneficiaries and/or minimize estate taxes. The trust only controls and disposes of the property to which it has legal title; the trust assets are not distributed to the named beneficiaries until the final obligations of the estate are satisfied.

Once the personal representative identifies all of the assets and determines the form of ownership, the next step is to ascertain how the decedent's property will pass to the survivors. As an example, let's look at how John Porter's estate passes upon his death:

PROPERTY OWNED BY JOHN & MARY PORTER

	Ownership	*Beneficiary*
Checking account	Joint with Mary	—
Money market fund	Joint with Mary	—
Savings account	John	—
Stocks and bonds	Living Trust	Mary/Children
Mutual funds	John	—
Automobiles	Joint with Mary	—
Furniture	Joint with Mary	—
Residence	Tenants by the entirety	—
Condominium	Living Trust	Mary/Children
Cash, jewelry	John	—
Life insurance	John	Mary
Profit sharing plan	John	Mary

John has a *pour over* Will that distributes his individually-owned property (i.e., savings account, mutual funds, cash and jewelry), after probate, to his living trust. His living trust, which owns his stocks and bonds and condominium, continues for the benefit of his wife, Mary, and their children. All of the property that is owned jointly with Mary passes to her directly by operation of law. She is the named beneficiary under John's life insurance and profit sharing plan and receives the proceeds directly.

PROPERTY PASSING AT JOHN'S DEATH

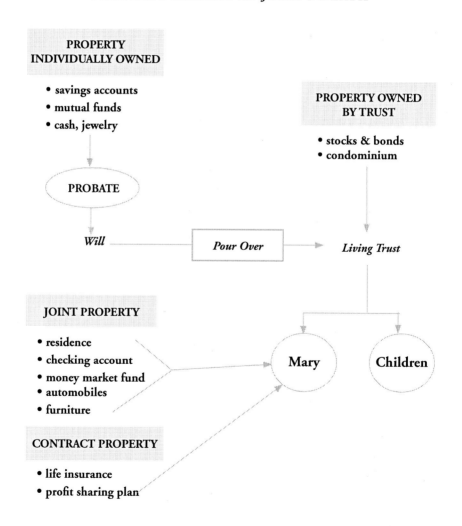

PROPERTY INDIVIDUALLY OWNED

- savings accounts
- mutual funds
- cash, jewelry

PROBATE

PROPERTY OWNED BY TRUST

- stocks & bonds
- condominium

Will · *Pour Over* → *Living Trust*

JOINT PROPERTY

- residence
- checking account
- money market fund
- automobiles
- furniture

CONTRACT PROPERTY

- life insurance
- profit sharing plan

Mary

Children

CHAPTER 4

Estate Transfer Procedures

Is Probate Administration Necessary?

KEY POINTS

- **The first step in settling an estate is to determine what property will be subject to probate.**

- **The next step is to determine what transfer procedure will be required, or used, if there are options.**

The term probate literally means the "proving of a Will." More commonly it is used to describe the court-supervised process of passing title of one's property, at death, to those legally entitled to it. Probate provides a mechanism for determining a decedent's heirs and settling his or her estate. Even if a decedent had no Will, his/her individually owned property may be subject to probate. It passes under the laws of intestacy of the decedent's state of domicile (i.e., his or her permanent home.) Whether an individual dies with or without a Will, the steps that must be taken to transfer property and settle the estate are essentially the same.

Property Subject to Probate:

Registered property—Property that is registered in a decedent's individual name, including property owned as a tenant in common, is subject to the probate laws. It includes checking and savings accounts, brokerage accounts, stocks and bonds, mutual funds, real estate, automobiles, and other property that has a legal form of registration. It does not include property that is registered as joint tenants, tenants by the entirety, (i.e., joint ownership between husband and wife), or property that designates a beneficiary under the terms of a contract.

Unregistered property—Virtually every estate, no matter what its size, includes tangible personal property. This category of assets includes jewelry, paintings, furniture, tools, stamp collections, antiques, clothing, appliances, memorabilia, etc. This property will also be included as part of the probate assets even though there is no formal registration indicating ownership. Also, any items that are referred to in a Will are indications of individual ownership and should be included as part of the probate estate.

What Property is In the Decedent's Own Name?

One of the most difficult and important tasks that a personal representative has to perform is locating, valuing and organizing the decedent's property by type of ownership. This requires going through all of the decedent's records and identifying everything the decedent owned outright and property that he or she had an interest in. Once the inventory is sorted by type of ownership (i.e., individually owned, jointly owned, contract property, etc.), the total fair market value of the individually owned property (i.e., probate property) will determine the probate procedures required to transfer the property to the decedent's heirs or beneficiaries.

The Probate Process

KEY POINTS

- **Probate administration is supervised directly or indirectly by the probate court in the state in which the decedent was domiciled.**

- **The process has several phases, which can take con-**

siderable time to complete.

- **Methodical planning is the key to efficient admin-istration. It should include an outline of the steps (phases) that will be taken to complete the process.**

Most people want to avoid a formal probate proceeding. It can be very expensive. In most states, the fee is a percentage of the value of probate assets. This is often defined as the gross value and not the net (i.e., gross value less the decedent's debts). In some estates, this fee can be sizeable and result in a smaller inheritance for heirs. Most courts also assess court fees for using their system to probate a decedent's estate.

Another reason to avoid probate is that it can take a long time to complete. Eighteen months to two years is not unusual for completing the process. In some cases it takes even longer. The personal representative is often blamed for the delay. Most people do not understand the process or the fact that the personal repre-sentative is required to complete the task in accordance with rules prescribed by law. These rules, both federal and state, can slow the process. Nevertheless the heirs will want their inheritance imme-diately and the personal representative must spend time explain-ing why they have to wait.

The process begins with petitioning the court for a hearing to probate the decedent's Will. It can take weeks and sometimes months to get a hearing, depending on the district and how backed up the court calendar is. Under an informal proceeding, this is much quicker and may not require a hearing. Until the hearing and/or formal appointment, the personal representative has no legal authority to conduct the affairs of the estate. As a practical matter however, if you intend to accept the personal rep-resentative position and are reasonably sure that the appointment will be made by the court, it is wise to begin gathering and safe-guarding the decedent's assets. Waiting months for a formal court appointment could jeopardize the proper handling of the estate. It is unlikely that the nominated personal representative will be criticized for using good judgment in protecting estate assets even before he or she is formally appointed.

Once appointed as personal representative, you must prepare an inventory of the decedent's assets. Itemize what the decedent owned at death and establish the fair market value of each asset. In most jurisdictions this inventory must be submitted to the court. As the personal representative you should publish notice to creditors in the legal notice section of a newspaper(s) for the period specified by local law. The public notice announces the death of the decedent and invites creditors to make claims for any outstanding debts. At the expiration of the notice period, creditors who are unknown to the personal representative are usually bared from making future claims.

During probate, you manage the decedent's estate as the personal representative and pay expenses associated with the settlement of the estate. The administration of the estate may include overseeing or being actively involved in the management of the decedent's business. If the decedent owned rental property, management will involve finding tenants, making repairs, paying operating expenses and collecting rents. Any stocks and bonds or other securities need to be evaluated to determine which ones, if any, need to be sold either to raise funds to pay taxes and expenses or to protect the portfolio against an extraordinary loss. You must see to it that all income that is due the estate is collected and all verified claims and other expenses are paid. Each of these activities must be recorded and accounted for. Accounting reports must be provided to the court and the beneficiaries prior to closing the estate.

If the estate owes any *federal estate tax,* the tax return must be filed and taxes paid no later than nine months from the date of death. A state inheritance tax may also be due. It is best not to file the return sooner than necessary. The estate will be much better off earning interest for as long as it can on the taxes due. This is one reason why it takes longer than a year to settle an estate. An estate is a separate taxable entity and must also file income tax returns to report and pay any taxes due on the income it receives. The probate court will not allow the closing of the estate and discharge of the personal representative until all taxes have been paid.

An accounting of the activities of administration is usually presented to the probate court for approval prior to closing. If the beneficiaries desire, or if ordered by the court, a master will be appointed to review the personal representative's records. The master's job is to perform an audit of the administration of the estate and report the findings to the court. If the review is satisfactory the master will recommend to the court that the accounting be approved. At this point the personal representative prepares to distribute the assets of the estate to the decedent's heirs. A distribution schedule is prepared listing the property each beneficiary will receive. The assets are then registered in the name(s) of the beneficiary (ies) and delivered to each.

Once distribution has been completed and receipts obtained from each beneficiary, you must submit a final accounting (also referred to as a supplemental final accounting) to the court along with the signed receipts. This demonstrates to the court that all tasks have been completed and the decedent's assets have been distributed to those who are legally entitled to them. At this point the court issues an order to close the estate and discharge you as the personal representative. Once the discharge has been ordered you are relieved of any further responsibilities with respect to the administration of the decedent's estate.

You've been named the personal representative under someone's Will. Now what?

Uncle Joe just died and before he passed away he told you that he had named you the personal representative under his Will. Once you discover what might be involved, you are not quite sure you want to serve or can handle the responsibility. However, you might feel that this is the least you should do for Uncle Joe. After all, you were the one person he was willing to trust to handle his affairs. Besides you should be honored that he chose you over other family members and friends. To serve or not to serve -that is always the question. While this can be an agonizing decision, it must be made within a reasonable period of time. Whether the choice is based on your willingness to make the time commitment, your ability to perform the role, or what you feel is a moral obligation, acceptance should be made as soon after the death as possible.

If your decision is not made promptly, it could cause unnecessary delays in settling the estate. If you decide not to serve, the court will appoint someone unless the decedent's Will designates an alternate personal representative. If you decide to serve, notify the attorney who drew the Will, or an attorney of your choice, to file the petition for probate with your acceptance noted.

To protect the interests of those who are entitled to payment of claims and of those who are legally entitled to receive the property, as personal representative, you are required to follow the instructions of the decedent's Will, or if there is no Will, the *laws of intestacy* in the state of jurisdiction. The laws of intestacy specify the lineal descendants (blood relatives) who legally inherit the decedent's property if there is no Will. An estate is subject to the jurisdiction of the probate court in the state in which the decedent was domiciled.

The probate court issues *letters of administration,* where there is no Will, or *letters testamentary,* for a personal representative who has been named in a Will. This is your legal authority to act as personal representative. Once formally appointed, you assume all of the duties and responsibilities under local law. This includes identifying, taking control of, and safeguarding all probate assets. As mentioned earlier, an inventory of the decedent's assets needs to be prepared immediately and the property must be appraised at its fair market value as of the decedent's date of death. The appraisals are used for estate taxes, to determine the proper probate procedure, to establish cost bases, and for other matters related to the administration of the estate.

Administering an estate should be done in logical steps to insure that all of the legal requirements are met and the estate is managed efficiently. To do otherwise makes the process more difficult than it needs to be and invites criticism from heirs. The plan for administration should include the following steps:

- **Preparing for the Administration of the Estate**

- **Assembling and Protecting Estate Assets**

- **Preparing the Inventory and Acquiring Appraisals**

- **Managing Estate Property**

- **Estimating Cash Requirements and Raising the Needed Funds**

- **Paying Claims and Expenses**

- **Filing Tax Returns**

- **Making Tax and Other Elections**

- **Accounting for the Administration of the Estate**

- **Distributing Assets and Closing the Estate**

SETTLING THE ESTATE

Locate the Will

Review Will for funeral
and other special
instructions

**PREPARING
FOR
ADMINISTRATION**

Meet with attorney and
family members to
discuss will provisions

Confer with attorney
regarding duties and
responsibilities in
handling the estate

Search for all estate
assets

Take possession of
valuables

Take possession of keys
to residence

**ASSEMBLING AND
PROTECTING
ESTATE ASSETS**

Review insurance
policies to insure that
coverage is
adequate.

Change bank,
brokerage, etc.,
accounts to estate.

Review all documents
covering rentals,
investments and
business interests.

Obtain list of contents
in safe deposit box

Prepare inventory of all
estate assets

**INVENTORY
AND
APPRAISALS**

Arrange for appraisal of
real estate and personal
property.

Appraise businesses.

Value stocks, bonds,
mutal funds and other
securites.

Collet dividends, interests and other income due the estate.

Review investments and take action to preserve estate assets.

Arrange for the management and/or disposition of business interests.

MANAGING THE PROPERTY

File claims for insurance payable to the estate.

Manage cash in interest bearing account.

Arrange for management of real estate.

Estimate cash needs for bequests, claims, taxes and other expenses.

Select assets to be sold to meet cash requirements

SALE OF ASSETS

Review the need to sell assets not required to meet cash needs, i.e., assets that cannot be distributed in kind.

Publish notice for creditors.

Defend estate against lawsuits

CLAIMS AND EXPENSES

Receive claims and ascertain their validity.

Pay valid claims and expenses.

File income tax returns for the decedent

File income tax returns for the estate during administration

TAXES

File the federal estate tax return, if required.

File state inheritance tax return, if required.

Prepare inventory for the court and beneficiaries during the period of administration

ACCOUNTING

Provide accounting of administration to the court and beneficiaries.

Distribute income to beneficiaries as appropriate.

Make distribution to beneficiaries upon receiving appropriate clearances.

DISTRIBUTION AND CLOSING

Prepare and file the final accounting with the court.

Obtain releases from the beneficiaries and/or discharge from the court.

Transfer By Affidavit

In some states, if the total fair market value of the decedent's individually owned property does not exceed a specified dollar amount, the property can be distributed to the beneficiary(ies) or heir(s) by affidavit. (*See Appendix I.*) This procedure usually applies to the transfer of personal property and usually does not involve the probate court. The heir signs an affidavit stating that he or she is legally entitled to the property and that the value does not exceed the limits specified by law for using this method. There are usually no costs involved in transfer by affidavit. There may be a small cost if an attorney is needed. For real estate, this procedure is usually not permitted and the transfer of title to a beneficiary is done through the probate court.

Small Estate, or Summary Administration

A small estate, or summary administration, proceeding is an informal process for smaller estates. The estate must be below a certain dollar threshold value under local law, (i.e., $10,000, $20,000, $30,000, etc.) in order to qualify for this procedure. You do not need an attorney; these estates are typically handled by or through the clerk of the probate court. The procedure is fairly simple and straightforward, requiring the personal representative or a family member to complete some forms provided by the clerk of the probate court. In some jurisdictions, the small estate pro-ceeding is used to transfer real estate to the decedent's heirs where there is no requirement for a formal probate proceeding.

Informal, Unsupervised, or Independent Proceeding

If the gross value of the decedent's probate assets is greater than the threshold for the affidavit and small estates procedure, an informal, unsupervised, or independent probate proceeding is either required or is an option in many states. Some states limit this procedure to a specific range of estate values; others make it an option for any size estate. This procedure, which many states have adopted through The Uniform Probate Code, is not directly supervised by the court. It simplifies the process and minimizes settlement costs. It is also designed to reduce the time it takes to settle the estate. Once appointed personal representative, you act independently from the court throughout the administration and settlement of the estate. Some states may require limited reporting to the court at the beginning, during, or upon completion of the settlement process. The cost is significantly less than a formal proceeding because an attorney is not required and court costs, if any, are minimal. At any time under this method, a personal representative, beneficiary or any interested party can elect to have the estate handled by the court in a formal proceeding. Although an attorney is not required, the personal representative should consider retaining counsel for advice on how these procedures work under local law.

Formal, or Supervised Proceeding

When a decedent's probate assets reach a certain value, many states require a formal, or supervised, probate proceeding. Whether the formal proceeding is required or is elected by those involved, an attorney is usually necessary and often involves extensive supervision by the probate court. Hearings are required throughout the proceeding and inventories, accountings and other reports must be filed with the court. Court costs and attorney's fees make the formal probate proceeding more expensive and it usually takes longer to complete. It is not unusual for the settlement for larger or more complex estates to take two to three years or longer.

Procedures vary from state to state and it is your duty as personal representative to find out what the local law requires and what options are available. An estate attorney can tell you or you can contact the clerk of the probate court for guidance. (See *Appendix I* for a general description of the procedures available in each state.)

CHAPTER 5

Preparing for the Administration of the Estate

KEY POINTS

- Organizing and preparing for the administration of the estate will make it easier to manage, minimize errors, and make the process more efficient.

- The personal representative, attorney and any other advisors need to agree on what responsibilities and tasks each will assume during the period of administration.

- The decedent's heirs should be told at the beginning what the will provided. They should also be given an estimated time frame for settling the estate.

The supervision and management of a probate estate can be complex. It requires a commitment of time, attention to detail and strict adherence to meeting deadlines. During the course of administration, unanticipated events can change a relatively simple estate settlement into a time consuming process. The decedent's heirs expect the estate to be settled quickly and efficiently. Organizing the process and keeping on top of things will save you a lot of time, aggravation and criticism from creditors and the decedent's heirs. Use a checklist *(see Appendix II)* to keep track of what needs to be done and when tasks should be completed.

When settling an estate, the key to keeping everyone happy is to keep them informed. Creditors and beneficiaries want to know what is going on and when they can expect to be paid or receive their inheritance. Whether the news is good or bad, they will usually want to hear from you. If there is a problem and the probate is inadvertently delayed, frequent communication will usually buffer any unhappiness among the beneficiaries.

Do not wait for the court to issue letters testamentary giving you legal authority as personal representative. This process may take several weeks or even months. The fundamental responsibility of protecting assets should begin immediately.

Locate the Original Will

You might hear of a decedent's death and your appointment as personal representative from a family member or, in some cases, learn of the death from an obituary notice. The decedent's attorney may also inform you because you are named under the Will. The most important and immediate step once you have been informed of the death is to locate and secure the decedent's original Will. Only the original Will can be presented to the probate court.

One of the obvious places to look is in the decedent's safe deposit box. A family member or the estate attorney should be present while the box is being searched for the Will. Financial institutions require one of their employees also to be present when the box is opened. Most banks will allow the removal of a Will from a decedent's safe deposit box when presented with a death certificate. The search of the safe deposit box is also an opportunity to collect information about other assets such as stocks, bonds, insurance policies, jewelry, etc. that may have to be probated or is otherwise part of the decedent's estate. Make an inventory of the box's contents.

You might also look for the original Will in the decedent's home among other important documents. Ask a family member to assist in this search. Like the opening of the safe deposit box, the search of the decedent's home is also an opportunity to begin developing an inventory. The original Will may also be held for safekeeping with the decedent's attorney, bank or other financial institution. Sometimes a business associate or friend will have possession of the original Will. The search for the Will must be thorough to assure that the most current Will and *codicils* (i.e., amendments) are presented to the probate court.

Another reason to locate the original Will as soon as possible after death is because it may contain burial and funeral instructions and/or directives regarding anatomical gifts. It is obviously critical to notify the decedent's physician, family, and attorney of any organ donations as soon as possible. Most organ donations must be made within hours of death or they may not have value.

Family members need to be notified of any funeral instructions so that burial arrangements can be made in accordance with the wishes of the decedent. The decedent may not have surviving family members and the personal representative may need to make the funeral arrangements if friends or acquaintances of the decedent are not inclined to assume this responsibility.

The original Will should be turned over to the attorney for filing with the court.

"Eddie was a simple man and, in the end, an eminently practical one."

Selecting the Attorney

Although some states may not require an attorney to represent the estate, as personal representative, you should consider retaining an attorney to guide you through the initial stages. Contrary to popular belief, it is the personal representative who has the responsibility for hiring the attorney to represent the decedent's estate. The personal representative will ultimately be held accountable. Therefore it behooves you as the personal representative to select an attorney who has the ability to take on the responsibility. Typically, the attorney who prepared the decedent's Will is the logical choice. He or she would be familiar with the decedent's expressed wishes and have some knowledge with respect to the decedent's family and financial affairs. However, if the Will was drawn many years ago, this familiarity may no longer exist. In addition, the attorney may not have an interest in doing this kind of work, or may not have the expertise to handle probate administration matters.

If you feel that the attorney is incapable of handling the estate or if there is a conflict of interest, select another attorney. Look in the yellow pages of the phone book for attorneys who specialize in estate planning and administration or contact the local bar association for references. A banker or accountant can also be a good reference. It is always a good idea to discuss this matter with the decedent's family and beneficiaries; they may have someone in mind. Do not, however, get talked into using a favorite uncle or family friend who does not have expertise in this area. An attorney whose practice does not include estate administration may also give the engagement a low priority. The attorney may have to devote the same amount of time and attention to the probate as the personal representative. Any delays caused by an attorney will become a problem for the personal representative who is answerable to the decedent's heirs and the court. Remember the personal representative is ultimately responsible for the services provided by the attorney or any other professional who is hired to assist in the administration of the estate.

Meet With the Attorney

Once you select the attorney, arrange an initial meeting to begin planning. If there is a co-personal representative named in the Will that individual should also be present at this meeting. If someone, other than you as the personal representative, is named trustee under the decedent's revocable living trust, that individual should participate in the discussion. Turn over the original Will to the attorney at this time for filing with the probate court. This first meeting should accomplish the following things:

- **Review of the decedent's Will and trust.**

- **Assign duties and responsibilities between the personal representative, attorney and trustee.**

- **Determine the need for special administration.**

- **Determine if there is a need for family and other allowances.**

- **Discuss the surviving spouse's elective right.**

- **Obtain the necessary documents and information to begin the probate process.**

- **Review the initial steps and time frames necessary for administering the estate.**

Review the Decedent's Will and Trust

A summary of the pertinent provisions of the Will and trust should be made. The summary will be helpful when discussing the provisions with the family and as a reference for planning. Specific bequests should be identified and any instructions regarding the payment of administration expenses should be noted. Identify the beneficiaries and determine if the Will is a *"pour over"* Will that names the decedent's trust as the residuary beneficiary. Review the trust to determine if it terminates or continues, if death taxes, debts and funeral expenses are payable from the trust, whether there is a marital and family trust split and whether there are any generation-skipping transfers.

Assign Duties and Responsibilities

At the first meeting, decide what duties and responsibilities you will assume as personal representative and what tasks will be handled by the attorney. The attorney's principal duty is to serve as legal advisor and counselor to the personal representative. The attorney is responsible for drafting all legal documents, representing the estate before the probate court, and advising the personal representative of your duties and responsibilities regarding the administration of the estate.

Some attorneys will file the estate tax returns and fiduciary income tax returns for the estate. Others prefer that an accountant or someone else who has specific expertise in this area handle these responsibilities. There may be legal issues that fall outside the expertise of the estate attorney and he or she may prefer that these matters be referred to attorneys who specialize in those areas. Other duties, such as preparing the inventory, maintaining accounting records, arranging for appraisals, managing the decedent's business interest, etc., can be handled by either the attorney, the accountant, or the personal representative. Remember though, the ultimate responsibility for seeing that these things get done rests with you as the personal representative.

It is very important that you have a clear understanding of who is doing what so nothing "falls between the cracks." A common problem in administering an estate is assuming the attorney has taken responsibility for a particular task while the attorney thinks that the personal representative is handling it. The solution is simple. Make sure that the assignment of responsibilities is clearly understood by everyone involved. The personal representative should keep a written record of these assignments and monitor the progress.

Determine the Need for Special Administration

You may have to take action to protect the decedent's property prior to receiving formal appointment by the court (i.e., issuance of letters testamentary). There may be a need to manage the decedent's business, attend to a bad investment, deal with pending litigation, or manage some other special situation that requires immediate action. You can apply for the appointment of a special administrator within a few days to deal with these matters. The formal appointment of a personal representative can take weeks, and in some cases, several months.

The attorney can help you decide whether special administration is necessary and should file the appropriate petition with the court. Once approved, the court will appoint a special administrator, which may not necessarily be you, and give that individual specific limited authority to deal with the particular issue.

Family and Other Allowances

Most states provide a decedent's surviving spouse and minor children with certain allowances from the estate, which is in addition to what has been provided for them under the decedent's Will or the laws of intestacy. These allowances generally fall into two categories. One is a monetary allowance, called a *family or homestead allowance,* for financial support during the period of administration. The other is a specific dollar value of property, called *exempt property,* which they can receive from the estate. Both types of awards are usually exempt from creditor claims against the decedent and the decedent's spouse. Although these allowances are nominal, you should discuss them with the spouse in terms of eligibility and to make arrangements for payment.

Surviving Spouse's Elective Right

Under the probate statutes in many states, a surviving spouse has the right to receive a specified amount of money or property instead of what has been provided, or not provided, under the decedent's Will. For example, on her death, Mary leaves all her property to her children. Her husband, John, can elect to receive a portion of the property even though Mary excluded him under her Will. This election against the Will, referred to as the *elective share,* is limited to probate assets in some states. In other states the right applies to the decedent's *"augmented estate,"* which includes all of the decedent's property, including trusts, joint assets, insurance policies, retirement plans, etc. It may also include property that the decedent had transferred to others prior to death. In some states, the amount of the elective share increases with the number of years of marriage. As the personal representative, you need to determine the amount and extent of this right and explain it to the surviving spouse who will decide whether or not to make the election. The court will require that a form be completed or that a petition be filed to exercise the election. In some states, a written declination is also required if the surviving spouse does not wish to take the elective share. Consideration should also be given to the tax and estate planning implications of making the election. For example, property received by a surviving spouse as a result of the election will normally qualify for the marital deduction unless it is a terminable interest. *Dower* and *curtesy* rights (i.e., the elective rights given to a wife in some states—dower, and the rights given to a husband—curtesy) are terminable interests that would not qualify for the marital deduction. If the elective share is a dower or curtesy interest, it may generate additional estate taxes in the decedent's estate. The surviving spouse should be advised to seek counsel before making this election.

Obtaining the Necessary Documents and Information for Settling the Estate

After finding the Will, the personal representative and/or attorney should collect the information necessary to begin the probate process as soon as possible. Information can be obtained from the decedent's family, friends, and personal records and should include the following:

- **Decedent's Social Security number.**

- **Decedent's home address.**

- **Decedent's date of birth.**

- **Decedent's date of death.**

- **Names, addresses, telephone numbers, and relationship of all beneficiaries named under the decedent's Will or heirs-at-law if there is no Will.**

- **Birth dates for all minor children.**

- **Birth dates of other individuals whose inheritance is contingent on the attainment of a specified age.**

- **Names and addresses of all witnesses to the Will.**

- **Preliminary list of assets that will be subject to probate (i.e., assets in the decedent's own name) and an estimate of their value.**

- **Preliminary list of non-probate assets (i. e., jointly owned property, trusts, IRA, pension and profit shar-**

ing plans, etc.), the names and addresses of co-owners and beneficiaries, and an estimate of their value.

- Preliminary list of life insurance policies owned by the decedent, their face value, and the beneficiaries named in the policies.

- Preliminary list of known debts of the decedent, including mortgages and other encumbrances on the decedent's real property, outstanding bills, credit cards, notes, etc., the amount owed, and account numbers.

- Copy of any trusts, including all amendments, which were created by the decedent, or that the decedent was a beneficiary of, the name and address of the trustee(s), and a list of the trusts assets and estimated value.

- Copy of deeds, leases, contracts, etc.

- Copy of pension, profit sharing, 401(k), IRA and other employee benefit plan documents.

- 3 years of income tax returns.

- Last gift tax return filed, if any. (i.e., if the decedent made gifts in excess of the annual exclusion amount of $10,000, or $20,000 for a married couple, in any one year, a gift tax return, Form 709, was required to be filed.)

Considerable effort could be involved in locating the decedent's heirs. Obviously, the first source should be family members and friends. If that fails, you should make a thorough search of the decedent's records, correspondence, address book, miscellaneous notes, etc.

If an address cannot be found among the decedent's records, you can publish a legal notice in a newspaper where the heir was last known to reside. You can also contact the county department of records or office of vital statistics for an address. Another good source is the Social Security Administration. Although they will not give you an address or phone number, the administration will contact the individual and ask him or her to contact you as the personal representative. As a last resort you can hire a professional to locate the missing heir. There are several companies across the country that provide this service. Most will not charge a fee unless the heir is found. The decision to hire a professional search firm should be based on the amount of the inheritance. While there is no common formula for making this determination, obviously the estimated cost of locating the heir should not exceed the value of the inheritance. Once an address is found, write a letter notifying the individual of the decedent's death. The letter should describe the interest the individual has in the decedent's estate and include a current address and telephone number where the personal representative can be contacted.

Reviewing the Initial Steps Necessary for Administering the Estate

The personal representative has the responsibility to locate and take possession of all assets that belong to the estate, pay all debts and expenses, distribute the assets to the beneficiaries that are legally entitled to receive them, and account to the beneficiaries and the court for these actions. This requires planning, both before the personal representative's formal appointment and throughout the entire administration. Careful planning will avoid delays and costly administration errors.

During the initial meeting with the attorney for the estate some key issues need to be discussed in preparation for the administration of the estate:

- **HIRING OF AN ACCOUNTANT, INVESTMENT ADVISOR, BANKER, APPRAISERS, BUSINESS AGENT, REALTOR, ETC.—** Although the personal representative may be able to handle many of the administrative tasks alone, you should obtain professional assistance where needed. Be mindful that you are responsible to the creditors and beneficiaries of the estate for any errors that occur, intentional or unintentional. The estate attorney can be a good source for recommending other professionals to assist in the administration of the estate.

- **OUTLINE KEY DUE DATES**—It is extremely important to anticipate and meet the various deadlines imposed on the estate. First set a target date for final distribution of the estate. Although this is a rough estimate, the target date gives you a point from which other estimates can be made. Establish estimated target dates for other aspects of administration, determine deadlines and a reasonable time frame for completing each phase. In the absence of target dates, the tendency is to focus on the most pressing problems first which, in turn, may cause delays in other phases of the administration. Setting target dates and identifying deadlines will keep the administration of the estate on track.

  Failure to perform the various administrative functions on time can be costly to the estate. Some of the dates that should be included in the plan for administration are:

EVENT	DUE DATE
1) Court hearing dates.	Set by the judge having jurisdiction over the probate proceeding.
2) Filing the inventory of probate assets.	Depends on state law; usually 30 days from the date of death.

3) Expiration of the Notice to Creditors.*	Depends on the law of each state, but usually 120 days after publishing first notice.
4) Alternate valuation date.**	6 months from the date of death.
5) Filing of the Federal Estate Tax Return.	9 months from the date of death.
6) Filing the decedent's final income tax returns.	April 15, following the year of death.
7) Filing the Fiduciary Income Tax Returns for the estate.	3½ months after end of selected tax year.
8) Period for IRS to respond to request for early determination of estate tax.***	9 months from the date the request is filed.

*The Notice to Creditors is a public notice that invites creditors to make claims against the estate for debts owed. Upon expiration of the notice, creditors are usually barred from making future claims.

**This is a provision under the Internal Revenue Code that allows the estate to use an alternate valuation date that could potentially reduce the estate tax liability.

***A personal representative may be held personally liable for additional estate taxes assessed against the estate. An early determination of the tax by the IRS protects against this possibility.

- REVIEW ISSUES THAT WILL REQUIRE SPECIAL ATTENTION—
  A Will contest can be disruptive to the administration
  of the estate. Although this is a legal issue that will be
  decided by the courts or settled among the disputing
  parties, as personal representative you may have to take
  a position on behalf of the estate. Pending or threat-
  ened litigation involving the estate may require hiring
  an attorney and deciding on a strategy to protect estate
  assets. If no one was designated to manage the decedent's business, you may need to decide on continuing
  the business or prepare it for liquidation. You should
  discuss these issues with the attorney for the estate and
  decide how they will be handled.

Meet With the Family

A meeting should be held with family members and other beneficiaries. If possible, the meeting with the attorney should take
place first so that the plan of administration can be discussed with
the heirs. The meeting should be attended by the estate's attorney
and trustee, if other than the personal representative. The meeting
should have several purposes:

- **To review the terms of the Will and trust.**

- **To explain the functions of the attorney, personal
  representative and trustee.**

- **To describe the steps that need to be taken to settle
  the estate.**

- **To outline the timetable for administration.**

- **To obtain information from family members.**

The heirs will want to know what Uncle Joe left them. One
of the first items on the agenda should be a "reading of the will"
by the attorney or personal representative. All bequests under the

Will should be described as well as the dispositive provisions of the decedent's trust. The decedent's Will may also contain *precatory* language (i.e., words or phrases in a Will or trust expressing that something be done, but not directing that it be done) that expresses the decedent's desires. These expressions should be paraphrased or read to the heirs. The family, and others who have an interest in the estate, are primarily interested in the terms of the Will. The reading should be thorough and delivered with compassion.

The personal representative and trustee are in charge of the decedent's affairs from the date of death through completion of the administration of the estate. The decedent may not have planned for meeting the immediate financial needs of his family and a determination should be made early in the conversation whether or not a need exists. Funds can be made available from a trust, through a family allowance if allowed under local law, or by obtaining a short-term loan.

This meeting is a good opportunity to gather information. It is important to explain the need for this information because some family members may be reluctant to provide it if they feel it is personal and unnecessary.

The personal representative or attorney should explain all of the legal rights that the heirs have with respect to the estate and/or trust. To the extent that any elections being considered have tax or estate planning implications, they should be discussed with the family members or their financial advisors.

It is important that you as the personal representative describe the process for administering the estate and provide an estimated time frame for completion. If the trust is a terminating trust, provide the heirs with an estimate for final distribution of the trust assets. This is probably of greater importance to the family than other estate matters. Spending the extra time to explain the process will go a long way toward making family members comfortable with your handling of the estate. The more they understand, the more helpful they can be.

Estate Administration Preparation Checklist

✓ Locate the original Will.

✓ Review the Will and trust with the estate's attorney.

✓ Develop a written agreement specifying the responsibilities the attorney, and other professionals will assume, and which duties the personal representative will handle.

✓ Is there a need for special administration?

✓ Determine if a family or homestead allowance is needed.

✓ Obtain declination or request for exercise of the elective share from surviving spouse.

✓ Obtain basic information such as names, addresses, and date of birth of beneficiaries, tax returns, and list of assets, etc.

✓ List and record key due dates.

✓ Meet with the family and attorney to review the provisions of the Will and the trust.

✓ Outline the probate process for the beneficiaries and give them an estimated time frame for completion.

CHAPTER 6

Assembling & Protecting Estate Assets

KEY POINTS

- **Identifying, taking possession of, and protecting, the decedent's property should all be given high priority.**

- **Appropriate steps need to be taken to protect the property during the administration of the estate.**

Assembling and protecting estate assets is one of the most important steps in settling an estate. In addition to locating and accounting for the decedent's property, as personal representative you are responsible for preventing the destruction, deterioration or disappearance of these assets. Even before the formal search has begun, items sometimes have a way of disappearing. A beneficiary, who does not understand the legal process for passing property at death, may take possession of the diamond ring or other valuables that "mother wanted me to have" when those items have been given to someone else under the decedent's Will. Taking possession of tangible assets should be done as soon after the decedent's death as possible to prevent them from getting into the wrong hands.

Where to Look

If you are lucky, the decedent will have left an inventory of the assets he or she owned, making the job of locating them a lot easier. The list may not be up to date, but it is a starting point.

More than likely there will be no list and you will need to begin the search. The best place to start is with the decedent's income tax returns. Here, assets that are associated with income from investments, business interests, rental properties, retirement plans, etc. can be identified. Property tax deductions indicate real estate holdings. Another good source is the decedent's checkbook. Deposits that are made to other bank accounts may be found here in addition to payments for insurance premiums, mortgages, investments, safe deposit boxes, vehicle registration fees, purchase of jewelry and other payments that can be traced to assets owned by the decedent. The decedent's mail is another source. Dividend, interest, rent, retirement and other checks are sources for locating assets. Friends and family members may also be able to help identify assets and their location. Statements covering brokerage, mutual funds and other investment accounts will give detailed descriptions of these assets.

If the decedent had a safe deposit box it should be inventoried. This can be done at the time the box is opened to retrieve the Will. The box may contain an inventory of assets, life insurance policies, stock and bond certificates, promissory notes, jewelry, cash, rare coins and legal documents. Assets located in the safe deposit box are obviously secure and need not be removed immediately.

Searching the Residence

The decedent's home should be searched for valuables such as jewelry, cash, paintings, art objects, etc. The decedent may have these valuables insured separately and an inventory identifying them (i.e., "scheduled property") may be attached to the insurance policy. The personal representative should take possession of these items immediately for safekeeping. Once the valuables have been safeguarded and the decedent's documents and other financial records have been collected the residence should be secured.

Protecting the Property

As personal representative you are responsible for the decedent's property and charged with preventing any destruction or deterioration of the assets. As mentioned at the beginning of *Chapter 5 Preparing for the Administration of the Estate*, this process needs to begin even before the personal representative is formally appointed. Tangible personal property, particularly jewelry and valuable artifacts, can be intentionally, or unintentionally "misplaced." Other steps that need to be taken include:

- **SECURING THE RESIDENCE.** The locks should be changed immediately, unless there is a responsible person, such as a relative or close family friend, who can occupy the decedent's residence and protect its contents. This is to make sure that no one with keys obtained from the decedent can gain access. In some cases, it may be necessary to hire a guard service to protect the property until other security arrangements can be made. If the home is a condominium or apartment, a resident manager might be able to assist in keeping an eye on things.

- **SAFEGUARDING PERSONAL ITEMS.** Consider renting a safe deposit box registered in the name of the estate to store small portable items such as jewelry. Take possession of other valuables and secure them in an appropriate storage facility until they are distributed to the beneficiaries.

- **PROTECTING AUTOMOBILES.** If the decedent's automobile was jointly owned, the surviving owner can have full possession and use immediately after the death. If owned by the decedent individually, it should be locked in the decedent's garage or secured in a storage facility until it can be legally transferred to a beneficiary or sold.

- **CHANGE THE MAILING ADDRESS.** The mailing address of the decedent should be changed immediately to that of the personal representative. Statements and other correspondence received in the mail will help you get a handle on the decedent's affairs. Checks representing income to the estate should be deposited to a separate bank account in the name of the estate.

- **GET AUTHORITY OVER BANK AND BROKERAGE ACCOUNTS.** Technically a personal representative must have letters testamentary from the probate court in order to exercise legal control over accounts that a decedent has with financial institutions. However, once these accounts have been identified you should notify the financial institutions that you will have authority over those accounts as soon as letters testamentary have been issued. If necessary you can obtain special letters of administration if something needs to be done immediately. All accounts should be re-registered in the name of the estate as follows:

  "Estate of (Name of the decedent), deceased, (Name of the personal representative), personal representative".

  All new accounts established for the estate should also be registered this way.

- **MAKE SURE THAT REAL ESTATE AND OTHER VALUABLE ASSETS ARE ADEQUATELY INSURED.** Contact the decedent's insurance agent and review the insurance coverage on all assets. As personal representative, you will be held responsible for any losses on assets not adequately covered. Pay particular attention to the coverage on real estate and valuable personal property such as jewelry and paintings.

- **EVALUATE SECURITIES AND OTHER FINANCIAL ASSETS.** Retain a professional investment adviser to help you review the decedent's financial assets and identify any securities that need to be sold to protect the estate. The review should also identify assets that are candidates for liquidation to pay debts and meet the other cash needs of the estate.

Managing the Decedent's Business

If the decedent owned a business, you should take whatever steps necessary to continue the business until it is sold or distributed to the beneficiary(ies) in order to protect its value. The decedent's partner, employee(s), family member or someone who has expertise in the field, may handle management of the business. In either case the personal representative should oversee the management of the business until it is sold or distributed. Depending on the nature of the business, you may need to hire a professional, such as an accountant, to help you monitor the operation. (*See Chapter 7 Administering the Estate—Managing the Property.*)

Checklist for Assembling & Protecting Estate Assets

SEARCHING FOR ASSETS:

✓ Review the decedent's tax returns.

✓ Review the decedent's checkbook.

✓ Inventory the safe deposit box.

✓ Review the decedent's mail. Look for account statements and correspondence that identify other assets.

✓ Conduct a search of the decedent's residence for personal records.

✓ Ask family and friends of the decedent about any assets that they know of that were owned by the decedent.

PROTECTING ASSETS:

✓ Change the locks on the decedent's residence.

✓ Collect and put in safekeeping all valuable personal items, such as jewelry, paintings, artifacts, etc.

✓ Secure automobiles in a garage or storage facility.

✓ Change mailing address to that of the personal representative.

✓ Re-register all banks, brokerage and other financial accounts into the name of the estate.

✓ Make sure that all assets are adequately insured.

✓ Evaluate the securities portfolio.

✓ Arrange for the continued management of the decedent's business or other enterprise.

CHAPTER 7

Administering the Estate

Inventory and Appraisals

KEY POINTS

- An inventory needs to be made of all assets owned by the decedent in his or her individual name. These are the assets that may be subject to probate.

- An inventory must also be made of the decedent's other assets such as jointly owned property and property subject to a contract. These assets must be accounted for and reported on the decedent's estate tax return.

- All of the decedent's assets must be valued as of the decedent's date of death.

- Penalties may be imposed by the IRS for assets that have been substantially undervalued.

The basis for the probate proceeding is that list that you have made of all assets that were in the decedent's individual name. This inventory may have to be filed with the probate court. In addition to the items mentioned in *Chapter 4 Estate Transfer Procedures,* other probate assets may include things such as installment sales contracts, powers of appointment, tax and other refund claims, insurance policies on the life of others, accounts receivable, social security benefits, veterans administration benefits, etc. Include unregistered personal property, such as jewelry, paintings, stamp collections, etc.

Joint tenancy and tenancy by the entirety property (see *Chapter 3 How Property Passes at Death—Jointly Owned Property*), while not subject to probate, must be inventoried for estate taxes. Other non-probate assets such as life insurance, retirement plans, IRAs, revocable living trusts, and property subject to a contract must be inventoried for estate taxes. While not part of the probate proceeding in the decedent's state of domicile, real property titled in the decedent's own name in other states must be accounted for as well. This property may be subject to an ancillary probate proceeding in the state in which it is located.

The descriptions on the inventory should be fairly specific. For each parcel, the real property description should include the property's address, land area, tax, city, county, state or other identification reference number, an indication of whether or not the property is improved or unimproved, a listing of all encumbrances and the date of death value. All lien holders should be described along with the nature of the lien and the amount that was owed at the decedent's date of death. Record the year, make, model and vehicle identification number for all automobiles owned by the decedent. For all checking, savings, brokerage and other accounts owned by the decedent, list the name of the institution, account number and date of death balance. Describe securities by the name of the company, number of shares owned and date of death value.

If the estate files a *Federal Estate Tax Return* (Form 706), it will be helpful to categorize the assets on the inventory in accordance with the asset schedules on the return:

Schedule A—Real Estate
Schedule B—Stocks and Bonds
Schedule C—Mortgages, Notes and Cash
Schedule D—Insurance on the Decedent's Life

Schedule E—Jointly Owned Property
Schedule F—Other Miscellaneous Property
Schedule G—Transfers During Decedent's Life
Schedule H—Powers of Appointment
Schedule I—Annuities

Valuation of assets

All of the decedent's assets must be valued at their *"fair market value"* on the decedent's date of death. The Internal Revenue Service generally defines *"fair market value"* as *"the price at which the property would change hands between a willing buyer and a willing seller, neither being under any compulsion to buy or to sell and both having reasonable knowledge of relevant facts..."* Where an organized market exists, such as the New York Stock Exchange, the market price on the decedent's date of death is the value for estate tax purposes. Valuations are based on a hypothetical sale where there is no actual sale in the market place. Valuation of some types of assets, such as a closely held business or a parcel of real estate, can be complex. Although formal appraisals are not required by law, the personal representative is responsible for substantiating all reported values. A personal representative should always obtain an appraisal by a qualified expert for assets that are difficult to value or whose value may be challenged by the IRS. Not all property needs to be appraised professionally. The rules for valuing specific types of property are straightforward and covered by IRS regulations:

TYPE OF PROPERTY	REQUIRED METHOD OF VALUATION
Bank Accounts	Account balance on the date of death.
Stocks and Bonds	The average (i.e., arithmetic mean) between the high and low trade price on the date of death.
Mutual Funds	The amount that would be received if the shares were redeemed on the date

of death (i.e., "bid" price or redemption value).

Real Estate	Fair market value
Tenants by the Entirety (husband and wife)	One-half of the fair market value
Joint Tenancy (other than spouse)	Entire value of the property less the original contribution of the survivor.
Life Insurance	Amount received by the estate (owned by decedent or by the beneficiary. on his/her life)
Life Insurance on Someone Else's Life	The cost of buying another policy, of the same value and same type on the (owned by decedent) same insured.
Annuity (joint & survivor contract)	The amount which the same insurance company would require for a single life annuity on the survivor.
Stocks of a Closely Held Company	Value is based on history and nature of business, economic outlook, book value, earnings capacity, dividend paying capacity, goodwill, recent sales of stock and similar publicly traded company's stock.
Mortgages and Notes	The amount of the unpaid principal plus accrued interest.

As personal representative, you should be aware that the IRS will assess a penalty for any asset that is substantially understated on the estate tax return (Form 706). Substantial understatement is a value that is fifty percent (50%) less than the amount determined to be the correct value.

Inventory and Appraisal Checklist

INVENTORY:

✓ Prepare an inventory of all assets owned by the decedent individually.

✓ Inventory all jointly owned property.

✓ Inventory all property subject to a contract.

APPRAISING THE PROPERTY:

✓ Value all assets as of the decedent's date of death.

✓ Follow the rules for valuing property prescribed by the IRS.

✓ Obtain professional appraisals for real property, business interests and other difficult-to-value assets.

Managing the Property

KEY POINTS

- A personal representative's primary responsibility is to preserve and protect estate assets until they are distributed to the decedent's heirs.

- It is not the personal representative's job to invest estate funds for the purpose of maximizing the heir's inheritance.

A personal representative is a temporary administrator whose responsibilities are limited in duration. They include collecting the decedent's assets, paying debts and distributing what is left to the heirs. Ordinarily the personal representative is not responsible for managing the decedent's portfolio during the period of administration, except for the temporary investment of cash. However, the personal representative does have the responsibility to preserve the assets for the beneficiary(ies) of the estate. Essentially this means that you must exercise reasonable care and skill to prevent any substantial loss to the estate from occurring. As personal representative, you will be judged by how you carry out the responsibilities in settling the estate and not on any measure of investment performance.

Securities portfolio

Contrary to popular belief, the personal representative is not responsible for "making money" for the estate and its beneficiaries. In addition to selling a security to raise cash, an investment should only be sold if it is apparent that it will lose substantial value if retained. If you are aware that a particular security will substantially diminish in value if held until it is distributed, as personal representative, you have a duty to sell it to prevent the loss. This is obviously a judgment call that requires careful analysis. In situations where the information about the investment is widely known and suggests that some kind of action should be taken, you should take whatever steps necessary to protect the estate against a loss. Sell a security in a situation where the probability of incurring a substantial loss is high. Again, the primary duty is to preserve what is there. Decisions regarding the management of the securities portfolio should be motivated entirely by the need to protect these assets.

Business interests

If the decedent owned a business, the personal representative has a responsibility to dispose of it unless the decedent's Will directs that the business be continued. As personal representative, you can be held liable for any losses that occur if the business is managed for retention without authorization. However, you do have a responsibility to protect the business by managing it until it is sold or distributed. If you do not have the skills to properly manage the business, hire someone with the right expertise. Review the financial statements of the business periodically or have a professional evaluate the operations and advise you of the financial condition of the enterprise. If the estate owns the majority, or all, of the outstanding shares of the company's stock, you should, as personal representative, get a seat on the board of directors, and/or be elected a corporate officer of the company, in order to maintain control of the business until it is sold or distributed to the heirs.

Real estate

The decedent may have owned residential or commercial real estate for investment. As with any other asset, the personal representative is responsible to preserve the value of these assets during the period of administration. This may entail maintaining rental cash flows, paying operating expenses and making repairs to the property. If a real estate agent manages the property, you should monitor the agent's activities including income collections, expenditures and the other functions that are required under the management agreement. An evaluation of current market rent and rates should be made to determine if the rent or lease needs to be adjusted. Again, as with any other estate asset, the personal representative is responsible for preserving and protecting real estate assets.

Investing cash

During the period of administration, income might be collected from a variety of different sources, including dividends, interest, rents, refunds, proceeds from the sale of assets, etc. Deposit these funds in an interest-bearing account. Operating cash (i.e., cash needed to pay day-to-day expenses) should be in a separate interest-bearing checking account. Funds that will not be needed for several months can be invested at higher interest rates in time certificates of deposit at a bank or savings and loan institution. The maturity date of these deposits should obviously coincide with the date the funds will be needed to pay expenses or for distribution to the heirs.

Asset Management Checklist

✓ **Invest all cash receipts in interest-bearing accounts.**

✓ **Sell only those assets that are needed to raise cash or prevent the estate from incurring substantial losses.**

✓ **If you lack the time or expertise to manage the decedent's property, hire a professional to perform the task.**

Cash Requirements

KEY POINTS

- **Determining how much cash will be needed to cover estate expenses should be given a high priority.**

- **Once the cash needs have been determined, the funds should be raised as soon as possible. Speculating on when to sell an estate asset to raise cash is dangerous.**

As personal representative, you must determine the cash needs of the estate at the earliest possible opportunity and decide what assets are to be sold to raise the needed funds. Debts, court costs, taxes, administration expenses, family allowance, funeral expenses, etc. will need to be paid on a timely basis. Estimating the cash needs of the estate and determining when the funds will be needed should be a high priority. Prepare a schedule similar to the following to assist you with this task:

	AMOUNT	DATE NEEDED
Funeral Expense	$_____	_____
Family Allowance	_____	_____
Creditors Claims	_____	_____
Mortgages & Liens	_____	_____
Court Costs, Publication Fees, Appraisal Fees & Other Administration Costs	_____	_____
Packing & Shipping Costs	_____	_____
Cash Bequests	_____	_____
Income Taxes	_____	_____
Probate Fees	_____	_____
Estimated Federal Estate & GST Tax	_____	_____
Reserve for Contingencies	_____	_____
TOTAL CASH NEEDS	$_____	

Timing is important. Cash may be needed immediately to cover payments such as the premiums on insurance coverage to protect estate assets. The decedent's spouse and children may also need access to cash through the family allowance if other funds are not available. Expenses such as estate taxes should not be paid until the taxes are due, nine months from the date of death. Estimating the timing of these expenses is important in determining which assets are to be sold and when they should be sold.

Raising the needed cash

A personal representative is authorized to sell estate assets to pay expenses and meet other cash needs either under the terms of the decedent's Will or local law. The typical language under a Will gives the personal representative fairly broad powers including the power to borrow funds:

> *"I authorize and empower my Personal Representative at any time prior to final distribution of my estate, without first selling personal property and without securing the prior approval of any court or judge, to sell and convey all or any part of my estate, real or personal, on such terms as it shall determine, and to borrow money and to mortgage, pledge or otherwise hypothecate to secure the same, any of the said property, in such amounts, at such rates of interest and upon such terms and conditions as it shall determine..."*

Once the cash requirements for the estate have been determined, the personal representative should identify the liquid cash that is available from checking accounts, savings accounts, money market funds, insurance, etc., to pay expenses. Identify assets that need to be liquidated to raise the remaining funds. As personal representative, you have the sole authority to select the assets that you deem appropriate for sale. However, you should consider reviewing the list with the beneficiaries. A beneficiary may have an attachment to a particular asset and may prefer that another asset be selected for sale. A beneficiary may also want to advance the needed funds to the estate instead of having the assets sold. The personal representative should not speculate on the timing of the sale of these assets; they should be liquidated as soon as practical. As an alternative to selling a security immediately, a stop-loss order can be placed with a broker to protect the estate against any downside risk from a drop in price. Other assets may have to be sold at a private sale by sealed bid or auctioned through open competitive bidding. The personal representative can select any method that is reasonable to obtain the best price.

Sale of Assets Checklist

✓ Make a list of all required cash disbursements and indicate the date the cash will be needed.

✓ Identify the assets that are to be sold to raise the needed cash and consider discussing the plan with the estate beneficiaries.

✓ Sell the assets as soon as practical.

Claims and Expenses

KEY POINTS

• Debts incurred prior to death represent claims against the estate.

• Expenses incurred in the administration of the estate are payable out of the estate property.

• If there are insufficient assets in the estate to cover claims and expenses, local law prescribes a priority for payment.

There are basically two categories of estate debts: debts that were incurred by the decedent prior to his or her death, such as credit cards, taxes, medical bills, household bills, etc., and expenses that are incurred in the administration of the decedent's estate. The latter category includes items such as personal representative fees, attorney fees, court costs, appraisal fees, publishing expenses, etc. Under normal circumstances, pay claims and expenses as soon as possible to avoid any late payment charges. However, as personal representative, you may need to postpone payment until you determine that there are sufficient funds to cover the expenses. You also need to determine if the decedent had insurance to cover credit cards, mortgages, consumer loans, medical expenses, etc. If the estate's assets are not sufficient to cover all of the claims and expenses, some creditors may not be entitled to full payment. Every state has established priorities for payment when debts and expenses exceed the estate assets available to pay them. The following is the priority prescribed by law in most states:

1) **Expenses of estate administration, including personal representative and attorney fees, publication expenses, appraisal fees, court costs, etc.;**

2) **Funeral expenses (must be reasonable);**

3) **Family allowance in accordance with local law;**

4) **Federal taxes;**

5) **Expenses of the decedent's last illness;**

6) **State taxes;**

7) **All other general debts and expenses (most claims fall into this category).**

If there is not enough money to pay all of the claims in a particular category, payment is made on a pro-rata basis with the amount available.

Notice to creditors

Local laws give creditors the opportunity to make a claim against an estate for amounts the decedent legitimately owed prior to death. This process takes two forms. One is a "notice to creditors" that is published in a newspaper of general circulation. The other is a direct notification by mail to those creditors who are known to have claims. The published notice to creditors advises unknown creditors of the death of the decedent and gives them the opportunity to submit their claims. It is published with a frequency and time period (i.e., once a week for 3 months, 4 months, etc.) specified under local law. The notice also gives instructions for submitting claims to the personal representative for payment. If unknown claims are received after the notice to creditors has expired, they are forever barred and payment should not be made. However, the beneficiaries may prefer that these claims be satisfied. Under these circumstances, the personal representative should obtain written direction from the beneficiaries to pay the claims.

Payment of claims

Sufficient information should be submitted with all claims so the personal representative can make a reasonable determination as to their legitimacy. The claim should include the name and address of the claimant, the amount owed, the due date, a copy of the bill and any other documentation to support the claim. Both known creditor claims and unknown creditor claims that are submitted within the notice to creditors period should be paid soon after the public notice to creditors has expired. If a claim is made that involves assets that were held as joint tenants with the decedent, an allocation of the expense incurred prior to and after death must be made. The decedent's estate pays the share of the expense that was incurred prior to death. The portion incurred after the decedent's death is the responsibility of the surviving joint owner(s).

If you reject a claim, you should immediately notify the claimant in writing. The claimant may be entitled to sue the estate if the suit is brought within the time period specified under local law. The personal representative usually has the authority to compromise and settle claims against the estate and this should be taken into consideration as an alternative to litigation.

Payment of expenses

Either through the decedent's Will, and/or state law, as personal representative, you have the authority to incur and pay all expenses out of the decedent's property that are incidental to the administration of the estate. These expenses include personal representative fees, attorney's fees, income taxes, estate taxes, real property taxes, appraisers fees, advisor fees, assessments, utility bills, insurance premiums, family allowance, court costs, etc. All of these expenses are expected to be paid in a timely manner. Disbursements for the family allowance should be made as soon as funds become available. Personal representative fees are usually paid just prior to completion of administration. Taxes should be paid only when they are due and not before. This is particularly important with respect to the payment of estate taxes. The tax can be very large and the estate should not lose interest on these funds if paid before the tax is due. Other expenses should be paid within a reasonable time after receipt of the bill and availability of funds.

Checklist for Payment of Claims and Expenses

✓ File a notice to creditors in accordance with local law.

✓ Verify that a claim is legitimate before payment is made.

✓ Generally, unknown claims that are submitted after the notice to creditors has expired should not be paid.

✓ Pay all expenses incurred in the administration of the estate promptly.

✓ If there are insufficient assets in the estate to cover all claims and expenses, refer to local law to determine the priority for payment.

Personal Representative's Fees

> ### KEY POINTS
>
> • **Personal representatives are entitled to charge a fee for their services.**
>
> • **Fees are usually approved by the probate court.**

Personal representatives are entitled to receive reasonable compensation for the services they perform and responsibilities they assume when settling a decedent's estate. The personal representative's fee is an administration expense and a proper charge against the estate. If the personal representative is also the sole beneficiary of the estate, charging a fee is a good way to distribute funds to the personal representative/beneficiary and have it taxed at a lower tax rate. This occurs because the fee is a deductible expense for estate tax purposes. The estate is usually in a higher tax bracket than the personal representative/beneficiary, and the payment of fees can reduce the tax on these amounts. The personal representative's fee is usually set by statute in each state and is often a percentage of the value of the estate assets (See *Appendix I*). Some states allow both a percentage-of-assets fee and a fee based on the income received by the estate. Other states allow the personal representative to receive "reasonable compensation" instead of a percentage. In these states, the fee will depend on local practice and is usually approved by the probate court. It is a good idea to keep time records to substantiate the charges for the court and/or the beneficiaries of the estate. You may also need these records to justify any extraordinary charges for handling unusual tasks during the period of administration.

In most states there are separate statutory provisions for trustees fees and the fees that personal representatives are entitled to charge. If the same person is both the personal representative of the decedent's estate and his or her trustee, fees can usually be charged under both statutory provisions for administering and managing the same property, unless there is an exception in the law.

Tax Returns

KEY POINTS

- The personal representative is responsible for filing a variety of tax returns during the administration of the estate.

- If a personal representative is not appointed, whoever has possession of the decedent's property is responsible for filing the returns. This could be a surviving joint owner or a trustee.

- The principal returns that must be filed are the decedent's final income tax returns, fiduciary income tax returns and, if the decedent's gross estate exceeds the exemption equivalent amount, an estate tax return.

As personal representative, you are responsible for filing tax returns on behalf of the decedent's estate. These include the decedent's final income tax returns, fiduciary income tax returns and the federal and state estate tax returns. This is an important responsibility. Penalties and interest can be incurred for failing to file these returns on a timely basis. The Internal Revenue Service also will hold a fiduciary personally liable for paying the decedent's debts, other than those that have priority over federal taxes (see section on *Claims and Expenses* in this chapter for priorities for payment), before paying federal tax obligations. The IRS Publication 559, "Survivors, Executors, and Administrators" and IRS Publication 950 "Introduction to Estate and Gift Taxes" can assist the personal representative with filing these returns. The publications can be ordered on the Internet at: *www.irs.ustreas.gov.*

If a personal representative has not been appointed because there are no probate assets, the *"executor"* for the purposes of filing these returns is *"any person in actual or constructive possession of any property of the decedent"* (Internal Revenue Code Section 2203). An individual who inherits the decedent's property as a surviving joint owner would have this responsibility under this section of the code, as would the trustee of a trust created by the decedent.

The personal representative will have a number of post-mortem tax planning opportunities when filing these returns and has an obligation to take advantage of them on behalf of the beneficiaries. These are usually very complex planning issues and the personal representative should seek competent advice from a tax attorney, CPA or other professional who specializes in this area.

The personal representative, or person having possession of the decedent's property, should file IRS Form 56, *"Notice Concerning Fiduciary Relationship,"* to inform the IRS of the capacity in which the person, who is representing the decedent's estate, is serving. The IRS will send all tax notices to this person once it receives the form.

The decedent's estate is a separate taxable entity requiring a federal tax identification number. The number is obtained by filing IRS Form SS-4, *"Application for Employer Identification Number."* The form can either be mailed or faxed to the I.R.S. The number can also be obtained by telephone with the requirement that the form be mailed or faxed within 24 hours after the call. This identification number is required for filing the estate's fiduciary income tax returns. The decedent's social security number is used as the identification number for the decedent's final individual income tax returns and the federal estate tax return.

Other IRS forms may need to be filed during the administration of an estate. They include:

FORM NO.	FORM NAME	PURPOSE
1040	U.S. INDIVIDUAL INCOME TAX RETURN	Used to file decedent's final income tax return
1041	U.S. FIDUCIARY INCOME TAX RETURN	To report income received by the decedent's estate
706	UNITED STATES ESTATE TAX RETURN	For reporting & paying the federal estate tax
709	UNITED STATES GIFT (AND GENERATION-SKIPPING TRANSFER) TAX RETURN	For reporting gifts made by the decedent
1310	STATEMENT OF PERSON CLAIMING TAX REFUND DUE A DECEDENT	To collect the decedent's income tax refund
2688	APPLICATION FOR ADDITIONAL EXTENSION OF TIME TO FILE U.S. INDIVIDUAL INCOME TAX RETURN	To obtain an additional extension of time for filing the decedent's income or gift tax returns
2758	APPLICATION FOR EXTENSION OF TIME TO FILE U.S. PARTNERSHIP, FIDUCIARY, & CERTAIN OTHER RETURNS	For extension of time for filing of the fiduciary income tax return for the estate
4768	APPLICATION FOR EXTENSION OF TIME TO FILE U.S. ESTATE TAX RETURN/OR PAY ESTATE TAX	For extension of time to to file the estate tax return
4810	REQUEST FOR PROMPT ASSESSMENT UNDER IRC SECTION 6501	To request an early assessment of the decedent's income or gift taxes
4868	APPLICATION FOR AUTOMATIC EXTENSION	For requesting a 4-month extension to

	OF TIME TO FILE U.S. INDIVIDUAL INCOME TAX RETURN	file the decedent's income or gift tax returns
5495	REQUEST FOR DISCHARGE FROM PERSONAL LIABILITY UNDER IRC SECTION 6905	For requesting an early determination of the tax and discharge from liability for the decedent's income or gift tax return

Decedent's final income tax returns

The personal representative is responsible for filing any tax returns that the decedent would have been required to file if living, including his or her final individual income tax returns. However, the surviving spouse shares this responsibility if a joint return is filed. Filing a joint return with the surviving spouse is an election that the personal representative must make. The following should be taken into consideration before the election is made:

- **Will splitting the income attributable to either spouse lower the tax bracket upon which the income is taxed?**

- **Is there an advantage to utilizing the decedent's medical expenses against the surviving spouse's income, assuming the decedent had not earned substantial offsetting income prior to death?**

- **Is there an advantage to utilizing the decedent's medical expenses against the surviving spouse's income, assuming the decedent had not earned substantial offsetting income prior to death?**

- **Does the decedent have operating losses or a capital loss carryover that can be used against the surviving spouse's income?**

- **Can the surviving spouse pay more than his or her share of the tax due in order to pass more of the estate on to children or other beneficiaries?**

Considerations for filing a separate return include:

- **Is there a reason to avoid joint and several (i.e., individual) liability with the surviving spouse by filing separately?**

- **Is faster response to a request needed for an early determination of the tax and release from liability?**

- **Will filing separately allow better utilization of medical, casualty loss and miscellaneous expense deductions by lowering the threshold amounts at which point these expenses become deductible?**

It may be necessary to file two sets (i.e., federal and state) of income tax returns if the decedent died before filing these returns for the previous year. For example, if the decedent died in March, but had not filed returns for the prior year, income tax returns will have to be filed for that year and the year of death. The decedent's final federal income tax return is due on the day the decedent would have been required to file the return, or on April 15. The decedent's social security number is used as the tax identification number on this return. The personal representative should file Form 5495 with the IRS to request an early determination of the tax and a discharge from personal liability.

Fiduciary income tax returns

The personal representative must file an income tax return for the estate for each year of administration. The estate is a separate taxable entity and, as previously mentioned, must have a separate tax identification number (i.e., employer identification number). In general, beneficiaries of an estate are taxed on any income that is paid out to them during the period of administration. All income that is retained during the estate's tax year is taxed to the estate, which has a separate rate schedule. The tax on estate and trust income is higher than for individuals. For example, taxable income in an estate that exceeds $8,650 is taxed at the maximum federal tax rate of 39.6% (year 2000 rates). For an individual, the maximum rate of 39.6% does not apply until taxable income exceeds $288,350 (year 2000 rates). Since any income in an estate that is not needed to pay estate expenses will ultimately be distributed to the beneficiaries, it almost always makes sense to distribute the excess income to the beneficiaries and avoid having it taxed at the higher rate. This can be done through payment of the family allowance or direct distributions to the beneficiaries.

For example, if an estate had one beneficiary and distributable net income of $20,000, the estate would pay $6,957 in taxes on that income if it were retained in the estate for the estate's taxable year. If the beneficiary has other taxable income of $30,000, files as a single taxpayer and received the entire amount of distributable net income from the estate during the year, the amount of tax on the $20,000 would be $5,600. The additional tax paid for keeping the income in the estate is $1,357. This example was based on year 2000 tax rates:

	KEPT IN ESTATE	DISTRIBUTED TO BENEFICIARY
Taxable income	$20,000	$20,000
Tax	$6,957	$5,600
Savings with Distribution to beneficiary		**$1,357**

In most states, early distributions to a beneficiary cannot be made until the notice to creditors has expired (i.e., during the period that claims can be presented for payment.) Some states may require prior court approval for any distribution. Distributions that are made prior to closing the estate must be authorized under the decedent's Will or local law.

The personal representative can select a tax year other than December 31 for the estate, for example, May 1 to April 30. This can have tax planning advantages; beneficiaries can defer taxes on any unusually high income during the period of administration. Taxes can also be reduced by the timing of the payment of deductible expenses. For example, if deductions exceed the estate's taxable income for any taxable year other than the final year of administration, the excess deductions are lost. However, if these excess deductions are incurred in the final year for the estate, they can be passed out to and deducted by the beneficiaries on their individual income tax returns.

If the administration of the estate goes beyond two taxable years from the decedent's date of death, the personal representative must make estimated tax payments based on the estimated taxable income projected for those years.

65-day rule

A personal representative can elect to treat distributions made within 65 days of the close of the estate's tax year as having been made on the last day of that tax year. For example, if the estate's tax year is December 31, 2000, income can be distributed in the first 65 days of 2001 and reported as if it had been paid in 2000. This rule makes it easier to distribute estate income to beneficiaries and minimizes the income tax liability. The 65-day rule allows the personal representative to determine with certainty if there would be an advantage to distributing the income to low-bracket beneficiaries in any one year.

Federal estate tax return

Generally, if an estate tax return is required, the personal representative or trustee is responsible for filing it. If the value of the decedent's gross estate exceeds the exemption equivalent (see Exemption Equivalent table under "Federal Estate and Gift Taxes" below,) a federal estate tax return is due no later than nine months from the decedent's date of death. The Federal Estate Tax Return, Form 706, can be a very complex return to prepare. A personal representative almost always needs to hire an attorney or CPA who specializes in this area of taxation to complete the return. It is important that the personal representative identify who will prepare the return, set deadlines for gathering information, obtain appraisals and begin the preparation of the return no later than 30 days from the due date of the return to allow for timely completion and filing.

A review of the estate's detailed inventory is the first step in determining whether or not an estate tax return must be filed. The IRS requires that fifty percent of all property that was owned jointly with the decedent's spouse be included in the estate for tax purposes unless the surviving spouse can prove he or she contributed more than fifty percent to the acquisition of the property. That amount is deducted from the total value of the asset and what remains is taxable in the decedent's estate. If the property was owned jointly with someone other than the surviving spouse, one hundred percent (100%) of the value is included. However, if the other owner can prove that he or she contributed to the acquisition of the property, the amount of the original contribution is excluded from the value.

When the value of the gross estate is close to the exemption equivalent, the personal representative should consider filing a return even if it does not appear that a return is required. If you do not file a return and the IRS later determines that the value was incorrect and a return was required, the IRS will assess penalties and interest. The decision to file a return, under these circumstances, should be based on whether or not the estate includes assets that are difficult to appraise, (i.e., real estate and business interests) and whose value could be called into question by the IRS. The personal representative could be held personally liable for the penalty and interest if a return is required and not filed.

The Federal Estate Tax Return is due nine months from the decedent's date of death. This can be extended under certain circumstances. Use the decedent's social security number as the tax identification number on the return. The surviving spouse's social security number cannot be used. If the decedent did not have a social security number, the personal representative must obtain one by filing Form SS-5 with the local Social Security Administration Office. An estimate of the tax should be made as soon as the necessary information is available to allow the personal representative to raise the needed funds. The following work sheet can be used for this purpose:

ESTATE TAX WORKSHEET

Gross Estate	$_____
Less: Administration expenses	(_____)
Debts, taxes and losses	(_____)
Adjusted Gross Estate	_____
Less: Marital deduction	(_____)
Charitable deduction	(_____)
Taxable Estate	_____
Add: Adjusted taxable gifts	_____
Tax Base	_____
Tentative Tax	_____
(calculate from the table below)	
Less: Gift taxes paid	(_____)
Tax before applying credits	_____
Less: Unified Credit	(_____)
Other Credits	(_____)
Net Federal Estate Tax	$_____

DEFINITIONS:

Gross estate = The fair market value as of the decedent's date of death of all property in which the decedent had an interest and which is required to be included in his or her estate.

Adjusted gross estate = The gross estate less allowable funeral expenses, administration expenses, debts, taxes and losses.

Taxable estate = The adjusted gross estate less the allowable marital deduction and/or charitable deduction.

Federal estate tax payable before credits = Determined by adding to the taxable estate any prior taxable gifts made by the decedent and applying the Unified Transfer Tax Rate Schedule to the combined amount. This establishes the tentative tax from which any gift tax that was paid by the decedent is deducted. The result is the estate tax payable before credits.

Net federal estate tax = The tax payable before credits, less the: 1. unified credit, 2. state death tax credit, 3. credit for foreign death taxes paid, 4. credit for tax paid on prior transfers.

FEDERAL ESTATE AND GIFT TAXES
(Unified Transfer Tax Rate Schedule)

IF TAXABLE ESTATE IS OVER	BUT NOT OVER	TENTATIVE TAX IS TAX	PLUS %	ON EXCESS OVER
$0	$10,000	$0	18%	$0
$10,000	$20,000	$1,800	20%	$10,000
$20,000	$40,000	$3,800	22%	$20,000
$40,000	$60,000	$8,200	24%	$40,000
$60,000	$80,000	$13,000	26%	$60,000
$80,000	$100,000	$18,200	28%	$80,000
$100,000	$150,000	$23,800	30%	$100,000
$150,000	$250,000	$38,800	32%	$150,000
$250,000	$500,000	$70,800	34%	$250,000
$500,000	$750,000	$155,800	37%	$500,000
$750,000	$1,000,000	$248,300	39%	$750,000
$1,000,000	$1,250,000	$345,800	41%	$1,000,000
$1,250,000	$1,500,000	$448,300	43%	$1,250,000
$1,500,000	$2,000,000	$555,800	45%	$1,500,000
$2,000,000	$2,500,000	$780,800	49%	$2,000,000
$2,500,000	$3,000,000	$1,025,800	53%	$2,500,000
$3,000,000	$10,000,000	$1,290,800	55%	$3,000,000
$10,000,000	$21,040,000	$5,140,800	60%	$10,000,000
$21,040,000		$11,764,800	55%	$21,040,000

YEAR	UNIFIED CREDIT	EXEMPTION EQUIVALENT
2000	$220,550	$675,000
2001	$220,550	$675,000
2002	$345,800	$1,000,000
2003	$345,800	$1,000,000
2004	$555,800	$1,500,000
2005	$555,800	$1,500,000
2006	$780,800	$2,000,000
2007	$780,800	$2,000,000
2008	$780,800	$2,000,000
2009	$1,455,800	$3,500,000
2010	$0	$0

The personal representative (or trustee) is personally liable for correctly filing the estate tax return and paying any taxes that are due. To get relief from this exposure, the personal representative should make a request to the IRS for an early determination of the estate tax and discharge from personal liability. This is a procedure permitted under Internal Revenue Code Section 2204. The request should be submitted at the same time that the federal estate tax return, Form 706 is filed. The following sample letter can be used for this purpose:

Internal Revenue Service

(Appropriate district office)

Gentlemen:

Subject: Estate of John Doe, deceased

> *In accordance with Section 2204 of the Internal Revenue Code, I request an early determination of the amount of tax due on the subject estate in order to relieve me from personal liability.*
>
> *Please acknowledge receipt of this request by indicating your receipt on the copy of this letter and return it to me in the envelope provided.*

Sincerely,

Personal Representative
Estate of John Doe, deceased

The IRS has nine months from the date the request is received to make a final determination that the amount of the tax reported on the return is correct and the personal representative is no longer liable. If the IRS does not respond within the nine-month period, any additional tax liability will be the responsibility of the beneficiaries and not the personal representative. Take care when making distributions of the estate's assets to beneficiaries prior to receiving the early determination of the tax. As personal representative, you should withhold sufficient funds to cover any potential additional assessments until the early determination has been received from the IRS or the nine-month period has lapsed.

Right of recovery of estate taxes

In general, if a surviving spouse's estate includes a Marital Trust (i.e., Estate Trust, Power of Appointment Trust, QTIP Trust or

Qualified Domestic Trust) that he or she was a beneficiary of, the estate is entitled to recover the estate tax attributable to the trust from the trustee. If the personal representative or trustee does not recover the tax, the amount of the tax will be treated as a gift unless the surviving spouse's Will, or trust, provides that recovery of the tax is not to be made.

Flower bonds

Flower bonds are certain issues of U.S. Treasury Bonds that can be redeemed at their face value to pay federal estate taxes. These bonds pay very low interest and therefore can be purchased at a deep discount relative to their face or par value. If used to pay the tax, the savings is the difference between the discounted purchase price and the face value of the bond. Very few, if any, of these bonds are currently in circulation. They were purchased primarily by individuals who anticipated their death. If purchased just prior to death, the savings could be significant. If held too long this advantage would be eroded by the low interest the bonds pay relative to alternative investments.

State Death or Inheritance Tax Return

All fifty states have some form of estate tax. The majority bases their tax on the Maximum Credit for State Death Taxes claimed on the Federal Estate Tax Return:

MAXIMUM CREDIT FOR STATE DEATH TAXES

IF ADJUSTED TAXABLE ESTATE		CREDIT IS		
Is equal to or more than:	But less than:	Credit amount:	Plus %:	On excess over:
$0	$40,000	$0	None	$0
$40,000	$90,000	$0	0.8%	$40,000
$90,000	$140,000	$400	1.6%	$90,000
$140,000	$240,000	$1,200	2.8%	$140,000
$240,000	$440,000	$3,600	3.2%	$240,000
$440,000	$640,000	$10,000	4.0%	$440,000
$640,000	$840,000	$18,000	4.8%	$640,000
$840,000	$1,040,000	$27,600	5.6%	$840,000
$1,040,000	$1,540,000	$38,800	6.4%	$1,040,000
$1,540,000	$2,040,000	$70,800	7.2%	$1,540,000
$2,040,000	$2,540,000	$106,800	8.0%	$2,040,000
$2,540,000	$3,040,000	$146,800	8.8%	$2,540,000
$3,040,000	$3,540,000	$190,800	9.6%	$3,040,000
$3,540,000	$4,040,000	$238,800	10.4%	$3,540,000
$4,040,000	$5,040,000	$290,800	11.2%	$4,040,000
$5,040,000	$6,040,000	$402,800	12.0%	$5,040,000
$6,040,000	$7,040,000	$522,800	12.8%	$6,040,000
$7,040,000	$8,040,000	$650,800	13.6%	$7,040,000
$8,040,000	$9,040,000	$786,800	14.4%	$8,040,000
$9,040,000	$10,040,000	$930,800	15.2%	$9,040,000
$10,040,000	....	$1,082,800	16.0%	....

The way it works is that the claim that would otherwise be paid as federal estate tax (i.e., the amount of the credit) is paid instead to the state. This is referred to as a *pick-up* tax. Those states that have elected to receive the credit have a form (i.e., return) for this purpose that must be filed with the state's department of taxation. A few states have a separate inheritance tax that is imposed on individuals receiving property from an estate and also require that a return be filed.

Generation-skipping Transfer Tax (GSTT)

Personal representatives and trustees have the responsibility to report all generation-skipping transfers made by the decedent and pay any taxes that may be due. Generation-skipping transfers are those that are made to grandchildren, descendants who are at least two generations younger than the decedent and unrelated persons who are 37½ years or more younger than the decedent. These individuals are called "skip persons." In addition, transfers to trusts in which all interests (i.e., the right to receive income and principal) are held by skip persons are generation-skipping transfers. While all generation-skipping transfers must be reported, only amounts in excess of $1,030,000 (year 2000 GSTT Exemption) are subject to the generation-skipping tax, which is a flat 55% of the amount transferred to the skip person. The tax may be due immediately or sometime in the future, as is the case with transfers through a trust. Transfers that must be reported fall into three general categories:

Direct skip—a transfer, subject to federal gift or estate tax, of a property interest directly to a skip person.

Taxable distribution—a distribution from a trust (during its term) to a skip person.

Taxable termination—the termination of an interest in a trust which results in a distribution to a skip person.

A personal representative is required to file a gift tax return, Form 709, to report all pre-death direct-skip transfers that the decedent made and had not reported. A personal representative is also required to report any generation-skip transfers that occur at the decedent's death under a Will or trust on the estate tax return, Form 706.

Checklist for Filing Tax Returns

✓ Apply for a tax identification number (i.e., employer identification number) using Form SS-4.

✓ Make a list of the returns that need to be filed and their due dates.

✓ Estimate the amounts of the tax as soon as possible so the needed funds can be raised.

✓ Hire a tax attorney or CPA to complete the Fiduciary Income Tax Returns, Estate Tax Return (Form 706,) and State Death or Inheritance Tax Return.

✓ If the value of the estate is close to the exemption equivalent amount, consider filing the Estate Tax Return even though a return may not be required.

✓ At the time the Estate Tax Return is filed, request an early determination of the tax and relief from personal liability from the IRS.

Tax Elections &
Other Postmortem Planning Issues

KEY POINTS

- In settling an estate, making the right tax elections and selecting appropriate planning options can be beneficial. The personal representative has a responsibility to take advantage of these opportunities.

- Significant savings can be achieved through proper analysis and planning. This aspect of estate administration should not be overlooked.

- Tax planning for estates is complex. A personal representative should seek guidance from a CPA or tax attorney.

Personal representatives and trustees have a responsibility to take advantage of tax planning opportunities that will benefit the decedent's heirs. This process can involve lengthy tax analyses. A personal representative must consider the effect several tax elections will have on the estate. They include the allocation of administration expenses, medical expenses and casualty losses, the qualified terminable interest property (QTIP) election, allocation of the generation-skipping tax (GSTT) exemption, the alternate valuation election, the special use valuation, disclaimers and extension of time to pay estate taxes. Other issues that can affect a favorable tax result include making the right choice in handling income in respect of a decedent (IRD) and the qualified domestic trust election (QDOT).

Making the proper tax elections will affect the amount of income and estate taxes beneficiaries will have to pay and ultimately the size of their inheritance. Give great care to carrying out this task. Again, most individual fiduciaries do not have the skill and knowledge to handle this level of analysis. Unless the personal representative or trustee is a tax attorney or CPA, it would be foolish not to hire a professional tax advisor to assist.

Administration expenses, casualty losses and medical expenses

Administration expenses, such as fees paid to attorneys, accountants, appraisers, and the personal representative, can be deducted on either the estate tax return (Form 706) or the fiduciary income tax return (Form 1041). This option also applies to casualty losses. The estate tax will be reduced if these deductions are taken on the estate tax return and correspondingly the income tax liability will be higher. If taken on the income tax returns, the reverse is true. When making the decision as to where these deductions should be taken, consider these issues:

- **The relative estate and income tax brackets. The top fiduciary income tax rate is 39.6% and the effective estate tax rate begins at 37% with a maximum rate of 55%.**

- **The effect the election will have on the marital deduction. If the deduction is taken on the estate's income tax return, it will increase the amount of the marital deduction if a marital deduction formula bequest is used in the Will or trust.**

- **How *trust beneficiaries* are affected by the use of the deductions. These expenses are charges against principal and therefore paid by the remainder beneficiaries. If deducted on the estate's income tax return, this reduces the income tax paid by the estate. Since income taxes are charged against income, the income beneficiaries benefit at the expense of the remaindermen. If the expenses are used to reduce the estate tax, the remaindermen benefit, since estate taxes are charged against principal.**

Medical expenses can also be deducted on the decedent's final individual income tax return (Form 1040) or on the federal estate tax return. Normally, these expenses are deductible in the taxable year in which they were paid. However, medical expenses incurred before death can be deducted on the decedent's final return if paid within one year of the decedent's death. The personal representative should compare the tax savings effect, taking into consideration that medical deductions are limited to the excess over seven and one half percent (7½%) of adjusted gross income on an individual federal income tax return. If the deductions are claimed on the individual income tax return, the personal representative must file a waiver of right to claim the deduction on the estate tax return.

Qualified terminable interest property (QTIP) election

Property that passes to a surviving spouse is deducted from the decedent's adjusted gross estate *(marital deduction)* to determine the amount of federal estate tax. The IRS allows an unlimited marital deduction for property that passes directly to a surviving spouse or is used for the benefit of the surviving spouse. This does not eliminate the estate tax on the marital deduction assets; it simply defers the tax until the death of the surviving spouse. The most common types of qualifying marital deduction, other than direct transfers to a surviving spouse, are payments to a surviving spouse as a beneficiary of a life insurance policy or pension plan, assets that pass to a surviving spouse as a result of owning property jointly, and transfers of qualified terminable interest property (QTIP). QTIP transfers are usually done through a trust. For a trust to qualify for the marital deduction, four requirements must be met:

1) **the property must "pass" from the decedent;**

2) **the surviving spouse must be entitled to an income interest for life;**

3) **no other beneficiary may have any rights in the trust during the surviving spouse's lifetime; and**

4) an irrevocable QTIP election must be made.

The election is made on the estate tax return, which will qualify all or a fraction of the QTIP trust property for the marital deduction. This is done by listing the QTIP property on Schedule M of the estate tax return (Form 706). The advantage of the QTIP trust disposition is that it allows a partial marital deduction election. This permits the personal representative to elect an amount that will result in some tax being paid at the decedent's death, if it will be tax-cost effective to both the decedent's estate and that of the surviving spouse. Again, hiring a CPA to assist with this analysis is wise.

Allocation of the generation-skipping transfer tax (GSTT) exemption

As previously discussed, transfers to grandchildren may be subject to a generation-skipping transfer tax (GSTT). Every individual who transfers property subject to the GSTT is entitled to an exemption of $1,030,000 (year 2000.) The exemption can be allocated during the individual's lifetime or at death. The personal representative or trustee has the responsibility to allocate the GSTT exemption to any property transferred by the decedent to a "skip person." Where transfers are made by the decedent through a trust, the allocation needs to be coordinated with the trustee to allow proper funding of that portion of the trust to which the exemption has been allocated. Ideally, the allocation should be made to those assets that have the highest potential for growth since the appreciation will also be protected from the tax.

The GSTT exemption must be allocated at the time of death and no later than the due date of the Gift and Generation-skipping Tax Return (Form 709) for gifts that were unreported prior to the decedent's death. For transfers made under the decedent's Will or trust, the exemption is required to be allocated no later than the due date for the estate tax return (Form 706). With respect to QTIP trusts that distribute assets to "skip persons" at the death of the surviving spouse, the spouse is considered the transferor of these assets for GSTT purposes, which could "waste" the decedent's exemptions. The personal representative can remedy this by making a *reverse QTIP election* on the decedent's estate tax return which has the effect of treating the decedent as the transferor of the funds instead of the decedent's spouse.

If the personal representative does not make an election, the GSTT exemption is first allocated to direct skips made by the decedent prior to death, then to generation-skipping transfers made at death and finally to trusts created by the decedent that will result in generation-skipping transfers. The allocation of the GSTT exemption to trusts is further discussed in *Chapter 9 Preparing the Trust for Administration—Tax and Other Elections.*

Alternate valuation

A personal representative can elect to use an alternate date for valuing the decedent's assets to determine the federal estate tax. This alternate date is six months from the decedent's death. This election gives relief to estates that experience a decline in value of assets shortly after the decedent's death. If the decline is large enough, the estate could have difficulty paying the tax. The election has the effect of lowering the estate tax by allowing the use of the lower market value upon which the tax is based. Using the lower value for estate taxes also lowers the cost basis on the property inherited by the heirs. If the alternate value is used, the result will be a higher income tax upon sale of these assets at some future date. If property is sold or distributed within six months of the decedent's death, the asset(s) will be valued as of the date of sale or distribution if the alternate (i.e., six month) valuation election is made. The election can only be made if it has the result of reducing the gross estate and estate tax. This is to prevent the use of the election to gain a higher cost basis for the heirs in estates that have little or no estate tax liability. The personal representative may not "pick and choose" the assets for the alternate valuation election. All assets must be valued if the election is made.

Special use valuation

A personal representative can elect to value real property that is used for farming or other trade or business at its current use value rather than at its highest and best use value. For example, if a farm were located in an area that could presently or sometime in the future be used for residential, commercial or industrial development, the highest and best use value would be considerably higher than its current use as a farm. There is a limitation, however. The total value of the property may not be decreased from its fair market value by more than $770,000 (year 2000.) This provision permits a lower value to be used for estate tax purposes and is intended to allow the decedent's family to continue operating the business rather than forcing its sale to pay taxes. To qualify for the special use valuation (Internal Revenue Code Section 2032A) option several conditions must be met:

1) **The decedent must have been a U.S. citizen or resident at the time of his or her death.**

2) **The property must be located in the U.S., passed by the decedent to a "qualified heir" and used for a "qualified use."**

3) **The value of the business (i.e., the real property plus supplies, equipment, etc.) must comprise fifty percent (50%) or more of the decedent's gross estate adjusted by any mortgages or other indebtedness on the property ("adjusted value").**

4) **The real property, by itself, must be twenty-five percent (25%) or more of the adjusted value of the gross estate.**

5) **The property must have been used by the decedent, or a member of his or her family, for a qualified use (i.e., farming or a trade or business) for five of the eight years prior to the death of the decedent.**

6) **The decedent or a member of his or her family must have "materially participated" in the operation of the business for five of the eight years preceding the decedent's death.**

7) The heir(s) must receive a present interest in the property.

8) The personal representative must make the irrevocable election on the Estate Tax Return, Form 706.

9) Anyone with an interest in the property must sign an agreement accepting personal liability for any taxes that may be due as a result of the failure of the property to qualify for the special use valuation.

10) One or more of the decedent's heirs must continue to meet the material participation requirement for at least ten years.

The instructions for the estate tax return, Form 706, contains a checklist for this election that should be used by the personal representative, or the preparer of the return, to ensure that all of the requirements for the election have been met. In making the election, the personal representative needs to take into consideration the effect this option has on other elections and tax planning opportunities:

• Even if there is no tax due in the decedent's estate, the special use valuation election may reduce the estate tax in the surviving spouse's estate. However, the personal representative must be sure that the surviving spouse will meet the material participation test.

• Another election available to a decedent's estate concerns the payment of taxes on a closely held business interest. If the closely held business interest represents more than thirty-five percent (35%) of the decedent's adjusted gross estate, the estate tax attributable to the business can be paid over fourteen years (Internal Revenue Code Section 6166). This tax can also be paid at a favorable interest rate. Making the special use valuation election could disqualify the estate from making use of this option because it may lower the value of the closely held business below 35%. The benefits of each choice must be weighed.

- **If the value of the decedent's incorporated business is thirty five percent (35%) or more of the adjusted gross estate, the IRS allows favorable tax treatment for sale of the company's stock to pay the estate tax (Internal Revenue Code Section 303). The special use valuation election could disqualify this option by reducing the value below the 35% threshold. Again, the personal representative needs to compare the benefits of each option before making the choice.**

Disclaimers

If an heir legally declines his or her inheritance under a Will, trust, life insurance policy or as a survivor on jointly held property, that interest passes to someone else. The use of disclaimers is primarily an estate tax-planning election, but they are also used to correct drafting errors in Wills and trusts and to achieve other dispositive objectives. Someone making a qualified disclaimer of property is deemed to have predeceased the decedent and the property interest passes to the successor in interest under a decedent's Will or trust, by operation of law, under the terms of a contract or under the laws of intestacy. For example, John's Will says that his entire estate is to go to his wife, Mary, if she survives him. If she does not survive John, then his estate is to go to their two children. If Mary disclaims her interest under John's Will, she is deemed to have predeceased John and the children inherit John's estate. A qualified disclaimer removes the ownership of the property from the estate of the person disclaiming the interest, and can reduce the estate tax for the person making the disclaimer. A disclaimer is an irrevocable refusal to receive an interest in property. It must satisfy four requirements to qualify (Internal Revenue Code Section 2518):

1) The refusal must be in writing.

2) It must be received by the appropriate party (i.e., personal representative, trustee or legal representative) within nine months after the date on which the transfer creating the interest (usually the date of death) was made.

3) The person disclaiming the property must not have accepted the interest or any of its benefits prior to making the disclaimer.

4) The interest must pass to someone, other than the disclaimer, without any direction on the part of the disclaimer.

A disclaimer can save taxes in a variety of situations. It can be used to pass property to someone without incurring a gift tax. In the above example, Mary, in effect, has made a tax-free gift to her children by disclaiming her interest under John's Will. Assuming that John's estate is under the exempt amount (i.e., $675,000 in the year 2000) and therefore no estate tax is due, his property would pass tax free to the children. If Mary took her inheritance, then gave it to the children, she would have to pay a gift tax on the amount over the annual gift tax exclusion of $10,000 per child.

Correcting adverse conditions is another use of disclaimers. For example, if the special use valuation would be beneficial to the decedent's estate, but the property does not qualify because it passes to a non-qualified heir, the heir can disclaim the interest and qualify the property to minimize the estate tax. Another example might be where a beneficiary is entitled to income for life from a charitable remainder trust and does not need the income stream. He or she can disclaim the income interest in the trust. This would terminate the trust and accelerate the bequest to the charity. The full value of the property, instead of the discounted remainder interest value, would be deductible in the decedent's estate in determining the federal estate tax.

To maximize sheltering assets from federal estate tax in the estate of the second to die, the family trust should be funded with the exemption equivalent (i.e., $675,000 for year 2000.) Under-funding can occur if most or all of the assets in the decedent's estate are owned jointly. For example, if a decedent had $400,000 in his revocable living trust and the rest of his assets, valued at $700,000, were owned jointly with his wife, his credit shelter trust would be underfunded. In other words, if the exemption equivalent amount is $675,000 (year 2000) the trust would be underfunded by $275,000 ($675,000 less $400,000.) She could disclaim enough of her interest in the joint assets (i.e., $275,000) to fully fund the trust. Those assets would be deemed to be his alone at the time of his death and would pass under his "pour-over" Will to fund the family trust for the full amount of the exemption equivalent.

Disclaimers can also be used to correct drafting errors in Wills and trusts. For example, a marital-deduction trust will not qualify for the marital deduction if it allows either income or principal to be paid to someone other than the decedent's spouse. If a trust, for example, permits distributions to the decedent's children, they could disclaim their interest in the trust to correct the problem and qualify the trust for the marital deduction.

If a surviving spouse is the trustee of a family trust (i.e., "credit shelter" trust) and the trust provides that the surviving spouse can distribute principal to herself in accordance with an "ascertainable standard" (i.e., health, education, maintenance and support,) the trust assets are not subject to estate taxes upon her death. How-ever, if the "ascertainable standard" language is flawed because it contains a disqualifying word, the surviving spouse could disclaim her right to receive a distribution under that word thus correcting the flaw.

A qualified domestic trust (QDOT), discussed below, requires that, if a surviving spouse is a co-trustee, he or she cannot have the power to make principal distributions to himself or herself. If a QDOT gives the co-trustee spouse this power, it can be dis-claimed to qualify the trust and allow deferral of the estate tax until the death of the surviving spouse.

Disclaimers can also be used to terminate a trust. For example, if a beneficiary has an interest in a trust which terminates upon death, he or she can cause an early termination by disclaiming the interest. At that point, the assets would be distributed to the remainder beneficiaries.

Income in respect of a decedent (IRD)

Income earned by a decedent, but not actually or constructively received by the decedent prior to death is called income in respect of a decedent, or IRD. Examples of IRD include unpaid salary, deferred compensation, retirement plan benefits, accrued interest and dividends on securities, royalties, installment obligations and accounts receivable. This income is not reported on the decedent's final income tax return (Form 1040), but instead is reported on the estate income tax return (Form 1041) or the individual income tax return of the beneficiary who receives the IRD. IRD is also included in the decedent's estate for estate taxes, but does not get a step-up in basis as other assets do. However, an offsetting income tax deduction is allowed for the estate tax that is attributable to the inclusion of IRD in the decedent's gross estate.

The personal representative, and trustee, should attempt to distribute IRD to lower tax bracket beneficiaries or to satisfy a charitable bequest. If a trust is involved in the decedent's estate plan, the personal representative could distribute an interest in IRD, before it is received, to the trust. The trust, in turn, could, if the trust permitted, distribute the IRD to multiple beneficiaries who may be in lower tax brackets. The income tax deduction for the estate tax paid on the IRD can be passed through the trust for use by the trust's beneficiaries.

The income tax impact on IRD can be reduced by choosing an appropriate tax year for the estate. If the receipt of IRD is known, you can split the income between two or more tax years. This might result in less tax than if the income was reported in one year. Taxable IRD can also be offset by electing to take deductions on the estate's income tax return instead of the estate tax return.

The taxation of IRD can also be minimized by timing deductible expenses to coincide with the receipt of IRD.

Accrued interest on Series E and EE U.S. Savings Bonds, which is normally reportable upon redemption of the bonds, is IRD. The personal representative can elect to report the accrued interest on the decedent's final income tax return, thereby eliminating it as IRD. If the decedent's final return has a small amount of income and/or large deductions, including this interest on the decedent's final return could significantly reduce the overall tax liability. A comparative analysis of the various options is necessary to determine the right course of action.

Qualified domestic trust (QDOT)

As previously mentioned, the estate tax marital deduction is nothing but a postponement of the estate tax on marital assets. The intent is to have these assets taxed at the death of the surviving spouse. The marital deduction is not allowed if the surviving spouse is not a U.S. citizen. From the government's point of view, if the marital deduction were allowed in this case, the non-U.S. citizen surviving spouse could move back to his or her country and the tax on the marital assets would be difficult, if not impossible, to collect. There are two ways to achieve the marital deduction if the surviving spouse is a non-U.S. citizen:

1) **The deduction will be allowed if the surviving spouse is a resident at all times following the death of the decedent and becomes a citizen before the decedent's estate tax return is filed.**

2) **The deduction is also available if the marital deduction property is transferred to a qualified domestic trust (QDOT) by the decedent's Will or trust or if the QDOT was designated as a beneficiary under property subject to a contract. The surviving spouse can also transfer to the QDOT any property that he/she received as a joint owner or beneficiary, if the transfer is made before the decedent's estate tax return is filed.**

The basic requirements for qualifying a power of appointment trust, QTIP trust and charitable remainder trust for the marital deduction also apply to the QDOT. However, there are other requirements that specifically apply to the QDOT:

1) **The trust must require that at least one trustee be a U.S. citizen or domestic corporation.**

2) **The trust must require that no distributions of principal be made unless the trustee who is a citizen or a domestic corporation has the right to withhold the estate tax on the distribution.**

3) **The personal representative must make the QDOT election on the decedent's estate tax return.**

A partial QDOT election cannot be made. The election is made by listing the QDOT property on Schedule M, Form 706, and providing the name and address of every trustee, a description of each transfer of property to the QDOT and the tax identification number of the QDOT.

Sale of closely held stock

If an estate owns a closely held company, liquidating the stock can have adverse consequences. If a closely held stock is redeemed to pay estate taxes, it will be treated as a dividend and subject to ordinary income tax. However, if the closely held stock represents more than 35% of the adjusted gross estate, less certain allowable deductions, and only enough shares are redeemed to pay estate taxes, funeral and administration expenses, the redemption will not be considered a dividend. This is called a *Section 303 stock redemption*, which is a reference to the Internal Revenue Code section that allows the exclusion (IRC Section 303.) If the redemption represents all of the decedent's holdings, or if after the redemption the estate will own less than 50% of the voting power of the company, the sale will be tax-free. This exception is covered under Section 302 of the code.

Partnerships

If the estate owns a partnership interest, an election (IRC Section 754) can be made on the partnership return that allows the "internal partnership account value" to receive a step-up in basis. This will be advantageous for the individual or trust that receives the partnership interest from the decedent's estate in terms of depreciation and the allocation of future partnership earnings. The "outside ownership value," or the value that is carried by the individual or trust that inherits the partnership interest, is the value (date of death or alternate value) reported on the decedent's estate tax return. If no return is required, then it is the date of death value. This value also is the cost basis to determine gain or loss upon sale of the partnership interest.

Extension of time to pay estate taxes

The federal estate tax is due nine months from the decedent's date of death. However, there are four provisions under the Internal Revenue Code that allow the personal representative to defer the payment, which may be useful if the estate or trust has assets that cannot be easily liquidated:

1. **The personal representative may apply for an extension of twelve months for the amount of cash shortage in the estate to pay the tax. The request may be granted only for a "reasonable cause," as to why the tax cannot be paid when due.**

2. **If the personal representative can show "reasonable cause," an extension of ten years may be granted for the payment of the tax. However, the extension will only be granted for one year at a time. (IRC Section 6161).**

3. **If the decedent's estate is entitled to a reversionary or remainder interest in property, the personal representative can elect to postpone the tax attributable to that interest until six months after the present interest in the property terminates. (IRC Section 6163)**

4. **If the estate owns a closely held business interest (15 or fewer shareholders/partners or 20% or more voting ownership) which represents more than thirty five percent (35%) of the adjusted gross estate, the personal representative can elect to have the tax attributable to that interest paid over fourteen years. The estate can make interest-only payments for the first five years, but must begin making principal payments after that. (IRC Section 6166).**

These elections require a thorough analysis of the interest costs associated with deferring the payment of the tax. For some deferral elections, such as the deferral of tax on a closely held business interest, a special interest rate is available. Other elections assess a higher interest rate. The personal representative may also want to elect for deferral so assets that need to be sold to pay the tax can be liquidated in a timely manner. Obviously, the economic benefit of deferring the sale of assets should be evaluated before any election is made.

Tax Elections Checklist

✓ Determine which tax issues and elections apply to the estate and trust:

• Allocation of administration and medical expenses and casualty losses.

• QTIP election.

• Allocation of the GSTT election.

• Alternate valuation.

• Special use valuation.

• Disclaimers.

• Taxation of IRD.

• QDOT election.

• Section 302 and 303 stock redemption.

• Partnership step-up in basis election.

• Extension of time to pay estate taxes election.

✓ Determine the marginal estate and estate income tax rates.

✓ Obtain the marginal income tax rate of all beneficiaries.

✓ Discuss the elections with a CPA or tax attorney.

✓ Evaluate the cost/benefit of each option.

✓ Discuss the choices with the beneficiaries and/or their financial advisors.

✓ Make the appropriate election.

Accounting for the Administration of the Estate

> **KEY POINTS**
>
> - **The personal representative has a responsibility to keep and maintain accurate records covering the administration of the estate.**
>
> - **The personal representative may be required to file accountings with the probate court.**
>
> - **Estate income must be accounted for separately from estate principal.**
>
> - **Beneficiaries and creditors are entitled to receive a record of all estate transactions.**

The personal representative must maintain and make available to beneficiaries and other interested parties, such as the estate's creditors, a detailed record of all activities pertaining to the administration of the estate. The court may also require an accounting for its approval. Most jurisdictions have a prescribed format for court accountings. Although a court accounting is a matter of public record and available to interested persons, it is primarily prepared for review by the court.

One of the unique characteristics of estate accounting is the need to distinguish income from principal. The decedent's Will and/or state law will determine how the personal representative accounts for and separates the two. Most states have adopted the Uniform Principal and Income Act in one form or another. The purpose of the Act is to standardize the accounting rules for estates and trusts.

The decedent's Will is the first source of authority for how transactions are accounted for. If the Will is silent with respect to how a particular accounting transaction is to be handled, the personal representative should look to state law and the Uniform Principal and Income Act for guidance. Although an individual's Will may have some specific directives on how particular transactions are handled, accounting rules for estates have some common characteristics:

- **All income accrued but not received prior to the decedent's death must be allocated to principal.**

- **For any property specifically bequeathed under a Will (or trust,) net income earned after the will maker's death belongs to the beneficiary. This is true even if the property is not distributed until the estate is settled. Income and expenses that are associated with the property should be accounted for separately from the other estate assets.**

- **Where a sum of money is bequeathed under a Will (i.e., a pecuniary bequest) the beneficiary is not entitled to the income earned during the period of administration. That is, if a bequest of $10,000 is made, the beneficiary gets $10,000, not $10,000 plus interest.**

- **All expenses incurred in connection with the settlement of the estate, including debts, funeral expenses, family allowances, attorneys fees, personal representatives fees, accountants fees, court costs, estate taxes are charges against principal.**

- **Generally, the beneficiary who receives what is left after specific bequests, payment of expenses, etc. (i.e., the *residuary estate,*) is entitled to the income earned during the period of administration.**

- **If a decedent bequeaths his or her residuary estate to a trust, the income earned during the administration**

of the estate is allocated to and becomes attributable to the trust.

Estate accounting covers only those assets that are under the direct control of the personal representative (i.e., probate assets) and all receipts and disbursements in connection with the administration of the estate. Joint assets and property subject to a contract (i.e., life insurance, trust assets, retirement plans, etc.), although inventoried for federal estate tax purposes, are not part of the decedent's probate estate and therefore not included in the estate accounting. The inventory of assets owned by the decedent individually is the basis of the probate estate. It must reflect all changes that take place during the course of administration. The inventory will change as new assets are discovered, property is sold to raise funds to cover expenses and when distributions are made to beneficiaries.

All financial activities that take place during the administration must be reported to the probate court, the estate's beneficiaries and other interested parties. Income and principal transactions are reported separately. In preparing the estate accounting the personal representative should obtain the reporting format required by the probate court that has jurisdiction over the estate. Although the format may differ slightly from state to state, estate accountings do have a common structure. The following is an example of an estate accounting:

ASSETS OF THE ESTATE

	Date of Death Value
Cash:	
Bank of N.Y. – checking account	$ 1,125.25
Citibank – CD	10,000.00
Merrill Lynch – money market	25,000.00
Decedent's cash	152.30
TOTAL	$ 36,277.55
Securities:	
550 shs. America Online	$ 26,675.00
100 shs. Bank of America Corp.	5,400.00
300 shs. Lucent Technologies	16,725.00
250 shs. Pfizer, Inc.	11,281.25
125.16 shs. Fidelity Magellan Fund	15,604.57
$10.000.00 N.Y. City Sewer Imp. Dist.,	
5 ½%, Due 4/15/2015	9,675.00
TOTAL	$ 85,360.82
Real Property:	
123 Chestnut Ave	
Long Island, N.Y.	**$ 675,000.00**
Tangible Personal Property:	
1 diamond ring	$ 3,250.00
1 pearl bracelet	535.00
2 paintings (artist unknown)	150.00
1 antique chair	100.00
TOTAL	$ 4,035.00
TOTAL VALUE OF PROBATE ASSETS	$ 800,673.37

SUMMARY OF RECEIPTS & DISBURSEMENTS

	Principal	Income	Total
Receipts	$ 29,400.00	$ 776.00	$ 30,176.00
Disbursements	17,907.50	726.20	18,633.70
TOTALS	$ 11,492.50	$ 49.80	$ 11,542.30

INCOME RECEIPTS AND DISBURSEMENTS

Date		Receipts	Disbursements
1/24/2000	Dividend – America Online	$ 375.00	
2/15/2000	Dividend – Lucent Technologies	126.00	
4/15/2000	Fiduciary income taxes		$ 126.20
10/15/2000	Interest – N. Y. City Sewer Imp. Dist., 5 ½ %, Due 4/15/2015	275.00	
11/1/2000	Fred Porter – distribution		300.00
	Susan Porter – distribution		300.00
	TOTALS	$ 776.00	$ 726.20

PRINCIPAL RECEIPTS AND DISBURSEMENTS

Date		Receipts	Disbursements
1/15/2000	Withdraw money market fund	$ 10,000.00	
2/16/2000	Bob's Mortuary		$ 1,750.00
2/18/2000	Clerk of the Court – probate fees		92.50
3/5/2000	Henry Swanson – real estate appraisal		65.00
5/16/2000	Sold 400 shs. America Online	19,400.00	
6/25/2000	Julia Morgan – Personal representative fees		16,000.00
	TOTALS	$ 29,400.00	$17,907.50

Consider hiring an accountant who is familiar with the accounting rules for estates to assist in performing this function. It may also be necessary to consult an attorney with regard to a beneficiary's entitlement to income, the allocation of a particular expense to income or principal or any other unusual accounting issue that will affect a beneficiary's interest in the estate. Fees for these services are generally chargeable to principal.

Accounting Checklist

✓ Identify all assets and sources of income that will be subject to probate.

✓ Determine if an estate accounting must be filed with the probate court and obtain the court's required accounting format.

✓ Review the decedent's Will, Uniform Probate Code and Uniform Principal and Income Act in the jurisdiction where the estate is being administered for guidance in maintaining the accounting records.

✓ If necessary, retain a qualified accountant.

✓ Establish a tickler to provide periodic accounting reports to the beneficiaries of the estate.

Distributing Assets

KEY POINTS

• Final distribution of the estate assets should be made only after all expenses and debts have been paid. A partial distribution can be made earlier if the expenses and debts are known and sufficient assets are retained to cover them.

• Different methods can be used to distribute personal items to minimize arguments and assure fairness.

• The terms per capita, per stirpes and per capita at each generation in a Will define how property passes if a beneficiary does not survive the decedent.

> • **A personal representative will not be discharged until all administration responsibilities have been completed and the remaining estate assets have been distributed to the beneficiaries.**

Estate assets can and should be distributed to the decedent's beneficiaries as soon as estate expenses have been paid. However, if there is the possibility of additional taxes as a result of an audit of the estate tax return, you should withhold sufficient funds to cover the estimated assessment. The reason for this should be obvious. If there is an additional estate tax and the personal representative cannot collect the tax due from the beneficiaries he or she is personally liable for the tax. As mentioned earlier, a request for early determination of the tax should be made at the time the federal estate tax return is filed. If the Internal Revenue Service does not respond within nine months from the date of the request, the personal representative is relieved of personal liability. Make partial distributions before the clearance is received if it is unlikely there will be an additional tax, but retain sufficient assets to cover unpaid expenses.

Non-probate assets, such as jointly owned property, insurance proceeds, trust assets, retirement plan proceeds, etc. pass by the terms of the contract or by operation of law. If they are not subject to creditor claims and not needed to cover debts, administration expenses and taxes, they should be allowed to pass to the surviving owner(s) or beneficiary(ies). Personal effects and certain specific bequests can also be distributed shortly after death if they will not be needed to pay expenses.

Joint assets

Joint assets must be valued for estate tax purposes. Once this is done, the personal representative should assist the surviving owner(s) to transfer the asset into the name(s) of the new owner(s). The property should be re-titled so the survivors can sell or otherwise take full control of the property. Present a certified copy of the death certificate to the bank, brokerage firm or other financial institution where the account is located. If the property is shares of stocks and bonds, the death certificate is sent to the transfer agent for the company that issued the stock or bond along with the certificate. Real property is transferred to the surviving joint owner(s) by recording a certified copy of the death certificate with the local real property recordation office.

Contract property

If the decedent's estate is named as a beneficiary under a contract, the personal representative is responsible for making the claim. The role of the personal representative, if someone other than the estate is named, is to inform the beneficiary that he or she is the beneficiary and, if needed, assist with making the claim. To make claims on life insurance policies, the beneficiary needs to obtain and complete a claim form from the insurance company that issued the policy. Every insurance company has its own form and will usually require that the insurance policy and a certified copy of the death certificate accompany the completed form when the claim is submitted. It is a good idea to submit it by registered or certified mail. Keep a copy of the claim form. Other types of property subject to a contract, such as retirement plans, may also require a claim form and a certified copy of the death certificate. The beneficiary should contact the plan administrator for the forms and claim procedures. You may need to evaluate several payment options under a retirement plan. A beneficiary should consult with a tax advisor before selecting an option and making the claim.

Personal effects

As a practical matter, unless otherwise specified in the decedent's Will, household items are considered the property of the surviving spouse or other joint owner of the decedent's residence. However, a decedent's Will usually provides for the disposition of this property. The following is a typical Will provision covering personal property:

"I give all my personal and household effects such as jewelry, clothing, automobiles, furniture, furnishings, silver, books, pic-

tures and any insurance on such property, to my wife, if she survives me, or if she does not survive, I give my tangible personal property to my children who survive me in equal shares as they shall agree, or if they do not agree as my personal representative shall in my personal representative's discretion determine."

Distributing personal property to the decedent's surviving spouse under the above dispositive language is a non-event since she would already have possession. Valuable items, however, do need to be inventoried for tax purposes. In the event that the spouse does not survive, the above language calls for distributing the decedent's personal property to the children in equal shares as they agree. Distributing assets this way does not usually present any problems. The personal representative can minimize disagreements and assure fairness by handling the distribution using the following methods:

- **PICK AND CHOOSE.** Under the above provision the children are given the right (i.e., "as they shall agree") to pick and choose the assets they want. Even without this specific direction they should be allowed to select the items they want. The value of the items selected should be tallied and adjustments made to the share of each beneficiary so that each receives an equal value.

- **AUCTION.** The pick and choose method works only if all of the beneficiaries agree on who gets what. If the items have substantial value, or if there is disagreement, the personal property can be auctioned among the beneficiaries. The highest bidder would receive the item and the bid amount would be deducted from that beneficiary's inheritance.

- **SALE.** The items that have not been selected should be sold and the proceeds distributed in equal shares to each beneficiary.

Unwanted items (i.e., property with little or no value) can be donated to a charity or given away to friends of the family by the surviving spouse, the children, a family friend or by the personal representative.

Specific bequests

A decedent's Will may direct that an individual or charity be given a particular item or a specified dollar amount. These are referred to as specific bequests. Examples:

"I give, devise, and bequeath to my daughter, Sally, my 15 carat diamond engagement ring."

"I give my son, John, $25,000.00."

"I give $100,000 to the University of Pennsylvania to provide scholarship assistance for deserving young men and women as the University shall determine in their discretion."

Unless the specific bequest is needed to pay debts, administration expenses and taxes, distribute it to the beneficiaries as soon as practical. If the specific bequest asset is income producing, such as a rented apartment or stock paying a dividend, the beneficiary is entitled to all of the income attributable to the asset from the decedent's date of death. If the bequest is a specific dollar amount, called a pecuniary bequest, the personal representative may have the option to satisfy the bequest by making a distribution in kind (i.e., distributing property). However, the property must have a value equal to the dollar amount of the bequest at the time the distribution is made. Income earned during the period of administration on the amount of the pecuniary bequest is not payable to the beneficiary.

The residuary estate

The property that remains after distributing specific bequests, paying estate debts, administration expenses and taxes, is referred to as the *residuary estate*. The decedent's Will may instruct that the residuary estate be distributed to a single individual, several individuals, a trust or to one or more charitable organizations. The beneficiaries of the residuary estate may receive a specific dollar amount, a percentage of the residue or a combination of the two. The decedent's Will may also direct that distribution of the residuary estate be made *per capita, per stirpes* or *per capita at each generation.* These are terms that define how property passes if one or more named beneficiaries does not survive the decedent. The personal representative must understand these terms to assure that the decedent's property is distributed to the right persons and in the right amounts:

PER CAPITA. A per capita provision in a decedent's Will distributes property equally to all beneficiaries living at the time of the decedent's death, share and share alike. This means that the surviving descendants will inherit equally, regardless of their generation. For example, let's assume that a decedent had three children, John, Sally and Fred. John had one child (Kerry); Sally had two children (Ron and Mary) and Fred had three children (Judy, Mike and Ruth). If Sally predeceased her decedent father, John, Fred and Sally's two children (Ron and Mary) would receive an equal share of the estate.

PER CAPITA

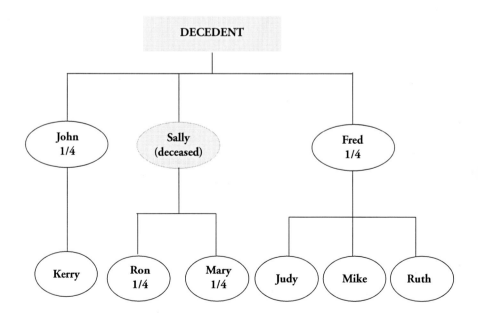

PER STIRPES. A per stirpes provision first divides property among the first generation beneficiaries (i.e., children of the decedent) with a deceased child's share passing to that child's children (i.e., the decedent's grandchildren) and so on down the line. In other words the property passes along blood lines in each generation by right of representation. Using the above example, Sally's share, under a per stirpes provision, would pass to her two children, Ron and Mary, each receiving half of Sally's one-third share, or one-sixth share each.

PER STIRPES

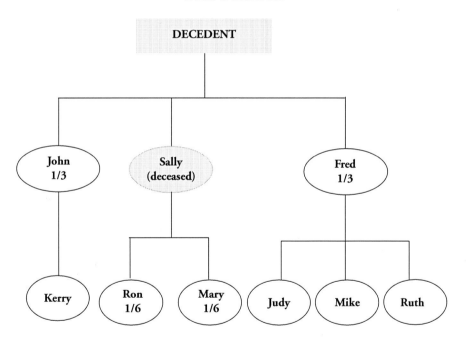

PER CAPITA AT EACH GENERATION. A per capita at each generation provision requires that grandchildren whose parents have predeceased the decedent share equally among surviving grandchildren instead of taking their deceased parent's share. If a Will is silent, local law may require this method of succession. Let's assume that John and Sally did not survive their deceased parent. Under this scenario John and Sally's combined two-thirds share will be split equally among their children, each receiving a two-ninths share.

PER CAPITA AT EACH GENERATION

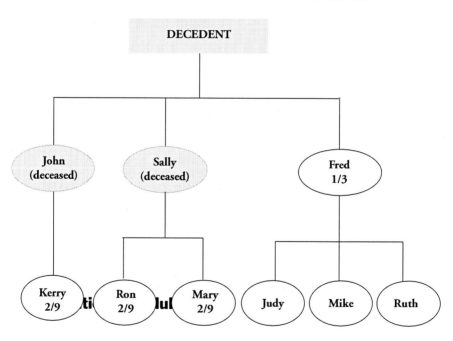

Figuring out which beneficiaries get what assets, especially if the beneficiaries have preferences for certain assets, can be confusing, if not approached in a methodical way. Preparing a distribution schedule will make it easier and minimize errors. The schedule should describe the specific assets to be distributed. Discuss the schedule with the beneficiaries before finalizing. The schedule helps to organize the plan and, if permitted, gives the beneficiaries the opportunity to request certain assets over others. The distribution schedule should describe the specific assets that each beneficiary will receive, show the adjustments for partial distributions, distributions of personal property, cash distributions and reflect the net value of each beneficiary's inheritance:

DISTRIBUTION SCHEDULE

	Total Value	Bill Doe 1/3 share	Jane Doe 1/3 share	Harry Doe 1/3 share
25 shs. ABC, Co.	$ 12,520.00	8 shs. $ 4,006.40	8 shs. $ 4,006.40	9 shs. $ 4,507.20
500 shs. XYZ,Co.	80,658.20	167 shs. 26,939.84	167 shs. 26,939.84	166 shs. 26,778.52
	93,178.20	30,946.24	30,946.24	31,285.72
Cash	28,320.60	9,440.20	9,440.20	9,440.20
Personal property	10,230.00	4,750.00	2,730.00	2,750.00
	131,728.80	45,136.44	43,116.44	43,475.92
Cash to equalize		-1,226.84	+793.16	+433.68
	131,728.80	43,909.60	43,909.60	43,909.60
Less: partial distribution	-6,000.00	-1,000.00	-3,000.00	-2,000.00
Total	$125,728.80	$ 42,909.60	$ 40,909.60	$ 41,909.60

The distribution schedule is used to figure out how many shares of stock each beneficiary is to receive and how much of the remaining cash each is to be paid. The cash balance is first allocated in accordance with what each beneficiary is to receive under the Will. Adjustments are then made (additions and subtractions of cash) to equalize the shares. Deduct any partial distributions that were made during the course of administration to arrive at the amount distributable to each beneficiary.

Distributing the property

The personal representative does not usually need authorization to distribute estate property, although some jurisdictions may require approval of the plan for distribution (i.e., the distribution schedule) by the court. Once the assets are ready for distribution (i.e., assets re-titled in the name of the beneficiaries) delivery can proceed. Securities should be delivered in person, by registered mail or through the beneficiaries' bank along with a schedule of the cost bases of the property, which is the value used for estate tax purposes (i.e., date of death or alternate value). If an estate tax return was not required, the cost basis is the date of death value. Most banks will arrange for their customers to receive assets from an estate upon request by the personal representative. If a beneficiary lives out of state or in a foreign country, this is a way to assure that the property is delivered to the right person and that the estate receipt will be signed and returned. The personal representative should obtain a receipt and release from each beneficiary, which should be prepared by an attorney. The following is an example of a Receipt and Release:

RECEIPT AND RELEASE

The undersigned, being one of the beneficiaries of the estate of (name of the decedent), hereby acknowledges receipt of the balances of income and principal distributable to me under the terms of the last Will and testament of (name of decedent). The said balances consist of:

(itemize securities, cash balances in income and principal and other assets that are being distributed)

Further, in consideration of the payment to me of the balance of the estate assets, I hereby release and discharge the personal representative of any further liability in connection with the estate or its administration.

In witness whereof I have executed this instrument the ___ ___ day of _____, 20___, with the intention of being legally bound.

_____

Distributions to a minor must also be made to the child's guardian. If a beneficiary is incompetent, the distribution must be made to a conservator or guardian (appointed by the court) of the property (or estate) of the incompetent person. If a beneficiary cannot be located, the probate court will determine the disposition of the property payable to that beneficiary and issue instructions to the personal representative.

Closing the Estate

The last step in administering the estate is to prepare a final accounting and close the estate. The probate court may require that a final accounting be submitted to the court, along with receipts from the beneficiaries before it discharges the personal representative. Each state has its own closing procedures, which may or may not involve a court proceeding. However, before this final step is taken the personal representative should check to see that all of the required administration tasks have been completed:

- **Have all debts, administration expenses and taxes been paid?**

- **Have all required tax returns been filed?**

- **Has the early determination of the federal estate tax been received or the nine-month period for an IRS response lapsed?**

- **Has the final accounting been prepared and copies provided to the beneficiaries and other interested parties?**

- **Have all the assets been distributed and receipts and releases obtained from all beneficiaries?**

Some states allow an informal closing. Under this procedure the personal representative files a statement with the court that the administration of the estate is complete and an accounting has been provided to the beneficiaries and unpaid claimants, if any. After a specified period from the filing date (usually one year under local law), the personal representative is discharged from any further responsibility.

In a formal proceeding, the final accounting is submitted to the probate court for approval. A *master* (auditor) may be appointed by the judge to review the accounts and advise the court as to whether or not the estate was properly administered. The appointment and expense of the master can usually be avoided if all beneficiaries approve the accounting prior to the hearing and waive their right to have a master appointed. If the court is satisfied that all of the requirements for settling the estate have been completed and the administration has been handled properly, it will issue an order of discharge relieving the personal representative from any further responsibility. The order of discharge is the formal closing of the estate.

Distribution Checklist

✓ Make partial distributions to beneficiaries prior to closing. Retain sufficient assets to cover debts and expenses.

✓ Distribute personal assets to family members. Conduct an auction for these items, if necessary.

✓ If a beneficiary does not survive a decedent, ascertain whether his or her share will be distributed per capita, per stirpes or per capita at each generation.

✓ Prepare a distribution schedule. Discuss with the beneficiaries before finalizing.

✓ Do not make final distribution of the remaining assets until the request for early determination of the estate tax has been received or the nine months period from the date of the request has lapsed.

✓ If a beneficiary resides outside the city where the estate is being administered, distribute that beneficiary's share through his or her bank.

✓ Obtain a Receipt and Release from every beneficiary.

✓ If required, submit the final accounts and receipts to the court and request the court to issue an order for discharge.

MANAGING
TRUSTS

CHAPTER 8

Trustee Responsibilities

KEY POINTS

- An individual who is nominated to serve as trustee is not obligated to accept the position.

- Being a trustee has many responsibilities and can require a significant commitment of time.

- A trustee is responsible for carrying out the purpose of the trust which includes minimizing estate taxes, managing property in the event of incapacity, protecting family members and distributing property to the decedent's heirs.

The Nature of Trusts

Trusts come in many different forms, as described in *Chapter 1 Serving as a Personal Representative and/or Trustee*. They are legal arrangements that allow someone to manage property for the benefit of others. A trustee essentially steps into the shoes of the creator *(settlor)* of the trust either before or after the settlor's death. This is not always an easy thing to do. The settlor may have left legal and financial problems that would challenge even the most knowledgeable and experienced individual. Managing the trust can require an extraordinary commitment of time and could also expose the trustee to personal liability. How a trustee manages the trust will determine the ultimate outcome of the estate plan. Understanding the general structure of a trust is a key first step to proper trust management. Regardless of the type of trust, they all have the same basic components:

CREATOR. The creator of a living trust (i.e., revocable living trust and irrevocable trusts established during one's lifetime, such as, children's gift trusts, irrevocable life insurance trusts, GRIT's, GRAT's, GRUT's, QPRT's, charitable remainder trusts, etc.) is referred to as the settlor, grantor, trustor or donor. The creator of a trust under a Will is the author of the Will, called the testator (male) or testatrix (female).

TRUSTEE. The person or institution (i.e., bank or trust company) that takes title to property and agrees to manage it, subject to the terms of a trust agreement or trust provisions under a Will.

INCOME BENEFICIARY. The person(s) for whose benefit the trust was created and whose interest is limited to the income earned by the trust assets.

PRINCIPAL BENEFICIARY. The person(s) for whose benefit the trust was created and whose interest is in distributions of principal.

REMAINDERMAN. The remainderman is the beneficiary, individual or organization, who receives the property upon the termination of the trust.

INCOME. Income is the return on trust property, such as, dividends, interest, rents, profits, royalties, etc., as opposed to principal.

PRINCIPAL. Principal is the property of the trust, other than the income from the property. Principal is also referred to as corpus or capital.

A trustee's responsibilities may differ from trust to trust, depending on the type of trust and the particular circumstances under which the trust is being managed. For example, the settlor of a revocable living trust may appoint a trustee to manage his or her trust because the settlor may lack management expertise, wants to travel or simply does not want to be bothered with the management of his or her property. In this situation, the trustee usually manages the trust property under direction of the settlor. The trustee is typically limited in the amount of discretion he or she can exercise. As a practical matter, the trustee's responsibilities parallel that of an agent. The settlor has the power to amend or revoke the trust and therefore retains total authority and dominion over the trust and the trustee. The primary difference between a true agency and trust relationship is that the trustee holds title to the trust property and has an obligation to act even without receiving direction from the settlor if failure to act would be harmful to the settlor.

Should the Settlor become incapacitated, the successor trustee is responsible for taking control and managing the trust property for the benefit of the settlor. At this point, the trustee makes all of the decisions and must observe the standards of care that would be expected of a prudent person dealing with the property of another. The trustee must manage the trust solely for the benefit of the incapacitated settlor and not the settlor's heirs. This level of responsibility continues until the settlor recovers or until the settlor's death. Managing a trust in this situation is discussed in greater detail later in this chapter.

On the death of the settlor, the trust becomes irrevocable. Like any other irrevocable trust, the trustee has total authority and responsibility at this point to carry out its provisions. While similar to managing a trust for an incapacitated settlor, the trustee's responsibilities under an irrevocable trust are far greater.

On the other hand, the decedent may have lived a somewhat normal life and management of his or her affairs might be relatively straightforward. There are as many different types of trust situations as there are people who create them.

Potential conflicts of interest should be evaluated to determine whether or not they will interfere with the management of the trust. No one is obligated to serve as a trustee or, once accepted, obligated to continue to serve for the term of the trust.

"...a fiduciary is not required to act at his peril; he need not eat the doubtful vegetable in order to ascertain if it is a wholesome mushroom or a poisonous toadstool..."

—*Judge Brockenbrough Lamb*

The assets and obligations of the decedent should be evaluated to ascertain if there are any problems that would make management difficult. Environmental problems, like contamination from a leaking fuel storage tank, can be especially challenging for a trustee and could expose the trust to liability. The trustee should conduct a preliminary environmental inspection of all real estate owned by the trust before accepting the trusteeship. If obvious environmental hazards exist, this is not a situation that most sane people want to step into.

The management of trusts is a serious responsibility and will be difficult if the trustee does not understand the basic rules. As trustee you may put yourself at risk and jeopardize the purpose and intent of the trust if you do not figure out what the duties are. In order to successfully carry out the provisions of a trust, you should possess good financial and business skills and/or hire financial advisors to provide needed expertise. If you accept the role of a trustee without fully understanding the responsibilities, you not only expose yourself to personal liability, but could also bring harm to the beneficiaries you serve. This chapter will outline the fundamental duties and responsibilities of a trustee.

Responsibilities of a Trustee

KEY POINTS

- **A trustee is expected to adhere to established standards of conduct in carrying out his or her responsibilities.**

- **The law contemplates that a trustee will exercise care, skill, prudence and diligence in managing a trust.**

- **A trustee should be pro-active in managing the affairs of the trust and avoid not performing a task because of a lack of understanding or time.**

As discussed in *Chapter 2 Fiduciary Standards and Limiting Liability*, every trustee has certain responsibilities under the law. In carrying out these responsibilities, trustees are subject to established standards of conduct under common law and the principles of equity. Most states incorporated these rules, in one form or another, under their local statutes. These rules focus on the trustee's fundamental duty to carry out the directions of the trust's creator. The standards of care that apply to trustees have deep roots that can be traced to biblical times. Courts have been fairly consistent in describing and upholding the concept of prudent standards for trustees. In an 1883 court case (Speight v. Gaunt) the presiding judge, Lord Blackburn, articulated the standard for trustees:

> *"as a general rule a trustee sufficiently discharges his duty if he takes in managing trust affairs all those precautions which an ordinary prudent man of business would take in managing similar affairs of his own .... It would be both unreasonable and inexpedient to make a trustee responsible for not being more prudent than ordinary men of business are."*

Whether or not a trustee has been reasonable in carrying out his or her responsibilities generally is not based entirely on the particular action taken by the trustee, but on the standards of care that ordinary prudent persons are expected to perform under similar circumstances. In managing the trust's affairs, a trustee will be held accountable for failure to apply the standards of care and skill. The standard of care that applies to trustees is often referred to as the *prudent person rule.* The Uniform Trustees' Powers Act, which many states have adopted, defines a prudent person as:

> *"a trustee whose exercise of trust powers is reasonable and equitable in view of the interests of income or principal beneficiaries, or both, and in view of the manner in which men of ordinary prudence, diligence, discretion and judgment would act in the management of their own affairs."*

This does not mean that a trustee can speculate with trust funds because he or she speculates with his or her own investments. Safeguarding income and principal, as ordinary persons of prudence would do, is what is expected. Being honest and well intentioned is not sufficient and will not excuse a trustee who does not apply prudent practices in administering the trust.

A trustee must understand that he or she cannot personally profit from the administration of the trust. The duty of loyalty is perhaps the most important rule for trustees. It mandates, among other things, a full and frank disclosure of any transactions in which the trustee may have a personal interest.

A trustee must keep beneficiaries informed by providing them with accurate accounting records and other information that is pertinent to their interests.

In administering the trust, a trustee must be impartial. This is fundamental and perhaps one of the most difficult responsibilities a trustee has. A trustee cannot favor current beneficiaries over remainder beneficiaries or one beneficiary over the other. When making investment decisions, distributions of income and principal, paying expenses and in other decisions in which the trustee uses discretion, he or she must be fair to all beneficiaries. This does not mean that distributions of income and/or principal to beneficiaries must be equal. The trustee must consider the individual needs and interests of each beneficiary and distribute funds in accordance with those needs and the terms of the trust. A trustee is usually given the authority under the trust document to sell, invest and reinvest the principal of the trust. To remain impartial between current beneficiaries and remainder beneficiaries and to protect the trust property, the trustee has a responsibility to distribute the risk of loss by diversifying the assets of the trust. When allocating deductible expenses between the federal estate tax return and the fiduciary income tax returns, the impartiality duty also comes into play. The remainder beneficiaries benefit if the deduction is taken on the estate tax return. If taken on the fiduciary income tax returns, the income beneficiaries do. This will be described in more detail later in this chapter. Discretionary decisions should take into consideration what is equitable for all beneficiaries and in the best interest of the trust as a whole. If a trust document gives the trustee discretion in crediting a receipt or charging an expenditure to income or principal, the trustee needs to make the allocation with the duty of impartiality in mind.

Trustees are expected to be proactive and use initiative in managing the trust. To remain passive or take no action at all is not defensible if something goes wrong with a trust transaction. It is also imperative that a trustee seeks qualified professional assistance where needed and makes informed decisions regarding the management of the trust.

There are several areas of trust administration that trustees need to understand to properly carryout their responsibilities and limit their liability exposure. These are the subjects of this chapter and include, making tax and other elections, funding the marital, family and generation-skipping trusts, managing trust investments, managing real estate assets, managing business interests, making discretionary distributions to beneficiaries, maintaining fiduciary accounting records, fiduciary income taxes and other filing requirements and termination of the trust and making final distribution of the trust assets.

Checklist of Responsibilities

✓ Avoid transactions in which the trustee has a personal interest.

✓ Keep beneficiaries informed.

✓ Do not favor one beneficiary over another. Distributions should be based on individual needs.

✓ Seek qualified professional help where needed.

✓ Be proactive in managing the trust.

Incapacity

KEY POINTS

- A revocable living trust provides for continued management of the settlor's financial affairs upon his or her incapacity.

- Upon the incapacity of the settlor, a successor trustee takes over the management of the trust property.

- The successor trustee is responsible for making decisions regarding the use of the trust property exclusively for the benefit of the incapacitated settlor.

A revocable living trust provides for the management of the settlor's financial affairs in the event that the settlor becomes incapacitated. Without a trust, a court supervised guardianship, or conservatorship, would be necessary to handle the financial affairs of the incapacitated person. A durable power of attorney (i.e., one that remains in effect upon incapacity) can also be used for this purpose, but only for the property that is not in a trust. A trust provides significant advantages over a guardianship proceeding. It is more flexible because handling financial transactions for the incapacitated person does not require the court's permission. Costs are lower because there are no attorney fees or costs for filing accountings in court. Upon the settlor's death, the trust also avoids probate and may reduce or eliminate estate taxes. These financial and estate planning opportunities are not available in a guardianship or conservatorship situation.

Every revocable living trust document names a successor, or back-up, trustee. If the settlor, who is the initial trustee, becomes incapacitated, the successor trustee takes over. The trust provision that brings the successor trustee into the picture upon the settlor's incapacity may read as follows:

"The determination of whether the Settlor is competent, for the purposes of this trust, shall be made by two physicians licensed to practice medicine in the state of the Settlor's residence, one of whom shall be his or her family physician stating that the Settlor is incapable of physically or mentally managing his or her financial affairs and is expected to remain so unable indefinitely or for the foreseeable future."

Older trust documents may not contain this language or make any reference to incapacity at all. However, it would be reasonable for a trustee to rely on a medical doctor's statement that the settlor is incapacitated and unable to manage his or her financial affairs as sufficient authority to step in as successor trustee.

On the incapacity of the settlor, the trustee must follow the terms of the trust and exercise the standards of care that apply. At this point, the trustee should not take any directions from the settlor in managing the trust.

Once the successor trustee assumes the trusteeship, he or she has the authority, right and power to do anything and everything that the settlor could do before his or her incapacity. The trustee is

166 / Trustee Responsibilities

now acting in a fiduciary capacity and must use the trust property exclusively for the benefit of the settlor and individuals who relied on the settlor's support before he or she became incapacitated. Expenditures can be made for any purposes that the trustee determines are suitable and proper.

The administration of the trust during the period of the settlor's incapacity is similar to managing an irrevocable trust. The trustee's responsibilities take effect immediately upon acceptance of the trusteeship and include:

- **Taking control of all trust property;**

- **Collecting, holding, managing, investing and reinvesting the assets of the trust;**

- **Paying the legitimate obligations of the settlor;**

- **Using the trust property for the exclusive benefit of the settlor.**

As in any other fiduciary role, the trustee is expected to observe the standards of care that would be observed by a prudent person dealing with someone else's property. The trustee must keep the trust property separate from all other property of the settlor and maintain records of all transactions during the period of the settlor's incapacity.

As long as the settlor is incapacitated, the trustee is responsible for the management of the trust, unless the trustee resigns and a successor trustee takes over or the settlor dies. Should the settlor die, the trustee carries out the provisions of the trust, which will either call for the trust to terminate or continue. If the settlor recovers and is no longer incapacitated, the trustee can continue to manage the trust at the settlor's direction or can resign and turn the management of the trust back to the settlor or an alternate trustee.

Incapacity Checklist

✓ Ascertain how the settlor's incapacity is determined under the terms of the trust.

✓ Obtain a physician's written statement that the settlor is unable to handle his or her financial affairs.

✓ Use the physician's statement and a copy of the trust document to take possession and control of all trust assets.

✓ Inform caregivers and vendors to submit all invoices to the successor trustee for payment.

✓ Do not rely on the settlor's instructions regarding management of the trust property. The successor trustee is responsible for all decisions concerning the supervision and use of the trust property for the benefit of the settlor.

Revocable Living Trusts That Terminate At Death

Managing a trust that terminates at death is significantly different than one that continues beyond the death of the settlor. As mentioned in *Chapter 1 Serving as a Personal Representative and/or Trustee,* under a terminating trust a trustee's responsibilities are similar to those of a personal representative, without the necessity of a probate proceeding. The administration of this type of trust has a relatively short duration.

Revocable living trusts that are established to provide protection in the event of incapacity, to avoid probate and to distribute property outright to heirs, usually terminate at the death of the settlor. This type of trust serves a similar purpose as a Will; its principal function is to distribute the trust property to the beneficiaries named in the trust document upon the death of the settlor. Using a trust instead of a Will has the added benefit of avoiding probate and avoiding guardianship in the event of incapacity.

Although the trust is the principle means of passing property to heirs, a Will is also used to distribute personal belongings and handle any property that was not transferred to the trust prior to death. In this case, the Will is drafted as a companion to the revocable living trust and is commonly referred to as a *"pour over"* Will. Such a Will transfers any assets in the decedent's individual name at death to the revocable living trust for ultimate distribution to the decedent's heirs. Hopefully, the value of the personal property and the property in the decedent's own name is small enough to avoid a probate proceeding.

The trustee's responsibilities under a revocable living trust that terminates at death include:

- **Assembling and protecting trust assets;**

- **Preparing an inventory and acquiring date of death appraisals of the trust property;**

- **Providing limited management of the trust property;**

- **Estimating cash requirements and raising the needed funds;**

- **Paying claims and administration expenses;**

- **Filing the required tax returns and paying any taxes due;**

- **Making tax and other elections;**

- **Preparing a distribution schedule;**

- **Preparing the accounting covering the administration of the trust; and**

- **Making final distribution of the trust assets to the beneficiaries and closing the trust.**

The personal representative of a decedent's estate is usually the same person as the trustee under his or her revocable living trust. In a well-planned estate, all of the individually owned assets will have been placed in the trust and, therefore, there will be no probate. The trustee, in this case, has control of the decedent's property and is responsible for settling the affairs of the decedent. These include filing the decedent's final income tax returns, filing fiduciary income tax returns, filing the estate tax return, paying the decedent's final bills, taking possession of and distributing the decedent's personal property and dealing with other financial matters. (Refer to the estate settlement checklists in *Chapter 7 Administering the Estate.*) If there is a probate, some of these functions, such as filing the estate tax return, need to be coordinated with the personal representative.

The major benefit in handling someone's estate through a revocable living trust is that the trustee does not have to deal with the probate court. In most states, court hearings or filings are not necessary if all the decedent's property is in his or her trust. This means that the estate can be settled quicker. However, the time that it takes to settle any estate depends on whether or not federal estate taxes are payable, the nature of the assets owned, and the decedents instructions regarding the handling of his affairs.

If the decedent has a taxable estate, the federal estate tax return (Form 706) is not due until nine months after death. The trustee has an obligation to wait until the due date before filing the return and paying the tax; interest can be earned on the amount of taxes for the full nine-month period. This of course means delaying settlement of the estate until then. Settlement might also be delayed if the decedent leaves specific instructions to sell a particular asset. If the trust owns a business, commercial real estate interest, limited partnership interest or some other illiquid asset, it could take additional time to consummate the sale. Matters that are being litigated or disputes among the heirs can also delay distribution and the closing of the trust.

The following steps should be covered when managing a terminating trust:

1. Notify the beneficiaries that the trust has terminated and describe the provisions of the trust that relate to their inheritance. This should be done as soon after the settlor's death as practical.

2. Publish a notice to creditors.

3. Obtain security reissue instructions from all beneficiaries including how the securities are to be registered, current address, social security number and name and address of a local bank through which delivery can be made if assets cannot be delivered in person locally.

4. Value the securities, real estate and other assets for the purpose of ascertaining any estate tax that may be due and the amount to be distributed to the beneficiaries.

5. Prepare a distribution schedule and tax cost bases schedule and review them with the beneficiaries before finalizing.

6. Have the attorney for the trust prepare new deeds for any real property distributable to beneficiaries.

7. Arrange for the preparation and filing of the decedent's final individual income tax returns.

8. Arrange for the preparation and filing of Fiduciary Income Tax Return(s).

9. If required, arrange for the preparation and filing of the federal estate tax return and state inheritance return.

10. Re-register all securities in accordance with the instructions of the beneficiaries.

11.   **Prepare an accounting for the period from the settlor's date of death through and including all transactions prior to making final distribution of the assets to the beneficiaries.**

12.   **Deliver the assets and obtain approval of the final accounting, receipts for delivery of the assets and a signed release of liability from all beneficiaries. The following is an example of a combined approval of account, receipt and release:**

APPROVAL OF ACCOUNT RECEIPT & RELEASE

I, the undersigned, being a beneficiary of the (name of trust), for the purpose of receiving distribution without a court order:

I. Acknowledge that I have examined the account of the trustee for the period from _(beginning date)__ to and including _(ending date)_ and approve the same, which approval shall have the same effect as if the account had been approved by the court;

II. Acknowledge receipt of income and principal as itemized therein, and release and discharge the Trustee from any liability in connection with the above trust or its administration;

III. Agree to indemnify and save the Trustee harmless against all liability, loss, or expense (including but not limited to costs and counsel fees) which may ever be incurred as a result of the settlement of its account and/ or the distribution herein referred to upon this Receipt and Release.

In witness whereof I have executed this instrument this _____ day of _____, 20___, with the intention of being legally bound.

_____

13. Prepare a supplemental final accounting from the end date of the last accounting through and including the final distribution of assets and cash. Provide each beneficiary with a copy of the supplemental final accounting.

Like a probate estate, as soon as the expenses, taxes, and other obligations of the trust have been satisfied, the assets can be distributed to the beneficiary(ies). Once the assets have been distributed and the supplemental final accounting has been delivered to the beneficiaries, the trust can be closed. Unlike a probate proceeding, in most jurisdictions the trustee is not required to seek a discharge from the court. The trustee can submit accountings to the court if the trustee wants to have the court approve the administration. However, having the beneficiaries approve the accountings and sign a release is less costly and allows the trust to close sooner. The final distribution of assets and closing of the trust effectively terminates the trustee's responsibilities.

REVOCABLE LIVING TRUSTS
THAT TERMINATE AT DEATH

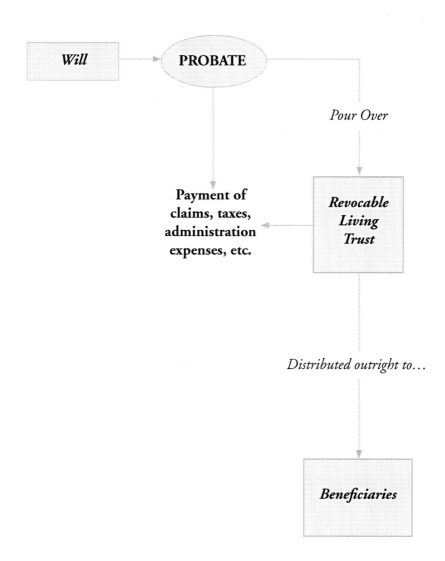

Revocable Living Trusts That Continue After Death

The responsibilities under a continuing trust are significantly greater than under a terminating trust and extend over a much longer period. Revocable living trusts that continue after death fall into two general categories. The first is the trust that is designed to protect a beneficiary(ies) for a period beyond the settlor's death. Some individuals desire to control their wealth after death by denying their heirs direct access to their fortunes. Others have a nobler objective of protecting those they feel need to be protected. Instead of directing the trustee to distribute the trust's assets outright at death, as in a terminating trust, this type of trust continues until the beneficiary(ies) reach a certain age or sometimes until the beneficiary's death. The trust may require the trustee to exercise discretion in distributing income and principal for the benefit of the beneficiary(ies) for the term of the trust. Upon termination, the trust property is distributed to the named remainder beneficiaries.

The other category of continuing trust is probably the more common. This is a revocable living trust that has as one of its primary purposes the reduction or elimination of the federal estate tax. The key feature under this type of trust is the so-called credit shelter or by-pass trust. Also referred to as the family trust or "B" trust, the credit shelter trust is a separate trust created under the terms of the revocable living trust upon the settlor's death. It is funded with assets having a value equal to the unified credit exemption equivalent amount (i.e., $675,000 for the year 2000.) The income and principal from this trust are used primarily for the benefit of the surviving spouse and often includes the decedent's children. The credit shelter trust is also referred to as the Family trust, where children and grandchildren are included, because it benefits all family members. Typically, on the death of the surviving spouse, the credit shelter trust terminates and the assets are distributed to the children, grandchildren or other named beneficiaries. Under the Internal Revenue Code, this trust will not be subject to estate tax in the surviving spouse's estate. In other words, the assets in this trust avoid estate taxes altogether and pass directly to the children, or other named beneficiaries. Hence it is sometimes referred to as the by-pass trust.

The assets that are not transferred to the credit shelter trust are either distributed outright to the surviving spouse or retained in the marital trust, another type of trust created under the decedent's revocable living trust. The marital trust qualifies for the marital deduction thereby avoiding any estate tax in the estate of the first to die. Although there is no tax on the marital trust assets at the first death, the tax is merely postponed. The marital trust assets will be included in the surviving spouse's estate.

The surviving spouse gets the benefit of the marital trust for life. On the death of the surviving spouse, the assets will either pass as the surviving spouse directs in his or her Will or as the settlor directs in the trust. In either case, the assets usually will be distributed to the children. The marital trust must direct that all of the trust income be paid to the surviving spouse in order to qualify it for the marital deduction. The trust may provide that principal be paid to the spouse in the discretion of the trustee or at the surviving spouse's direction. Upon the death of the surviving spouse the assets of the marital trust are included in his or her estate for federal estate tax purposes. If the marital trust along with the other assets owned by the surviving spouse exceeds the exemption equivalent amount, the excess will be taxed.

In a continuing trust, the trustee's initial responsibilities are the same as with a trust that terminates at death. That is, the final affairs of the decedent's estate must be settled. Then the trustee must:

- **Review and exercise tax and other elections.**

- **Set up the trust(s) for administration.**

- **Fund the Marital and By-pass trusts.**

Once these initial steps have been accomplished, the trustee will be responsible for managing the trust until it terminates. The trustee's duties will include:

- **Managing the trust's investment portfolio.**

- **Managing real estate assets.**

- **Managing business interests.**

- **Making discretionary distributions to beneficiaries.**

- **Maintaining fiduciary accounting records.**

- **Filing fiduciary income tax returns for the trust(s).**

- **Making final distribution of the trust assets upon its termination.**

Trusts can continue for many years and it is important that the trustee be aware of and understand these on-going responsibilities. To accept the trusteeship of a continuing trust without this knowledge is foolhardy and does nothing but put a trustee at risk. Familiarity with the standards of care and the basics of trust administration discussed in this chapter is essential for a trustee of a continuing trust.

REVOCABLE LIVING TRUSTS
THAT CONTINUE AFTER DEATH

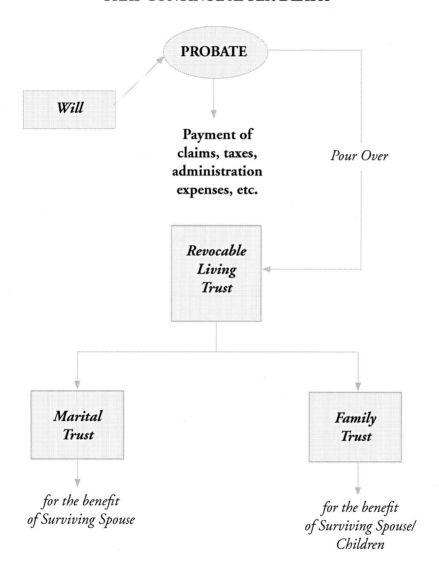

CHAPTER 9

Preparing the Trust for Administration

As with any other business activity, a well-established plan will help manage the numerous administrative tasks of a trust more efficiently. Organizing, collecting and establishing proper trust records in the beginning will minimize administration problems later on. There are several initial steps necessary to properly set up a trust for administration. Once these steps have been taken, a plan for administration should be developed and a sound management system established.

Initial Steps

Many of the initial steps can be performed concurrently with the settlement of the decedent's estate. The following are some of the things that need to be addressed in the setup:

- Examine the trust document and determine if the trust is terminating or continuing.

- Determine if income accrued to the date of death but not received as of the date of death is payable to the estate of the settlor.

- Are estate taxes payable from the trust?

- Are medical, funeral and other debts associated with the death of the settlor payable from the trust?

- Have an initial conference with the beneficiaries and/or notify them of the trust provisions that affect their interests. A copy of the trust should also be provided to the beneficiaries.

- Identify and take control of all assets belonging to the trust.

- Arrange for safekeeping of all tangible assets.

- Prepare an inventory of all trust assets using the values as of the date of death.

- Apply for a tax identification number by completing IRS Form SS-4, Application for Employer Identification Number.

- Arrange for transfer of securities, bank accounts, brokerage accounts and other registered property into the name of the trustee:

  "(name of trustee), Trustee of the (name of trust), dated (date original trust was signed)"

- Identify all encumbrances and liabilities.

- Acquire appropriate insurance coverage for all real estate assets and other trust property such as jewelry, paintings, coin collections, etc. If the property is covered by an existing policy, review the policy to see that the amount of the insurance is adequate.

- Collect any life insurance proceeds payable to the trust.

- If rental property is an asset of the trust, notify tenants to mail all future rent payments to the address of the trustee.

- Notify all debtors to mail future payments to the trustee.

- Notify, or have the attorney for the trust inform, the surviving spouse of her legal rights with respect to the trust.

- Determine if there are any alien or non-resident beneficiaries. Arrangements will have to be made with regard to delivery of assets, income and principal distributions and the withholding of U.S. tax, if required.

- Determine how much needs to be reserved for taxes and other expenses.

- Carry out any initial instructions in the trust document, i.e., a directive to sell a specific asset, payment of specific bequests or allowances, etc.

Establishing A Plan

Before administration of the trust begins, develop a plan of action that includes how specific administrative tasks are to be performed and by whom. Some of the more important issues to be addressed in the planning process include:

- Will a division of the trust into a marital, credit shelter and/or generation-skipping share be necessary? If so, who will advise the trustee how the splits are to be made and what assets will be used to fund the trusts?

- Who will handle the trust's investments?

- Who will handle the management of any real property owned by the trust?

- Who will maintain the accounting records for the trust and prepare accounting reports for the trustee and beneficiaries?

- How often will accounting statements be sent to the beneficiaries?

- If there are individuals referred to in the trust that are to be consulted with regard to investments, an agreement should be established outlining the procedures that will be followed.

- Once the income needs of the trust and short, intermediate and long-term cash requirements have been determined, an investment policy with goals and objectives needs to be established. Who will do this and when?

- How often will the investments be reviewed and when?

- Who will prepare the fiduciary income tax return(s) for the trust?

- The investments of the trust need to have an initial review by a qualified investment professional to determine if immediate action needs to be taken with respect to any individual securities in order to protect the portfolio. Who will do this and when?

- If the trust owns closely held stock, does the owner-ship interest warrant the trustee serving as a member of the board of directors and/or an officer of the company?

- What tax elections need to be made and who will be retained to advise the trustee in this regard?

- If there is a co-trustee, agree in writing on the division of duties and the procedures that are to be followed in the joint exercise of discretionary decisions.

- What will be required of beneficiaries when considering discretionary payments? These requirements should be communicated to the beneficiaries as soon as practical.

Establishing Trust Records

Keeping good records is essential to the efficient administration of a trust. There is probably no other aspect that is more important for minimizing errors and maintaining management control. Trust record keeping falls into three general categories. First is the creation and maintenance of the "document" or "pertinent information" file. The second is the "correspondence" or "work" file and the third is maintenance of accurate accounting records.

The document file is a critical reference of the pertinent records of the trust that will be referenced throughout the entire period of administration. This file should contain the following documents:

- A copy of the original trust document and all amendments.

- **A copy of the decedent's original Will.**

- **A certified copy of the death certificate.**

- **A copy of all real estate deeds.**

- **A copy of the federal estate tax return (Form 706), if one was filed.**

- **The date-of-death inventory of trust assets.**

- **A family tree.**

- **Other documents that are important to the on-going administration of the trust.**

In addition, a synopsis of the trust should be prepared and included in the document file for quick reference. The synopsis should contain information that will be frequently referenced:

- **A quote of the provision that covers distribution of income from the trust.**

- **A quote of the provisions that pertains to the distribution of principal.**

- **A list of the current beneficiaries, their addresses, birth dates, marginal (highest) tax bracket, social security number, and interest in the trust.**

- **A quote of the provision that triggers the termination of the trust.**

- **A quote of any provision that prohibits a particular action.**

- **A quote of any provision that requires the trustee to take a particular action.**

- **A list of the remainder beneficiaries.**

The correspondence, or work file, should contain all correspondence and other written materials related to the day-to-day administration of the trust. This file should also contain memorandums that outline and document important phone calls and meetings. The more documentation you have, the better. Trusts can last for many years and without good historical records, it will be difficult to recall the details of a particular action taken during the course of administration.

Fiduciary trust accountings are records that cover all of the financial transactions of the trust. These accountings are permanent records and can be useful as a reference and guide in handling future transactions. As will be discussed later in this chapter, one of the important functions of fiduciary accounting is to keep income and principal funds separate. All trust documents make specific reference to how, when, and under what circumstances income and principal are to be distributed to the beneficiaries of the trust. It is essential that these records be accurate in order to properly identify the interests of all beneficiaries at any given point. Accountings are also the tool needed to monitor investment performance, evaluate income production, plan payments from the trust and assess how the financial resources of the trust can meet the current and future needs of the beneficiaries.

Set-Up / Planning Checklist

✓ **Complete the initial steps outlined in this section.**

✓ **Establish a plan for administration of the trust. (Refer to the checklist in this section.)**

✓ **Establish trust records. (See recommendations in this section.)**

Tax and Other Elections

KEY POINTS

- Making the proper tax elections can result in significant tax savings for beneficiaries.

- If there is no probate, and therefore no personal representative, the trustee will have the responsibility for making these choices.

- Many tax elections will directly affect the trust and its beneficiaries.

- The disclaimer election can be used to correct drafting errors in a trust.

As discussed in *Chapter 7 Administering the Estate–Tax Elections and Other Postmortem Planning Issues,* the personal representative and/or the trustee is required to make tax elections that are advantageous to the beneficiaries. Proper post mortem tax planning can result in significant tax savings. The planning process may involve close coordination with the personal representative. If there is no probate, tax elections will be the responsibility of the trustee. Those that specifically affect the administration of trusts will be discussed further in this section.

The QTIP election

The Qualified Terminable Interest Property or QTIP election allows the use of certain qualified property as a marital deduction in determining the decedent's estate tax. A trust can qualify for the marital deduction if the following requirements are met:

1) the property must "pass" from the decedent;

2) the surviving spouse must be entitled to an income interest for life;

3) no other beneficiary may have any right in the trust during the surviving spouse's lifetime; and

4) an irrevocable QTIP election must be made.

A trust that requires all of its income to be distributed to a surviving spouse and no one else would qualify for the QTIP election, assuming that principal is not available to anyone other than the surviving spouse during her lifetime. Under the typical QTIP Trust, a surviving spouse is not given the right to direct who receives the principal of the trust at her death. Instead, the trust is usually distributed to the children upon the spouse's death.

Under the Internal Revenue Code, a partial QTIP election can be made, giving the trustee, or personal representative, a great deal of tax planning flexibility. For example, a partial election could be made to have some estate tax paid at the first death. This could have a beneficial effect if the surviving spouse's estate will be in a high tax bracket. Many estate-planning attorneys recognize the advantages of having this flexibility and will include a provision in the trust that directs the trustee to make the appropriate election. The following is an example of such a provision which gives the trustee fairly specific direction:

"The trustee(s) of the Qualified Terminable Interest Property Trust are hereby authorized, in the trustee(s)' sole discretion, to determine whether to elect (under Section 2056(b)(7) of the Internal Revenue Code) to qualify all or a specific portion of the Qualified Terminable Interest Property Trust created herein for the federal estate tax marital deduction. The trustee(s) of the Qualified Terminable Interest Property Trust, in exercising such discretion, shall attempt to minimize, or eliminate if possible, the federal estate tax payable by my estate at the time of my death.

If, however, the trustee(s) of the Qualified Terminable Interest Property Trust determine that it is in the best interest of the persons who may receive any assets after my death and my spouse's death to pay some federal estate tax in my estate, taking into consideration any other tax that is to be paid because of my death and my spouse's death, and any income tax liability that may be affected by the election, the trustee(s) of the Qualified Terminable Interest Property Trust may elect to take a marital deduction that does not reduce the tax to zero if the payment of the tax will not jeopardize the ability of the Qualified Terminable Interest Property Trust to provide my spouse with the level of support and maintenance contemplated by this Declaration of Trust. The decision of the Qualified Terminable Interest Property trustee(s) to make this election shall be final and binding on all persons."

Even without specific language like this, the trustee must take whatever actions necessary to reduce taxes and preserve the trust property for the benefit of the beneficiaries and other interested parties who would be affected by payment of the tax. Obviously, this election involves some sophisticated tax planning, including an analysis of the surviving spouse's estate tax liability, an evaluation of whether or not there would be any advantage to paying some tax now (i.e., at the first death), the impact of the election on the beneficiaries' interest in the trust and the overall tax and economic benefits of the various alternatives.

Disclaimers

The use of disclaimers can achieve significant tax advantages and can also be used to correct trust agreements that contain drafting errors. Once an interest is disclaimed, the person disclaiming the interest is considered to have predeceased the settlor, in the case of a trust, and the interest passes to the person (s) who would be legally entitled to receive it. For example, let's say that a settlor provided in his living trust that his surviving spouse was to receive income for life if she survived him, and if she did not survive him, the income would be paid to the settlor's children. If the surviving spouse disclaimed her interest in the trust, she would be considered to have predeceased the settlor and the income would be paid to the children. This is a good way to transfer property, or an interest in property, to others. Gift taxes are avoided because the person making the disclaimer, in this case the surviving spouse, is considered to have predeceased the settlor and therefore is not making a gift to children.

As explained in *Chapter 7 Administering the Estate,* making disclaimers can also be used to maximize the amount that can be sheltered through the credit shelter trust of the first to die. If a decedent's credit shelter trust will hold less than the allowable amount, and there are other assets such as jointly held property that passes to the surviving spouse by operation of law (automatically,) the surviving spouse can disclaim some of the joint property. This allows the credit shelter trust to be funded with the full value of the exemption equivalent amount. In *Chapter 7 Administering the Estate,* the following example was used: Say a decedent had $400,000 in his revocable living trust and $700,000 was jointly owned with his wife. The decedent's credit shelter trust would be funded with the $400,000. If the allowable exemption equivalent amount is $675,000 (Year 2000) the trust would be under-funded by $275,000 ($675,000—$400,000 = $275,000). If the surviving spouse disclaims $275,000 of the joint assets, that amount would flow into the trust under the decedent's Will bringing the amount of the credit shelter trust up to the full $675,000 exemption equivalent amount. Assuming that the additional $275,000 grew at an annual rate of 5% for ten years, the use of the disclaimer would have the result of saving anywhere from $165,740 (37%) to $246,370 (55%) in estate taxes upon the death of the surviving spouse. Conversely, if the surviving spouse did not disclaim the $275,000 it would grow, at 5%, to $447,946 in ten years and would be subject to tax in her estate.

If a trust is not drafted properly, it may fail to qualify for the marital deduction and create a tax liability in the estate of the first to die. The failure might be the result of the trust allowing distributions to individuals other than the surviving spouse during her lifetime, which would disqualify the trust for the marital deduction. This can be remedied by having the disqualifying person disclaim his or her interest. Before suggesting a disclaimer, the trustee should have the individual seek advice from a financial counselor or attorney to advise the beneficiary of the consequences of giving up their rights under the trust.

Disclaimers should be considered as soon after death as practical since the election must be made within nine months from the time the interest is created and it may take some time to complete the process. Also, the longer it takes to make the decision, the greater the chances are that the person having the interest will inadvertently receive benefits from the interest (i.e., income distributions) thereby disqualifying the person from making the disclaimer.

Generation-skipping transfer tax (GSTT) exemption

The generation-skipping transfer tax is assessed for all gifts and transfers to "skip persons" that exceed $1,030,000 (year 2000.) These transfers may occur after death through a credit shelter trust and/or QTIP trust. For example, a credit shelter trust might provide that the decedent's surviving spouse receive income and/or principal during her lifetime and upon her death continue for the benefit of her children. The trust might also provide for distributions to grandchildren for their education and upon the death of the last to survive of the settlor's children, that the remaining assets be distributed to the grandchildren as remaindermen. Any distributions to grandchildren ("skip persons") during the term of the trust, and distribution of the assets to the grandchildren upon termination of the trust, are generation-skipping transfers subject to the generation-skipping transfer tax (GSTT.)

The trustee needs to allocate the $1,030,000 GSTT exemption at the decedent's death in a way that maximizes, or leverages, its tax sheltering effect. Using the previous example, let's say that a decedent's estate is valued at $1,500,000 and that his revocable living trust splits into a credit shelter trust and a QTIP trust. The QTIP is for the benefit of his surviving spouse for her lifetime and upon her death is distributed to the credit shelter trust and continues for the benefit of their children and grandchildren. The surviving spouse is the primary beneficiary of the credit shelter trust, but the trust allows distributions to the children and grand-children, in accordance with their needs. Upon the death of the surviving spouse, the credit shelter trust continues for the benefit of the children and grandchildren and upon the death of the last to survive of the settlor's children the trust terminates and distrib-utes to the grandchildren, as remaindermen.

To maximize the effectiveness of the GSTT exemption, many trust documents direct the trustee to allocate the exemption in a way that leverages its use. This is accomplished by authorizing the trustee to create separate trusts that will allow full use of the exemption. The following is an example of such a provision:

> *"If a trust hereunder would be partially exempt from genera-tion-skipping tax by reason of an allocation of generation-skip-ping tax exemption to it, before the allocation the trustee in its discretion may divide the trust into two separate trusts of equal or unequal value, to permit allocation solely to one trust which will be entirely exempt from generation-skipping tax. In addi-tion, if a trust hereunder is entirely exempt or nonexempt from generation-skipping tax and adding property to the trust would partially subject it to generation-skipping tax, the trustee in its discretion may hold that property as a separate trust in lieu of making the addition. Except as otherwise provided in this trust, the two trusts shall have the same terms and conditions, but the trustee shall not make discretionary distributions from the income or principal of the exempt trust to beneficiaries who are non-skip persons so long as any readily marketable assets remain in the nonexempt trust."*

If the trust document does not contain language that permits the trustee to establish separate trusts for the purpose of allocat-ing the exemption, authorization may be given under local law in some states. If allocation is not permitted in the trust document or under local law, the trustee should file a petition in the probate court for authorization. In the above example, if a separate exemp-tion trust is not created, the allocation of the trust assets upon funding would be as follows:

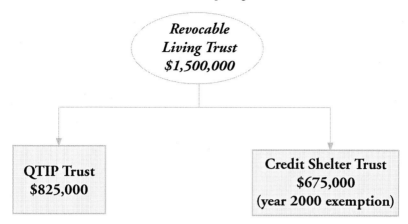

If the election to allocate the GSTT exemption is not deliberately made by the trustee at the time the trusts are established, the $1,030,000 exemption will be applied to distributions to the grandchildren when they are made, based on the then value of the distributions. However, if the trustee allocates the exemption to the trusts at the time the trusts are created, the assets in those trusts are "protected". That is, the amount allocated, plus the appreciation on the assets in the trusts, will pass free of the generation-skipping transfer tax. In the above funding scenario, $675,000 of the GSTT exemption would be allocated to the credit shelter trust since that is the trust that will be distributed to grandchildren and is likely to be invested for growth. The remaining $355,000 (i.e., $1,030,000—$675,000) of exemption cannot be allocated to the QTIP trust without specifically identifying and separating out assets that have an aggregate value equal to the $355,000. This can be accomplished by splitting the QTIP trust into two separate trusts. One trust would be called the "GSTT Exempt QTIP Trust" and would be funded with assets having a value that is equivalent to the remaining amount of the GSTT exemption, or $355,000. The other trust would be called the "Non-Exempt QTIP Trust" and would be funded with the balance of the QTIP assets, or $470,000 ($825,000 – $355,000.) This funding scenario results in the creation of three separate trusts that should be accounted for separately until they terminate:

All distributions to grandchildren, or any other "skip persons," should first be made from the "protected" GSTT Exempt QTIP Trust and Credit Shelter Trust since the assets in these trusts plus any appreciation in value are exempt from the generation-skipping transfer tax. Since the GSTT Exempt QTIP Trust will be subject to estate tax in the surviving spouse's estate, distributions to grandchildren should be made from this trust first and then from the Credit Shelter Trust.

The allocation of the exemption by the trustee in this way can result in significant tax savings for the remainder beneficiaries. If, for example, the $1,030,000 exemption that was allocated to the Credit Shelter Trust and the GSTT Exempt QTIP Trust appreciated in value by a conservative 5% annually, the amount of the appreciation alone after ten years would be $647,764. The generation-skipping transfer tax savings resulting from capturing the appreciation through the allocation of the exemption to these two trusts would be $356,270 at a 55% rate. A word of caution: the trustee should never allow additional assets to be deposited to these trusts once the allocation has been made. This could expose the trusts to the generation-skipping transfer tax.

The inclusion ratio

In the first example, where the QTIP trust was not separated into two separate trusts, part of the assets would be subject to the generation-skipping transfer tax. The portion of the QTIP trust subject to the tax is expressed as a percentage of the total QTIP trust assets and is referred to as the *inclusion ratio* under the Internal Revenue Code. The inclusion ratio is determined by dividing the unused portion of the exemption by the funding value of the QTIP trust and subtracting the result from 1 (one.) The inclusion ratio for the QTIP trust would be as follows:

$$1 - \frac{\text{Unused exemption (i.e., } \$1,030,000 - \$675,000 = \$355,000)}{\text{Value of QTIP trust upon funding}}$$

$$1 - \frac{\$355,000}{\$825,000} = .57 = 57\%$$

For every principal distribution made to a grandchild from the QTIP trust in this example, 57% (the inclusion ratio) of the amount distributed would be subject to the generation-skipping tax. All of the appreciation in the trust is also proportionately subject to the tax. A better way to allocate the exemption is to create separate trusts, as previously discussed, which would result in an inclusion ratio of one (1) for the Non-Exempt Trust and zero (0) for the GSTT Exempt and Credit Shelter trusts.

Tax Elections Checklist

✓ Determine what tax elections apply or affect the trusts that have been created by the settlor.

✓ Consult with a CPA or the trust's attorney regarding the tax options and their impact on the trust and its beneficiaries.

✓ Before making an election that will affect a beneficiary's interest, consult with the beneficiary and/or the beneficiary's financial advisor.

✓ Seek court authority to create separate trusts for the purpose of allocating the generation-skipping transfer tax exemption, if needed.

CHAPTER 10

Funding the Marital, Credit Shelter and Generation-Skipping Trusts

KEY POINTS

- A revocable living trust will typically contain provisions that direct the trustee to create one or more trusts upon the death of the settlor.

- These trusts are designed to qualify for the marital deduction and allow deferral of the federal estate tax until the death of the surviving spouse.

- A trustee should understand the characteristics of the particular funding clause that creates these trusts.

- As with other tax-related decisions, a trustee should seek professional help in funding the trusts.

The basic technique for deferring federal estate tax when the first spouse dies is to maximize the marital deduction. Property that qualifies for the marital deduction is not taxed until the surviving spouse's death. Transfers to a surviving spouse will qualify for the marital deduction if made outright, by specific bequest under a Will or trust, through joint ownership, under the terms of a contract such as a life insurance policy, profit sharing plan, 401(k), Individual Retirement Account (IRA) or through a qualifying trust. There are four basic types of trusts that qualify for the marital deduction—the estate trust, the power of appointment trust, the QTIP trust and the qualified domestic trust (QDOT).

Estate Trust

An estate trust, which is created by a provision under a will or trust, is one that does not require all of its income to be paid to the surviving spouse. However, in order to qualify for the marital deduction, the estate trust must provide that upon the death of the surviving spouse, all of the accumulated income and principal of the trust be distributed to the surviving spouse's estate. Unlike the other types of trusts that qualify for the marital deduction, the estate trust can be funded with unproductive property; that is, property that does not produce income.

Power of Appointment Trust

Until the QTIP trust was introduced in 1981 by the Economic Recovery Act, the power of appointment trust was the most commonly used form of marital deduction trust. Although the QTIP trust provides more tax planning options, the power of appointment trust is still used in many estate plans. In order to qualify for the marital deduction, the terms of the power of appointment trust must provide that all of the trust's income be paid to the surviving spouse for life. It must also give the surviving spouse a *general power of appointment* by which the surviving spouse, under his or her Will, can appoint the trust property to his or her estate or any other person(s) upon death. The power of appointment trust cannot allow any other person to benefit from the trust during the surviving spouse's lifetime. Unlike the estate trust, in a power of appointment trust the trustee must obtain consent of the surviving spouse to fund it with, or invest in, non-income-producing (i.e., unproductive) property. Also, an election is not required to be made on the estate tax return in order to include the trust for the marital deduction. Qualification and use of the power of appointment trust for the marital deduction is automatic.

QTIP Trust

The QTIP trust is a popular marital trust provision. Like the power of appointment trust, the QTIP trust income must be paid to the surviving spouse and no one else. However, unlike the marital trusts discussed above, a general power of appointment need not be given to the surviving spouse. This allows the settlor to decide the ultimate disposition of the property upon the surviving spouse's death. The surviving spouse is the only one who can receive principal during his or her lifetime. As with the power of appointment trust, the trustee cannot fund the trust with unproductive property unless authorized to do so by the surviving spouse. An election must be made on the estate tax return (Form 706) by the personal representative or trustee to use all or a portion of the trust for the marital deduction. Once the election is made it is irrevocable.

Qualified Domestic Trust (QDOT)

This type of marital deduction trust is used when the surviving spouse is not a U.S. citizen. It is the only way to obtain a marital deduction in this situation. To qualify for the marital deduction, at least one trustee must be a U.S. citizen or domestic corporation (i.e., bank or trust company). The trust must provide that all income be paid, at least annually, to the non-U.S. citizen spouse unless an estate trust is being used. No principal can be paid unless the U.S. trustee has the right to withhold from the distribution the estate taxes that would be due at the time the distribution is made. As with the QTIP trust, an election to use the trust for the marital deduction must be made on the decedent's estate tax return (Form 706).

The Credit Shelter Trust

As part of the plan to avoid estate taxes, the credit shelter trust provision is used to shelter the decedent's exemption equivalent amount (i.e., $675,000 for year 2000) from taxation in the surviving spouse's estate. Also referred to as the *"family trust"*, *"residuary trust"*, *""B" trust"*, or *"by-pass trust"*, the credit shelter trust typically will provide that the income and principal be used for the benefit of the decedent's surviving spouse and children. Unlike marital deduction trusts there is no requirement for the credit shelter trust to distribute income to the surviving spouse. Upon the death of the surviving spouse the assets of the credit shelter trust, including any appreciation in value from the date of funding to the date of death of the surviving spouse, are not included in the surviving spouse's estate. The trust passes estate tax free to the children or other named beneficiaries in the trust. One of the principal planning objectives in funding the credit shelter trust is to use assets that will appreciate in value over time since the initial value of the assets, plus the appreciation, will not be taxed in the surviving spouse's estate.

Funding the various trusts created under a decedent's revocable living trust can be a challenging task for a trustee. A decedent's revocable living trust may create a marital trust, credit shelter trust, generation-skipping trust or a combination of all three to facilitate the estate plan. There are many issues to be considered in funding these trusts. The decisions that are made will have income tax, estate tax and trust management implications. Certain facts must be gathered before funding can be performed. Funding will be based on the final determination of the values for estate tax purposes, the formula clause and the value of the surviving spouse's estate. This information will not be available for many months after the decedent's death. However, the trustee should fund the trusts as soon as possible to minimize any income tax consequences.

Division of the property between the trusts is only required if the decedent left a surviving spouse and the trust assets exceed the exemption equivalent amount. Generally, if the trust assets exceed the exemption equivalent amount (i.e., $675,000 for year 2000) the credit shelter trust is funded with $675,000. Amounts in excess of $675,000 fund the marital trust. If the value of the trust is under the exemption equivalent amount, all of the trust assets will end up in the credit shelter trust under the terms of the living trust. The marital trust, in this latter case, will not be established since no excess amount is available to fund it.

The marital and credit shelter trusts are funded after the estate tax return (Form 706) has been filed and the early determination of the tax has been received from the IRS. Waiting until the IRS has made a final determination of the tax allows the trustee to be sure he or she is using the right amounts to fund the trusts. There are two basic funding formula clauses under marital and credit shelter trust provisions. One is the *pecuniary formula clause* and the other is the *fractional formula clause*. It is important for the trustee to understand these formulas and their basic characteristics; it is also important to understand the consequences of the funding choices.

Pecuniary Formula Clause

The pecuniary formula clause is the most flexible of the two types of funding formulas and gives the trustee several planning opportunities. A pecuniary formula gives (i.e., bequeaths) a specific dollar amount to either the marital trust or the credit shelter trust. If the specific dollar amount is given to the marital trust, the excess trust asset value over this amount, or residue, is distributed to the credit shelter trust. If the specific dollar amount is given to the credit shelter trust, the residue is distributed to the marital trust. A pecuniary gift to the credit shelter trust is referred to as a *"reverse pecuniary bequest"*. Pecuniary formula clauses are used more often than fractional formula clauses because they are easier to administer and are more flexible. There are three funding methods under pecuniary formula clauses. The formula clause will specify the particular funding method that is to be used:

- "True worth" funding

- "Minimum worth" funding

- "Fairly representative" funding

All three variations allow the trustee to "pick and choose" the assets that will be used to fund the pecuniary gift trust, whether it is the marital or credit shelter trust. The trustee must read the terms of the trust carefully to determine what method is to be used in funding the trusts.

True worth funding

This is the most common and flexible of the three types of pecuniary funding variations. It gives the trustee the greatest latitude in choosing the assets that will fund each trust. A pecuniary formula clause that makes a gift to the marital trust with the residue going to the credit shelter trust is the most common type of true worth funding provision. This method guarantees that the surviving spouse, who is the beneficiary, will not be affected by any depreciation in value of the estate assets from the date of death to the date of funding since the amount that funds the trust is a fixed dollar amount. Also, any assets that have appreciated from the date of death can be allocated to the credit shelter trust, thereby avoiding taxation of those assets in the surviving spouse's estate. The following is an example of a gift (i.e., bequest) to a marital trust with a true worth pecuniary formula clause:

"The trustee shall retain and administer as the Marital Trust an amount equal to the settlor's gross estate for tax purposes, reduced by the maximum dollar amount that, without considering the federal estate tax marital deduction in effect at the time of the settlor's death, can pass free of estate taxation. The trustee shall hold the remaining trust estate as the Family Trust (i.e., credit shelter trust.) Each asset distributed in kind to the Marital Trust shall be valued at the date of distribution thereof."

The true worth pecuniary formula clause has several characteristics with income tax consequences that the trustee needs to understand before funding the trusts:

- **Assets used to fund the trusts must be valued as of the date of funding.**

- **Assets used to fund the pecuniary amount are considered a sale of those assets for income tax purposes. Therefore, all trust assets must be revalued as of the date of distribution. Capital gains will be realized on any asset used to fund the trust. For this purpose, the capital gain is the difference between the value used on the estate tax return (Form 706) and the date of funding value. The capital gains taxes are paid by the non-pecuniary trust, or the credit shelter trust, in the above example of a pecuniary formula clause. For this reason, the sooner the funding takes place, the better. The longer it takes to fund the trusts, the greater the potential capital gains.**

- **Distribution of assets to the marital trust carries with it any taxable income that is classified as distributable net income (DNI) and taxes it to the marital trust.**

- **Distribution of assets to the trust that represent income in respect of a decedent (IRD) accelerates the reporting of the IRD in the year the trust is funded. This results in the income taxation of the IRD. (Refer to** *Chapter 7 Administering the Estate–Tax Elections and Other Postmortem Issues.*)

There are other issues that the trustee must consider before funding the trust, including the type of marital trust that is being funded, the intended use of the assets, the income requirements of the surviving spouse and other beneficiaries, and the need to shelter assets from taxation in the surviving spouse's estate. To illustrate how funding decisions are made, let's look at an example:

ESTATE OF HAROLD BAKER

Revocable Living Trust	$900,000
IRA	275,000
Joint checking account	25,000
Gross Estate	**$1,200,000**

ESTATE TAX RETURN

Gross Estate		$1,200,000
Marital Deduction:		
IRA	$275,000	
Joint checking account	25,000	
Marital trust	225,000	525,000
Taxable Estate		675,000
Exemption (Year 2000)		675,000
Estate Tax		**-0-**

HAROLD BAKER REVOCABLE LIVING TRUST
TRUST ASSETS

	Fair Market Value at Date of Death (Tax Cost Basis)	Date of Funding Value	Gain or Loss
Residence (50% interest)	$ 175,000	$ 180,000	$ 5,000
Putnam Capital Appreciation Fund	360,000	445,000	85,000
Fidelity Government Securities Fund	100,000	105,000	5,000
500 shares ABC, Inc.	50,000	55,000	5,000
Note – Installment Sale	100,000	100,000	—
Bank CDs, Money Market Fund	115,000	115,000	—
Totals	**$ 900,000**	**$1,000,000**	**$100,000**

Let's assume that the trust document calls for funding the marital trust with a pecuniary amount and the pecuniary formula clause prescribes the true worth funding method. The trust is a general power of appointment marital trust and provides that the surviving spouse has the power to withdraw principal on demand. She owns the other half of the residence in her own revocable living trust and has indicated that she plans to sell it and move into an apartment. The following is one way the marital trust can be funded:

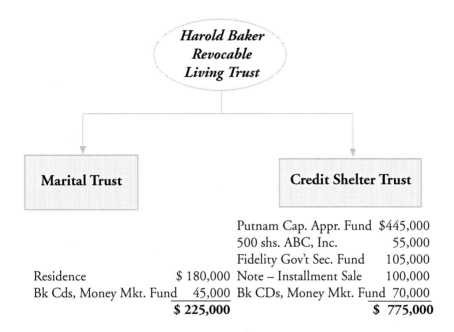

		Putnam Cap. Appr. Fund	$445,000
		500 shs. ABC, Inc.	55,000
		Fidelity Gov't Sec. Fund	105,000
Residence	$ 180,000	Note – Installment Sale	100,000
Bk Cds, Money Mkt. Fund	45,000	Bk CDs, Money Mkt. Fund	70,000
	$ 225,000		**$ 775,000**

The pecuniary amount that is gifted to the marital trust is the amount used on the estate tax return, or $225,000. Since the residence will be sold by the surviving spouse, and she has, in essence, control over the marital trust because of her right to withdraw principal, it makes sense to put the residence in the marital trust. A capital gain will be realized upon funding the trust, but the amount of the gain ($5,000) is relatively small. The balance of the pecuniary amount is funded with cash (i.e., money market fund). No capital gain is realized on this amount and when combined with the proceeds from the sale of the residence, it can be reinvested into bonds to provide income for the surviving spouse.

High growth assets should be distributed to the credit shelter trust to maximize the amount that will be sheltered and minimize taxes in the surviving spouse's estate.

The assets that are not used to fund the pecuniary marital trust will automatically fund, or fall into, the credit shelter trust. The reason this amount does not equate to $675,000 (i.e., exemption equivalent amount) is because it is being funded last—with what is left over of the trust assets after funding the marital trust amount. The assets that have grown, and are expected to grow in value in the future, have deliberately been allowed to fall into the credit shelter trust. This maximizes the estate tax sheltering effect of the credit shelter trust and also avoids triggering capital gains tax on the appreciation of these assets. The installment sale note is an IRD item and was allowed to fall into the credit shelter trust to avoid acceleration of the income tax. Also the note will have a greater value as principal payments are reinvested in growth assets over time. When they mature, the remaining assets (i.e., bank CDs and money market fund) can be invested in other growth investments or fixed income securities to produce income for the beneficiaries.

While these are not the only funding choices, they do address some of the tax and non-tax issues. The trustee needs to consider all of the tax and non-tax consequences in selecting the assets that fund these trusts. Seeking the advice of an attorney, accountant or other professional with experience in this area of administration is a prudent thing to do.

Some pecuniary formula clauses require that the credit shelter trust be funded first, with the residue passing to the marital trust. This so-called "reverse pecuniary" bequest is used primarily when the marital portion of the estate is expected to be very large and capital gains that may be incurred upon funding of the marital trust is a concern. A reverse pecuniary bequest might read as follows:

"If the settlor's spouse survives the settlor, then at the settlor's death the trustee shall retain and administer as the Family

Trust an amount equal to the maximum dollar amount that, without considering the federal estate tax marital deduction in effect at the time of settlor's death, can pass from the settlor's gross estate free of estate taxation, taking into consideration the value of all available credits against estate tax and all taxable transfers that pass outside of this trust."

The amount used to fund this trust is based on the exemption equivalent amount applicable at the decedent's date of death. The Taxpayers Relief Act of 1997 phases in an increase in the unified credit and the corresponding exemption equivalent amount through the year 2006:

YEAR	UNIFIED CREDIT	EXEMPTION EQUIVALENT AMOUNT
2000	$220,550	$675,000
2001	$220,550	$675,000
2002	$345,800	$1,000,000
2003	$345,800	$1,000,000
2004	$555,800	$1,500,000
2005	$555,800	$1,500,000
2006	$780,800	$2,000,000
2007	$780,800	$2,000,000
2008	$780,800	$2,000,000
2009	$1,455,800	$3,500,000
2010	$0	$0

Although a reverse pecuniary bequest likely would not be used in the above example, the following is one way to fund it if it were:

		91 shs. ABC, Inc.	$ 10,000
Residence	$ 180,000	Putnam Cap. Appr. Fund	445,000
409 shs. ABC, Inc.	45,000	Fidelity Gov't. Sec. Fund	105,000
Note—Installment Sale	100,000	Bank CDs, Money Mkt.	115,000
	$ 325,000		**$ 675,000**

Funding the credit shelter trust with the Putnam Capital Appreciation Fund shares will generate capital gains, yet it is a growth asset whose appreciation will escape estate taxation at the surviving spouse's death. Also, the capital gains taxes will be paid out of the marital trust, reducing the amount that will be taxed in the surviving spouse's estate. The shares of Putnam Capital Appreciation Fund used to fund the credit shelter trust will receive a new cost basis equal to their value on the date of funding. The note, as was pointed out earlier, is an IRD item, and is being allowed to pass as part of the residue to the marital trust to avoid acceleration of the income tax on this item. The balance of assets used to fund the credit shelter trust was selected because they generate little or no gain. Once the residence is sold, the proceeds allocable to the marital trust can be reinvested into income (non-growth) producing assets to generate more cash flow for the surviving spouse. In this example, the marital trust amount is $325,000 instead of $225,000 as in the previous example of a pecuniary bequest to the marital trust.

Minimum worth funding

The minimum worth funding method also allows the trustee to pick and choose the assets to fund the pecuniary bequest trust (marital or credit shelter.) In selecting the assets, the trustee must use the date of death value (or alternate value if it was used on the estate tax return) or date of funding value, whichever is lower. No capital gain is recognized upon funding because the assets used to fund the pecuniary bequest trust will never exceed their tax cost basis. The following is an example of a minimum worth funding provision:

"My trustee shall select and distribute the cash, securities, and other property, including real estate and interests therein, that will constitute the marital bequest, employing for the purpose of valuation the lesser of the adjusted basis of the asset for federal income tax purposes or current value of the asset at the time of distribution."

The following are characteristics of this type of funding formula:

- **No capital gain is realized upon funding of the trust.**

- **Only those assets that have diminished in value from the date of death need to be valued as of the date of funding. This formula avoids revaluing all of the assets and the time and expense of appraising difficult assets such as business interests and real estate.**

- **A capital loss cannot be used by the trust unless the funding is from an estate to a trust (i.e., testamentary trust).**

- **DNI is also taxed to the trust that is being funded with the pecuniary bequest amount and IRD issues associated with the true worth funding method also apply.**

- **This method gives the trustee the flexibility of favoring the surviving spouse by funding the marital trust with assets that have appreciated in value or underfunding it with depreciated assets.**

Using the Harold Baker estate example, the following is one way to fund a pecuniary marital bequest with a minimum worth formula clause:

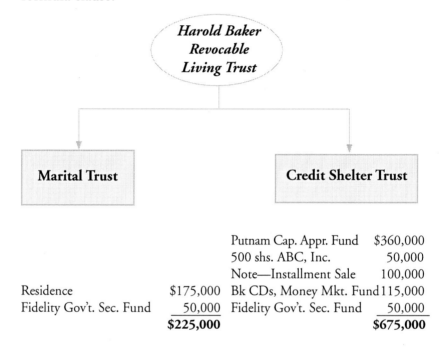

		Putnam Cap. Appr. Fund	$360,000
		500 shs. ABC, Inc.	50,000
		Note—Installment Sale	100,000
Residence	$175,000	Bk CDs, Money Mkt. Fund	115,000
Fidelity Gov't. Sec. Fund	50,000	Fidelity Gov't. Sec. Fund	50,000
	$225,000		**$675,000**

No capital gains will be realized upon funding. When it is sold, however, the residence will realize a gain, regardless of where the residence was placed. The growth assets were allocated to the credit shelter trust to shelter future gains. The note was not included in the pecuniary bequest, again, to avoid acceleration of the income tax on this IRD asset.

Fairly representative funding

This method of funding is also not as common as true worth funding, because it does not give the trustee as much flexibility. Although it allows the trustee to pick and choose assets to fund the trusts, this is limited because assets selected must be fairly representative of the gains and losses that have occurred from the date of death to the date of funding. The following is an example of a fairly representative funding formula clause:

"The trustee shall fund the Marital Trust with that pecuniary amount which is equal to the value of my estate as finally determined for federal estate taxes reduced by the largest amount, if any, which if allocated to the Family Trust would result in no increase in federal estate tax payable at my death. In funding the Marital Trust, the trustee shall distribute assets in such a manner that they have an aggregate fair market value fairly representative of the appreciation or depreciation in the value to the date or dates of distribution of all assets then available for distribution."

The following are characteristics of this type of formula:

- **The values used for funding are the values used on the federal estate tax return.**

- **No gain or loss is realized upon funding.**

- **Assets used to fund the bequest must be fairly representative of gains and losses from the date of death to the date of funding. Therefore, all trust assets must be valued as of the date of distribution to make this determination.**

- **DNI is carried out to the trust that is being funded with the pecuniary bequest resulting in tax at the trust level, although the amount is smaller than with the true worth funding method.**

- **Income will be accelerated on IRD assets that are used to fund the pecuniary bequest trust.**

In the Harold Baker estate, the trust assets valued at the date of funding include $100,000 of appreciation from the value reported on the estate tax return, Form 706. The appreciation represents 10% ($100,000 / $1,000,000) of the date of funding value. This funding method requires that date of death values be used and $22,500 of gains (10% X $225,000 = $22,500) be allocated to the marital trust. The following is one way the marital trust could be funded under this formula:

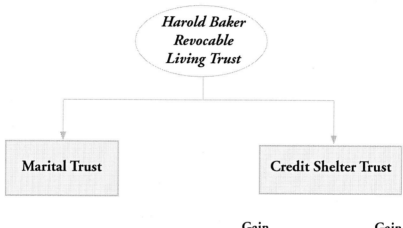

		Gain		Gain
Residence	$ 43,750	$ 1,125	$ 131,250	$ 3,875
Putnam Cap. Apr. Fund	90,000	19,125	270,000	65,875
Fidelity Gov't Sec. Fund	25,000	1,125	75,000	3,875
500 shs. ABC, Inc.	12,500	1,125	37,500	3,875
Note – Installment Sale	0	0	100,000	0
Bank CDs, M/M Fund	53,750	0	61,250	0
	$ 225,000	$ 22,500	$ 675,000	$ 77,500

No gains will be recognized upon funding. The residence, upon sale, will be subject to capital gains taxes. The note is allowed to pass as part of the residue to avoid acceleration of income taxes on this item.

Fractional Bequest Formulas

As noted above, one of the disadvantages of a pecuniary formula clause that uses the true worth funding method is that it generates capital gains upon funding, whether it is the marital or credit shelter trust. As with the minimum worth and fairly representative funding methods, this problem is avoided under a fractional bequest formula, which is one reason it may be used in a trust. Under a fractional formula the marital and credit shelter trusts receive a fractional share of the trust assets. The fraction is based on the values used on the decedent's estate tax return. The following is an example of a fractional bequest formula:

> *"The trustee shall retain as the Marital Trust a fraction of the trust property of which, the numerator shall be the largest amount, if any, that can pass free of federal estate tax taking into account the unified credit and the state death tax credit (provided use of the latter credit does not require an increase in the state death taxes paid) but no other credit, reduced by the value (as finally determined for federal estate tax purposes of all other property included in my gross estate passing thereunder, other than property which passes under this item which does not qualify for the federal estate tax marital deduction or charitable deduction, and by any charges to principal that are not deducted in computing the federal estate tax on my estate, and the denominator of which shall be the value of my residuary estate as finally determined for federal estate tax purposes"*

The following are the principal characteristics of this type of formula clause:

- **No gains or losses are realized when funding the marital and credit shelter trusts.**

- **Income is not accelerated on IRD items upon funding.**

- **DNI (taxable income) is taxed to the trust if the income is retained, or its beneficiaries if income is distributed to them.**

Fractional pro-rata formula

There are two variations of the fractional formula. One is a pro-rata method; the other allows the trustee to "pick and choose" the assets that will fund the trusts.

The pro-rata method allocates a fractional share of each trust asset to the marital and credit shelter trusts. The fraction is based on the value of the trust assets and the marital deduction used on the decedent's estate tax return. In the Harold Baker estate example, the formula would be determined as follows:

Marital deduction	$ 525,000
Less: marital deduction items other than the marital trust	300,000
Marital deduction attributable to trust	**$ 225,000**

$$\frac{\text{Marital deduction attributable to trust} = \$225,000}{\text{Date of death value of trust assets} \quad \$900,000} = .25 = \mathbf{25\%}$$

The marital trust would be funded with 25% of each trust asset. The assets that have not changed in value can be allocated at the discretion of the trustee. In total, 25% of the trust assets will fund the marital trust and the remaining 75% will go to the credit shelter trust:

	Marital Trust 25%	Credit Shelter Trust 75%
Residence	$ 45,000	$ 135,000
Putnam Cap. Appr. Fund	111,250	333,750
Fidelity Gov't. Sec. Fund	26,250	78,750
500 shs. ABC, Inc.	13,750	41,250
Note—Installment Sale	25,000	75,000
Bank CDs, M/M Fund	28,750	86,250
	$ 250,000	$ 750,000

Fractional "pick and choose" formula

The fractional "pick and choose" method begins with determining the fraction that applies to each trust, as in the previous example. That is, the fraction to be allocated is 25% for the marital trust and 75% for the credit shelter trust. The additional language that would allow a "pick and choose" fractional bequest might read as follows:

"Assets may be allocated to this fractional share by either pro-rata or non-pro-rata division, in cash or in kind..."

The following must be taken into consideration when using this method of funding:

- **Gains must be allocated proportionately between the two trusts in the same way that the pecuniary bequest—fairly representative funding—method requires.**

- **Each time a "pick and choose" asset is selected and allocated to the trusts the fraction must be re-computed. This is because the computation of the fractional formula is based on the estate tax value and the "pick and choose" asset is allocated at its date of funding value.**

Generation-Skipping Trusts

In addition to funding the marital and credit shelter trusts, an allocation of the generation-skipping exemption may also have to be made. (Refer to *Chapter 9 Preparing the Trust for Administration—Tax and Other Elections.*) The basic division is first made to the marital and credit shelter trusts. From here, the marital trust can be split into the Non-Exempt Marital (or QTIP) Trust and the GST Exempt Marital (or QTIP) Trust. Generally, all of the issues that relate to the funding of the marital and credit shelter trusts described above also apply to the generation-skipping exempt trust. Allocating growth assets to the generation-skipping trusts (i.e., GST Exempt Marital and Credit Shelter Trusts) will have the advantage of creating greater leverage of the exemption because all of the appreciation of these trusts, in addition to the original amount that funded the trusts, will not be subject to any generation-skipping tax. Funding or not funding the trusts with assets that will appreciate, of course, must take into consideration the beneficiary's need for income.

There are income tax-planning issues, in addition to the obvious estate and generation-skipping tax sheltering opportunities, which the trustee must consider. Funding decisions must also consider the kind of assets being allocated. For example, special use valuation property should be allocated to the marital trust to qualify for the special use valuation in the surviving spouse's estate. These are complex planning issues and the trustee would be well advised to seek competent professional advice before funding these trusts.

Funding Checklist

✓ **Determine the type of funding formula under the trust and review the formula's characteristics.**

✓ **Do not fund any of the trusts until a final determination of the federal estate tax has been made, unless there will only be a credit shelter trust.**

✓ **Consult with the surviving spouse, and/or the surviving spouse's financial advisor, regarding the surviving spouse's potential estate tax liability.**

✓ **If the marital trust will be funded with non-income producing (i.e., unproductive) assets, obtain a written consent from the surviving spouse.**

✓ **If the trusts will create generation-skipping transfers and there is no provision in the trust to create a generation-skipping exempt trust, petition the court for authority to create a separate trust.**

✓ **Seek professional assistance from a CPA or the attorney for the trust.**

CHAPTER 11

Managing Trust Investments

KEY POINTS

- Trustees are expected to exercise reasonable care, skill and caution in managing the trust's investments.

- Trustees are required to invest trust assets exclusively for the benefit of the beneficiaries of a trust.

- Trustees should adhere to the investment standards under the "Prudent Investor Rule" and Uniform Prudent Investor Act.

- A trustee has a greater investment responsibility under a continuing trust than under a terminating trust.

A trustee has the responsibility for managing the investments during the life of a trust, until the assets are ultimately distributed to the beneficiaries. The trustee must manage the trust's portfolio in accordance with the needs of its beneficiaries, the terms of the trust and local law. The trustee's authority for investing trust assets varies from trust to trust. The trustee may be given sole authority under the trust document or may be required to consult with a designated individual in making investment decisions. Even if the trust document directs the trustee to consult with others before making investment decisions, the trustee is responsible, unless language in the trust document protects the trustee from liability that may result from a consultant's advice. The trust document may direct the trustee to invest in specific stocks or restrict investments to certain asset categories such as insured bank deposits or U.S. Treasury obligations. If a trust document is vague or does not give a trustee sufficient powers, the trustee must look to local law for guidance.

The investment responsibility of a trustee falls into two general categories, or situations. One is managing investments in a terminating trust where the investment responsibility is relatively passive. The other is the responsibility under a continuing trust, which requires on-going management of the portfolio.

Investment Responsibilities under a Terminating Trust

A trustee's investment responsibilities under a trust that terminates at the death of the settlor are the same as for a personal representative. The trustee has the responsibility to preserve the assets and raise the cash needed to pay estate expenses, taxes, cash bequests, etc. as soon as is practical. If investments are to be sold to raise cash, an analysis needs to be made to determine which securities are the best candidates for liquidation. Preserving the assets does not require the trustee to manage the investments for the purpose of making more money for the beneficiaries. Preservation, in this context, means that the trustee should take whatever action is necessary to prevent known and obvious losses from occurring, beyond those that are the result of normal market fluctuations. For example, let's say a particular stock's value is rapidly dropping because the company's president has been fired, or the company is being sued for a billion dollars and it is obvious that the company is not likely to recover from these events anytime soon. The trustee should consider selling the stock to preserve what is left of its value for the beneficiaries. Obviously, this is a judgment call and the trustee should seek the advice of a competent investment professional before any action is taken.

Investment Responsibilities under a Continuing Trust

In a continuing trust the trustee's investment duties are active and on going. The duty extends for the entire life of the trust. The on-going management must take into consideration the terms of the trust, the income requirements of the beneficiaries, the need to make distributions of principal and other circumstances of the trust that affect investment decisions as they occur. The trustee of a continuing trust must manage the portfolio faced with the inherent conflict between the objectives of the current income beneficiaries and the remaindermen. The income beneficiaries want the trustee to invest in securities that will maximize current income and the remaindermen want maximum growth. Balancing these objectives presents special challenges for trustees. The trustee must produce enough income to meet the needs of the income beneficiaries and cover administration expenses and also provide some growth to the portfolio as a hedge against inflation to protect the interests of the remaindermen. This chapter focuses primarily on managing investments under a continuing trust.

Investment Standards for Trustees

Trustees must adhere to certain investment standards when managing trust assets. The origins of these standards date back to the early 1800s. The so called *Prudent Man Rule* statutes were developed from the Harvard v. Amory (1830) case in which the court described how trustees should conduct themselves when managing the trust's investments. The court said that:

"All that can be required of a trustee to invest is that he shall conduct himself faithfully and exercise a sound discretion. He is to observe how men of prudence, discretion, and intelligence manage their own affairs, not in regard to speculation, but in regard to the permanent disposition of their funds, considering the probable income, as well as the probable safety of the capital

to be invested."

Under the law of trusts (The Restatement of Trusts 2d (1959)), the same theme prevails as in the Amory case:

"In making investments of trust funds the trustee is under a duty to the beneficiary... to make such investments and only such investments as a prudent man would make of his own property having in view the preservation of the estate and the amount and regularity of the income to be derived...."

The standard measures a trustee's actions against the actions of others. That is, the law asks the question, "did the trustee behave in a way that other trustees would have behaved under similar circumstances?" The rules of trust law are default rules. This allows the creator of a trust to direct the trustee, under the terms of his or her trust, to manage the trust in a manner that would not necessarily be permitted under the standards of prudence. However, absent any specific investment directive, a trustee is expected to follow the standards of conduct established under the law.

Uniform Prudent Investor Act

The National Conference of Commissioners on Uniform State Laws has drafted suggested language to bring uniformity to the standards of conduct laws that apply to trustees in each state. The Uniform Prudent Investor Act, which reflects the "new" guidelines for trustees under the Restatement of Trusts 3d: Prudent Investor Rule, has been enacted by several states. It recognizes that the old rule is outmoded and describes a modern portfolio theory standard for managing trust assets. Although the Uniform Prudent Investor Act is a default rule, that is, the trust document can alter or abrogate the rules under the Act, trustees should refer to it as a guide in managing trust assets as long as the terms of the trust do not give a contrary directive.

Uniform Prudent Investor Act

Section 1. Prudent Investor Rule

(a) Except as otherwise provided in subsection (b), a trustee who invests and manages trust assets owes a duty to the beneficiaries of the trust to comply with the prudent investor rule set forth in this [Act].

(b) The prudent investor rule, a default rule, may be expanded, restricted, eliminated, or otherwise altered by the provisions of a trust. A trustee is not liable to a beneficiary to the extent that the trustee acted in reasonable reliance on the provisions of the trust.

Section 2. Standard of Care; Portfolio Strategy; Risk and Return Objectives.

(a) A trustee shall invest and manage trust assets as a prudent investor would, by considering the purposes, terms, distribution requirement, and other circumstances of the trust. In satisfying this standard, the trustee shall exercise reasonable care, skill, and caution.

(b) A trustee's investment and management decisions respecting individual assets must be evaluated not in isolation but in the context of the trust portfolio as a whole an as part of an overall investment strategy having risk and return objectives reasonably suited to the trust.

(c) Among circumstances that a trustee shall consider in investing and managing trust assets are such of the following as are relevant to the trust or its beneficiaries:

> *(1) general economic conditions;*

> *(2) the possible effect of inflation or deflation;*

> *(3) the expected tax consequences of investment decisions or strategies;*

(4) the role that each investment or course of action plays within the overall trust portfolio, which may include financial assets, interests in closely held enterprises, tangible and intangible personal property, and real property;

(5) the expected total return from income and the appreciation of capital;

(6) other resources of the beneficiaries;

(7) needs for liquidity, regularity of income, and preervation or appreciation of capital; and

(8) an asset's special relationship or special value, if any, to the purposes of the trust or to one or more of the beneficiaries.

(d) A trustee shall make a reasonable effort to verify facts relevant to the investment and management of trust assets.

(e) A trustee may invest in any kind of property or type of investment consistent with the standards of this [Act].

(f) A trustee who has special skills or expertise, or is named trustee in reliance upon the trustee's representation that the trustee has special skills or expertise, has a duty to use those special skills or expertise.

Section 3. Diversification. *A trustee shall diversify the investments of the trust unless the trustee reasonably determines that, because of special circumstances, the purposes of the trust are better served without diversifying.*

Section 4. Duties of Inception of Trusteeship. *Within a reasonable time after accepting a trusteeship or receiving trust assets, a trustee shall review the trust assets and make and implement decisions concerning the retention and disposition of assets, in order to bring the trust portfolio into compliance with the purposes, terms, distribution requirements, and other circumstances of the trust, and with the requirements of this [Act].*

Section 5. Loyalty. *A trustee shall invest and manage the trust assets solely in the interest of the beneficiaries.*

Section 6. Impartiality. *If a trust has two or more beneficiaries, the trustee shall act impartially in investing and managing the trust assets, taking into account any differing interests of the beneficiaries.*

Section 7. Investment Costs. *In investing and managing trust assets, a trustee may only incur costs that are appropriate and reasonable in relation to the assets, the purposes of the trust, and the skills of the trustee.*

Section 8. Reviewing Compliance. *Compliance with the prudent investor rule is determined in light of the facts and circumstances existing at the time of a trustee's decision or action and not by hindsight.*

Section 9. Delegation of Investment and Management Functions.

(a) A trustee may delegate investment and management functions that a prudent trustee of comparable skills could properly delegate under the circumstances. The trustee shall exercise reasonable care, skill, and caution in:

> *(1) selecting an agent;*

> *(2) establishing the scope and terms of the delegation, consistent with the purposes and terms of the trust; and*

> *(3) periodically reviewing the agent's actions in order to monitor the agent's performance and compliance with the terms of the delegation.*

(b) In performing a delegated function, an agent owes a duty to the trust to exercise reasonable care to comply with the terms of the delegation.

(c) A trustee who complies with the requirements of subsection (a) is not liable to the beneficiaries or to the trust for the

decisions or actions of the agent to whom the function was delegated.

(d) By accepting the delegation of a trust function from the trustee or a trust that is subject to the law of this State, an agent submits to the jurisdiction of the courts of this State.

Section 10. Language Invoking Standard of [Act]. *The following terms or comparable language in the provisions of a trust, unless otherwise limited or modified, authorizes any investment or strategy permitted under this [Act]: "investments permissible by law for investment of trust funds," "legal investments," "authorized investments," "using the judgment and care under the circumstances then prevailing that persons of prudence, discretion, and intelligence exercise in the management of their own affairs, not in regard to speculation but in regard to the permanent disposition of their funds, considering the probable income as well as the probable safety of their capital," "prudent man rule," "prudent trustee rule," "prudent person rule," and "prudent investor rule."*

The old "prudent man rule" statute places greater emphasis on specific security selection in the portfolio than the new Uniform Prudent Investor Act law does. The Uniform Prudent Investor Act applies the standard of prudence to an investment as part of the entire portfolio, rather than on the individual investment.

Total return

Most states have enacted the Uniform Prudent Investor Act in one form or another. It allows a trustee to make investments on a total return basis. The total return concept takes into account both the growth (capital appreciation) of an investment and the income earned (i.e., dividends and interest) to determine the merits of a particular investment or the portfolio strategy as a whole. For example a particular stock may pay a dividend which equates to a current yield of 1%, which on the surface may appear to be a poor investment. However, in a twelve-month period the stock may have increased in value by 15% or a total return (i.e., the dividend yield plus capital appreciation) of 16%. This gives the trustee the opportunity to earn a higher return for the trust than could be achieved by investing in a security with a high current yield, such as a bond or high dividend paying stock. In addition to being the best measure of investment performance, the total return approach gives a trustee more flexibility in managing the trust's portfolio.

Several states have adopted the "new" Uniform Principal and Income Act, which compliments the total return approach to investing trust assets. The act allows transfer of some of the appreciation from principal to income for distribution to the income beneficiaries. This provision is intended to assure that the trustee will distribute adequate returns to the income beneficiary even though the portfolio does not produce high income. The total return concept under the Prudent Investor Act gives a trustee more latitude in investment decisions than the old law. In managing the portfolio, trustees can take advantage of investment opportunities that rely primarily on returns from appreciation rather than from income. Trustees should review the trust document and local law before employing this technique.

Modern Portfolio Theory

Modern portfolio theory, which has been incorporated into the Uniform Prudent Investor Act, is evolving into law in most states and setting new investment standard for trustees. Generally, the theory holds that a trustee should purchase investments based on how a security is expected to perform relative to the risk and return of the entire portfolio, not necessarily how that investment will perform by itself. It allows a trustee to include riskier securities in a portfolio as well as conservative ones. The theory requires the trustee to carefully monitor the individual investments in the portfolio and how they influence the trust's overall investment strategy. Modern portfolio theory defines two types of risks, "compensated" and "uncompensated". A start-up company has greater risk to an investor than a large well-established corporation. Investing in this type of company offers a potentially higher rate of return for assuming the higher risk. In modern portfolio theory, this is referred to as compensated risk. A particular security, which if taken alone might be very risky, may be prudent when purchased in the overall context of the portfolio, under this theory.

Uncompensated risk is not investing in enough companies and industries within the trust portfolio (i.e., diversification) because the trustee is not being compensated by the company or market for the risk. Diversification of the portfolio minimizes uncompensated risk. Those states that have incorporated modern portfolio theory in their statutes emphasize that diversification within a trust portfolio is expected and a trustee must justify lack of diversification.

Modern portfolio theory continues to influence the evolution of investment standards for trustees. Trustees should review their state laws and understand the terms of the trust to make sure that he or she is in compliance with these new standards if they apply.

General Categories of Investments

Managing a trust portfolio involves the prudent allocation of investments that are suitable to the needs of the beneficiaries and investment objectives of the trust. The establishment of an investment policy and specific investment objectives serve as guides in making these asset allocation choices and help to avoid unsound decisions. These guides will be discussed later in this chapter. It is important for the trustee to understand the basic asset allocation choices (i.e., equities, fixed income and cash), the reasons for using a combination of each asset and the investment characteristics of each type. The trustee's job is to select and allocate a mix of equities, fixed income securities and cash to meet the investment objectives of the trust, while staying within acceptable risk levels.

Equities

Equities are investments in the common stock of a company. The investor holds an ownership interest and shares in the company's profits through shareholders' dividends. As the company grows and becomes more profitable, the investor is also rewarded through appreciation in the price of the company's stock. As a general rule, dividends that are paid on common stocks represent a relatively small part of the return on equity investments. Current dividend yields (dividend ÷ price of the stock) are typically in the 1%—2% range. The primary reason for investing in equities is the expectation of future appreciation in the price of the stock, which is driven by the profitability of the company. The justification for investing in equities is their record of long-term growth and earnings which, in addition to providing some income to the income beneficiaries, can help protect the portfolio from the eroding effect of inflation. Equity investments are not without risk. Stocks are subject to business, interest rate and market risks. However in most cases, using equities in a trust portfolio is a reasonable way to manage the investments.

The prudent investor standard, as defined in Section 227 of the Restatement (Third) of Trusts (1990) provides that an investment in equities can be a prudent investment decision:

> *"Ordinarily a trustee may also justify the relatively high principal risks associated with stock investments on the basis of a compensating prospect of long-term appreciation in share values. Thus, a primary and proper attraction of common stocks is that they offer trustees a hedge against loss of purchasing power and may even, in appropriate trust situations, contribute to a deliberate effort to increase the real value of the trust estate."*

The amount allocated to equities should, of course, take into account the need for income, liquidity requirements in the short, intermediate and long-term, estimated termination date of the trust, need to protect the portfolio from unnecessary risk, and overall investment objectives of the trust.

Types of stocks

Stocks fall into several categories and the terms used to describe them are the common jargon of investors. The *capitalization* of a company is determined by multiplying the number of shares outstanding by the price of the stock. For example, IBM has approximately 1,795,760,770 shares outstanding. As of 3/17/2000, the closing stock price was $109. Multiplying 1,795,760,770 by $109 equals a capitalization of over $195 billion. If a company has a capitalization over $5 billion, it is considered a large capitalization (i.e., *large-cap*) stock. A capitalization between $1 billion and $2 billion is a *mid-cap* stock and below $1 billion is considered a *small-cap* stock. Generally speaking, large-cap stocks are established companies that usually pay dividends. Also called "*blue-chip*" stocks, they tend to be more liquid. Mid-cap stocks, because of their size and maturity, have a little more risk than large-cap stocks. Small-cap stocks are the riskiest of the three categories. Their price tends to be very volatile and they have relatively few shares outstanding. This makes small-cap stocks less liquid.

Some stocks are purchased because the stock is selling at a bargain. These are called *value stocks*. They are purchased at their bargain price by investors looking for the stock to return to its fair market value. Value stocks are generally purchased by investors who are more conservative and willing to wait for a longer period of time to reap the potential rewards. *Growth stock* investors look for companies whose earnings will grow. As long as earnings keep growing, the price of the stock will increase. Growth stocks tend to be more volatile and usually have a higher risk than value stocks. Another category of stocks is *cyclicals*. These are stocks that react to changes in the economic cycle. For example, as the economy is expanding, new buildings and production equipment are needed. Companies that produce construction materials and sell manufacturing equipment will benefit. While these companies do well in an economic expansion, the price of that stock will be adversely affected when the economy begins to contract.

Fixed income

Fixed income securities are debt obligations issued by corporations and state, city and federal governments. These obligations are generally referred to as bonds, but include notes, debentures and mortgages. Bonds are purchased primarily for their interest income and the security of their full face value if held until maturity. The interest paid is generally considerably higher than the dividends paid on common stocks. Investments in fixed income securities are not without risk. Because the interest rate on a bond is fixed for the term of the obligation, any market interest rate fluctuations will affect the price, or value, of the bond prior to its maturity. Market interest rates have an inverse relationship to the price of a bond. If market interest rates are higher than the rate paid on a bond, the price of that bond will drop. If market rates are lower the price of the bond will be higher. However, if a bond is held to maturity, the investor gets the full face value back.

There are basically three types of bonds. Corporate bonds pay interest that is subject to federal and state income taxes. The interest from municipal bonds is federally tax exempt. If owned by a trust in the state or municipality that issued them, the interest is also exempt from local taxes. However, municipal bond interest paid to a beneficiary from a trust will only be dual tax exempt if a municipality in which the beneficiary resides issued the bond. Interest from U.S. Treasury obligations are subject to federal income tax and in some states are exempt from state income tax. In selecting any fixed income investment for the portfolio, the trustee should consider liquidity needs, income requirements and the marginal income tax bracket of the beneficiary(ies). If some or all of the income is retained and taxed to the trust, the tax bracket of the trust is another consideration.

The choice between a taxable bond and a tax-free bond is determined by converting the current yield on the tax-exempt bond (i.e., municipal bond) to its taxable equivalent. The following formula can be used for this purpose:

Non-taxable return (%) = **Taxable Equivalent**
(1—marginal tax bracket)

Example: Taxable bond yield—7%
Non-taxable yield—6%
Marginal tax bracket—28%

$$\frac{.06}{(1-.28)} = \frac{.06}{.72} = .0833 = 8.33\%$$

In the above example, the non-taxable bond has the higher taxable yield and is the better choice. The taxable bond would have to yield 8.33% to equal the before-tax return on the non-taxable bond.

U.S. Treasury obligations are generally viewed as having less risk than corporate and municipal bonds because they are backed by the full faith and credit of the federal government.

Cash equivalents

Cash equivalent investments are highly liquid and include interest-bearing savings and checking accounts, money market funds, some certificates of deposit (CDs) and short-term U.S. Treasury bills. These are used to meet known short-term cash needs and for temporary investment of funds awaiting investment in more permanent securities. The rate of return is usually lower than other fixed income investments because there is little or no risk and in the case of a checking account, savings account and money market fund, the full amount of the principal is available upon demand. The principal on other short-term vehicles such as CDs and treasury bills can be recovered in a short period, usually less than a year. Trustees cannot let cash sit idle and must keep trust funds properly invested at all times. Cash receipts should be invested in an appropriate short-term investment until the funds are paid out or more permanently invested in a longer-term vehicle.

Mutual funds

A mutual fund is a pool of money from individual investors that is invested in stocks, bonds, short-term money market instruments and a variety of other investments. Some mutual funds invest in a combination of these investments. A mutual fund provides on-going professional management and diversification to minimize investor risk. There was a time when investment in a mutual fund by a trustee could be viewed as an unauthorized delegation of the trustee's investment duty. At issue was the fact that the mutual fund manager, not the trustee, made the investment choices for the trust. In addition, the trustee could not closely oversee the activities or ratify the actions of the fund manager. Other issues included the unauthorized commingling of trust assets with others and double management fees. The trustee would be charging a trustee's fee based on the value of the trust assets, including the mutual fund, while the fund manager is charging the mutual fund investors a management fee.

This is not a problem, however, if the trust document authorizes the trustee to invest in mutual funds. If authority is not given under the terms of the trust, most state statutes allow trustees to invest trust moneys in mutual funds. Even if state statutes do not specifically authorize the use of mutual funds in trusts, Section 227 of the Restatement (Third) of Trusts (1992) indicates that such an investment is permissible:

"in the absence of restrictions imposed by statute or by the terms of the trust, mutual funds and other pooling arrangements are clearly permissible investments and that they tend to facilitate diversification."

When in doubt, the trustee should obtain written authority to invest in mutual funds from the beneficiaries of the trust. Also, if not specifically prohibited by state statutes, the trustee should not charge his or her trustees fees on mutual fund assets since a fee is already being charged by the fund manager.

Deferred Annuities

Although deferred annuities are not considered investments in the classical sense, they are viewed that way by many investors. A deferred annuity is a contract between the owner of the annuity and an insurance company. The owner invests a lump sum with the insurance company or makes payments over a period of time. The insurance company invests the funds and pays out a benefit to the annuitant for a specified time or the lifetime of the annuitant. There are two types of deferred annuities: a *fixed annuity* and a *variable annuity*. A fixed annuity pays a set rate, or payment, and is the more conservative investment of the two types. A variable annuity allows the owner to choose how the funds will be invested —usually from a group of mutual funds. The payout is based on the investment return...the better the return, the higher the payout—the lower the return, the smaller the payout.

The major advantage of deferred annuities is that the earnings are tax deferred until paid out to the annuitant. In a trust context, an annuity may not always be an appropriate investment. In general, if a non-natural person, like a trust, owns an annuity, the annuity may not receive tax-deferred treatment on its earnings. If a trustee purchases an annuity for a beneficiary, it may be viewed as favoring that beneficiary over other beneficiaries of the trust. This could be a violation of the duty of impartiality.

Minimizing Risk

A trustee has a responsibility to prudently manage the investment risk in a trust portfolio. This does not mean that the trustee can invest the entire portfolio in very safe investments, such as treasury bills, to avoid risk. In most circumstances, this would be considered imprudent. The trustee's responsibility is not to avoid risk entirely, but to assume a reasonable amount of risk to achieve the investment objectives of the trust.

There are several things that need to be considered in minimizing risk in the trust's portfolio. The trustee should avoid making improper investments. The terms of the trust will have an affect on how the portfolio is designed and the amount of risk assumed will depend on the types of investments selected. The trustee should also consider using diversification, dollar cost averaging and a ladder of maturities when investing in bonds to minimize risk to the portfolio.

Improper trust investments

Under the Uniform Prudent Investor Act, trustees are evaluated by the total performance of the portfolio and not necessarily by the results of a single investment. However, each individual investment that is made must still be prudent. Although the law of trusts maintains that any investment may be permissible under the right circumstances, certain investments should be avoided. A poor investment could materially affect the overall results of the portfolio and therefore might be deemed improper. Some investments that may be considered improper investments for trustees include:

- **investments in which the trustee has a personal interest;**

- **proprietorships and general partnerships;**

- **short term investments made for quick turnover and high potential profit;**

- **unproductive property;**

- **unsecured loans;**

- **investments whose value will diminish over time (i.e., wasting assets.)**

In general, while these investments, may be considered improper, they are not prohibited in all cases. Under certain circumstances their use would not be imprudent. For example, the use of family limited partnerships has become an important estate-planning tool. Holding these interests in a trust would not be considered imprudent assuming that the underlying assets in the partnership are reasonable investments.

Terms of the trust

The investment time horizon is an important factor in structuring and managing a trust portfolio. Most investment advisors agree that investing in stocks and bonds for a short time is considerably more risky than using those vehicles for the longer term. Stocks and even bond prices can drop substantially within a given year. If a trustee is forced to liquidate these assets in a down market, losses could be realized. As a general rule, the shorter the term of the trust, the less exposure it should have to equities. If a trust, let's say, will terminate in less than five years, the portfolio should be more conservatively structured to maintain stability and preserve value. While the construction of every trust portfolio takes into account the cash needs of the beneficiaries, capital gains, and other factors, the allocation of assets should also take into consideration the time frame of the trust.

INVESTMENT ALLOCATION OVER TIME   ☐ Stocks   ■ Bonds

Types of investments

Trustees are usually given broad authority to invest funds as the trustee deems proper for the trust. Although the prudent investor rule does not prohibit risky investments, it does suggest that some risk is appropriate in certain situations and not suitable at all in others. The trustee must decide the appropriate risk based on the purpose of the trust, its investment objectives, the expected termination of the trust and the needs of the beneficiaries. The trustee can then determine the types of investments that are suitable to the risk level and rate of return requirements of the portfolio. Understanding the characteristics of each type of investment and its respective risk level is essential to this decision-making process. The investment pyramid is a good place to start:

Investment Pyramid

Asset Allocation

The objective of asset allocation is to minimize the risk associated with market volatility yet meet the current return and long-term growth objectives of the trust. The trust's portfolio should be diversified among general asset categories (i.e., stocks, bonds, cash, etc.) consistent with the amount of income that needs to be generated for trust beneficiaries, the trust's long-term growth objectives, its liquidity needs and the income tax brackets of the beneficiaries and the trust. The trick in asset allocation is not to overweight the portfolio toward one asset category or underweight in another. The asset mix and weightings should be consistent with the overall investment objectives of the trust.

Diversification

In most states a trustee has a duty to diversify the investments in a trust portfolio. Diversification avoids concentrations in a particular type of investment, company or industry and minimizes the risk of loss if there is a downturn affecting that portion of the portfolio. Investments are affected by market temperament, interest rates, inflation, industry, company and world events, corporate earnings and other factors that influence security prices. Diversification minimizes the effects any of these elements have on the portfolio, reducing the possibility of large losses. A portfolio should be diversified by type of investment (i.e., stocks, bonds, cash, etc.), by investment class (i.e., small and large cap stocks, short, intermediate and long-term bonds, index funds, etc.), by industry (i.e., finance, transportation, technology, utilities, etc.) and by company (i.e., technology sector—IBM, Hewlett Packard, Apple, etc.). The important thing to remember is *don't put all of the trust eggs in one basket.*

Dollar cost averaging

Potentially, investing a large amount of cash all at once can result in paying the highest price for a particular investment. To minimize this risk, particularly with investments in common stocks, use the dollar cost averaging approach to investing cash. An equal amount of the investment is purchased over a period of time. It can be months or years depending on market conditions and the amount to be invested. Dollar cost averaging spreads the cost of the security over time, thereby spreading the risk of paying too much for the investment.

Ladder of maturities

As noted earlier, bond prices are affected by fluctuations in interest rates. The price of the bond will fall if interest rates rise relative to the rate paid on the bond. If interest rates are lower than the rate paid on the bond, the price of the bond will rise. The problem, of course, is that a loss can occur if the trustee is forced to sell a bond at a low price in order to meet a cash need such as a principal distribution to a beneficiary. If a bond is held until it matures there is no risk, since the entire amount of the principal is returned to the investor. If bonds are purchased so that they mature at different times over a period of years ("laddering") the risk of loss can be significantly reduced. Another advantage of laddering over shorter periods is to maintain current market interest rates of return in the portfolio. That is, as interest rates rise the proceeds of maturing bonds can be reinvested in bonds that pay current market rates.

The Investment Process

The prudent investor rule and Uniform Prudent Investor Act focus on the courts' long-held position that the way a trustee manages a trust portfolio is more important than the investment results that he or she achieves. A prudent trustee should have a process in place to manage the trust's portfolio. Policies and procedures should be established and all portfolio reviews and actions should be documented. The trustee must consider the duty of loyalty and impartiality to the beneficiaries in whatever actions he or she takes in managing the portfolio. While the investment process may vary slightly from one trust to another and from one trustee to another, it should contain those components necessary to effectively perform this function in accordance with the trust document, the needs of the beneficiaries and the prudent investor rule. The process outlined below contains some of these basic components:

The Investment Process

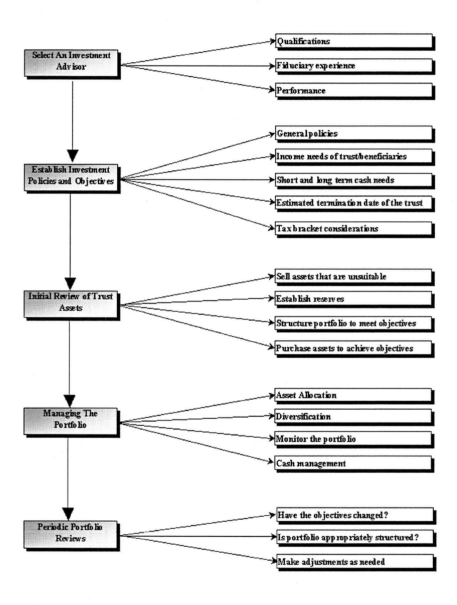

Select an investment advisor

Many people feel they know enough about financial matters to do a good job in handling their own investments. After all, this is the information age and whatever data is needed to make informed investment decisions is readily available. Some may also think that this knowledge is easily transferable to the management of a trust portfolio. This is a common perception particularly with individual trustees who see their responsibility as custodial and feel little need for a higher level of investment expertise. They assume that the deceased settlor's investment decisions were consistent with the intent and purpose of the trust and they are often reluctant to change the portfolio. They may also be unwilling to liquidate investments that have gone bad or purchase securities that are better suited to the objectives of the trust. This is a classic example of a trustee's failure to properly manage a trust portfolio, which could expose him or her to personal liability.

A trustee has a unique kind of responsibility when it comes to managing the assets of a trust. He or she serves two masters, so to speak. The trustee must produce sufficient income from the assets to meet the needs of the income beneficiaries and preserve the value (i.e., purchasing power) of the portfolio for the beneficiaries (i.e., remaindermen) who will inherit the property upon the termination of the trust. A trustee is expected to carryout these duties with "care, skill and caution." The general rule under common law is that a "trustee is under a duty to make such investments as a prudent man would make of his own property having primarily in view the preservation of the estate and the amount and regularity of the income to be derived."

The management of a trust portfolio is not a "part time" activity. A trustee must be able to respond to fast moving events in unpredictable securities markets and quick-changing economic conditions in managing the portfolio. This can be a full-time job. A prudent trustee should seek the assistance of a qualified investment professional. Commentators on the prudent investor rule have suggested that the rule encourages, and may even require, a trustee to seek expertise in managing the trust's portfolio.

The Uniform Prudent Investor Act (Section 9), the new law, encourages trustees to delegate the investment responsibility to others by providing that:

"A trustee may delegate investment and management functions that a prudent trustee of comparable skills could properly delegate under the circumstances."

However, the Act goes on to say that:

"The trustee shall exercise reasonable care, skill and caution in:

(1) selecting an agent;

(2) establishing the scope and terms of the delegation, consistent with the purposes and terms of the trust; and

(3) periodically reviewing the agent's actions in order to monitor the agent's performance and compliance with the terms of the delegation."

This means the trustee must act prudently in deciding to delegate the investment function to an advisor, but at the same time is required to supervise the agent.

Choosing an investment advisor can be daunting. There are literally tens of thousands out there. Begin the process with a clear understanding of what kind of advisor you need. You do not want someone who merely sells stocks and bonds, mutual funds or a particular investment program. Find an individual or institution that specializes in managing investment portfolios. An investment advisor can help to evaluate the investment needs of the trust and its beneficiaries, develop a specific portfolio strategy to meet the objectives of the trust, select specific investments that are suitable for the trust, monitor the portfolio on an on-going basis, monitor economic conditions and the securities markets, and conduct periodic reviews of the portfolio.

The key to selecting a good investment advisor is to ask questions, lots of them. The following are among those that should be asked during selection:

- How long have you been an investment advisor?

- What professional designations or certifications have you received (i.e., CFA, CFP, ChFc, etc.)?

- Are you a registered investment advisor?

- How many clients do you have?

- How much money do you manage?

- Are you familiar with the "prudent investor rule" and/or the Uniform Prudent Investor Act?

- How many trust portfolios do you manage?

- How do you charge for your services (i.e., commissions, management fee, or both?) How much?

- What has been your investment performance over the last year, 3 years, 5 years, 10 years?

- What is your worst performance for any 1, 3, 5, and 10-year period? Why?

- How much of your personal funds are committed to the investments you use?

Make sure you are compatible. The trustee should be sure the advisor's views are agreeable to his or hers. Check out the prospective advisor. Ask for a list of references including a list of clients. A bank is also a good place to check someone's reputation, as are other professionals such as CPAs, attorneys, insurance agents, etc. Another way to check out the prospective investment manager is to ask for a copy of ADV Form, Part II. This disclosure document, required by the Securities and Exchange Commission, outlines the individual's business history and any sanctions that were imposed against the advisor by regulators.

Establish investment policies and objectives

Investment policies articulate the general framework under

which the assets of the trust will be managed. The following should be among the items covered in the policy:

- **Whether or not an investment advisor will be retained and if one is hired to what extent will the advisor be used. For example, will the advisor provide assistance as needed or will the investment responsibility be delegated to the advisor?**

- **What quality standards will be applied to investments in stocks?**

- **What will be the minimum ratings for bonds that are purchased for the portfolio and what will be the maximum maturity or duration?**

- **If mutual funds are used will there be any restrictions regarding the use of "load" and "no-load" shares?**

- **What will be the maximum percentage of the portfolio invested in any one security?**

- **What general asset allocation weightings will be used?**

- **What will be the frequency of investment reviews for the trust?**

- **What benchmarks will be used to measure the portfolio's performance?**

Design a specific plan for meeting the needs of the trust beneficiaries, both income beneficiaries and remaindermen. Before these objectives can be formulated the trust document must be reviewed thoroughly. The terms of the trust may impose restrictions on investing trust assets or give directives that will affect how the funds are managed. For example, the trust may require the trustee to retain certain assets, restrict investments to specific kinds of securities, give preference to one or more beneficiaries, require that all of the income be paid to a beneficiary to maintain a specified standard of living, provide that certain amounts of principal be paid at specified times and other provisions that the trustee may need to consider in making investment decisions. In addition to reviewing the trust document, there are other issues to consider in developing the investment objectives for the portfolio:

- **The amount of income required to meet trust expenses and the needs of the beneficiaries.**

- **The ages of the beneficiaries.**

- **The income tax bracket of the trust and the beneficiaries.**

- **The estimated termination date of the trust.**

- **The short and long-term need for principal distributions.**

- **The amount of unrealized capital gains.**

- **The overall size of the trust, relative to the anticipated needs of the beneficiaries.**

- **The nature of the other assets (other than securities) of the trust.**

The investment objectives of the trust can by no means remain static. The nature of the trust and the needs of the beneficiaries will change over time and the investment objectives must be adjusted to accommodate those changes. For example, if the beneficiaries are very young with little or no need for income, the portfolio objectives can emphasize growth. When more income is needed, the portfolio objectives can be weighted toward fixed income investments to increase the current yield. If a total return strategy is used, the objectives must consider how much will be paid out to the beneficiaries each year.

Initial review of trust assets

Within a reasonable time after accepting the trusteeship, the trustee should review the assets of the trust. The review identifies those assets that are unsuitable for the trust and do not fall within the established policy guidelines. Once these assets have been identified, the trustee needs to take appropriate action. If there are large concentrations in a single investment and the beneficiaries do not want the investment liquidated, the trustee must ascertain whether retention is authorized by the terms of the trust document or local law. If not, the holding must be diversified. Another purpose of the initial review is to begin restructuring the portfolio to meet the investment objectives. This may involve selling some assets and purchasing others to achieve the desired asset allocation and positioning of the portfolio. Cash reserves need to be established for the trust to meet anticipated cash flow shortages and principal distributions. The portfolio strategy may also call for keeping some cash available for future investment. At the time of the initial review these cash needs should be identified, the funds raised and invested in a money market fund or other liquid short-term vehicle.

"To hell with a balanced portfolio. I want to sell my Fenwick Chemical and sell it now."

© The New Yorker Collection 1957 Richard Decker from cartoonbank.com. All Rights Reserved.

Managing the portfolio

As alluded to earlier in this chapter, managing a trust portfolio on a part-time basis and with limited investment knowledge is risky. Hiring an investment advisor substantially reduces the risk and allows the trustee to handle other trust matters more effectively. Establishing procedures for managing the assets of the trust and documenting investment decisions are good trust management practices. Part of the ongoing managing process involves maintaining the general asset allocation strategy for the portfolio. Fluctuations in the value of trust assets will affect asset allocation and the trustee may need to make adjustments to the portfolio to maintain the proper mix. Diversification of the portfolio can also be affected by changes in market values and yields. Changing circumstances within a given market or company can also affect diversification. Maintaining a well-diversified portfolio is important. As mentioned earlier, the portfolio should be diversified by asset type, industry and company to minimize the risk of loss to the trust.

The cash requirements of the trust and its beneficiaries can also change during the course of the year. This needs to be taken into account when managing the portfolio. As the need for cash arises, the funds should be raised as soon as practical without loss to the portfolio, if possible.

Under the Uniform Prudent Investor Act a trustee can delegate the investment responsibility for the trust to an agent (i.e., an investment advisor.) However, the Act imposes a duty on the trustee in selecting the agent, establishing the terms of the delegation and reviewing the agent's compliance with those terms. As part of the ongoing management of the trust, the trustee needs to communicate with, and regularly oversee the activities of the agent, whether or not the trustee delegates this responsibility under the Act or hires someone to assist in the management of the portfolio.

Periodic portfolio reviews

Review of the trust portfolio should take place at least every twelve months and more frequently if needed. The review determines if changes in the circumstances of the beneficiaries necessitate a change in the investment objectives or basic portfolio structure. The need for more income, for instance, may require a realignment of the portfolio toward fixed income securities. Or the need for income may have diminished, in which case the trustee might consider a shift to equities. Changes in the securities markets are frequent and portfolio reviews should take these events into account and if necessary appropriate adjustments in the portfolio should be made.

The review is also an opportunity to measure and evaluate how the portfolio and the investment advisor (agent) have done relative to meeting the investment objectives. The policies and objectives should also be reviewed and adjustments made where appropriate. Although communication with beneficiaries should be frequent and ongoing anyway, the portfolio review is a good time to discuss objectives, performance and other investment matters with them. It is important that the trustee not withhold information. Just because the trustee makes all of the decisions, is no excuse for not keeping the beneficiaries informed on how the trust is being managed.

Checklist for Managing the Trust's Portfolio

✓ Select an investment advisor (agent) to assist in evaluating and managing the portfolio.

✓ Review the trust document for any provisions that place investment restrictions on the trustee.

✓ Ascertain what investment standards (i.e., "Prudent Investor Rule", "Uniform Prudent Investor Act", etc.) apply under local law.

✓ Review the portfolio immediately to determine if any of the securities are illegal, substandard or unsuitable trust investments. Liquidate all inappropriate investments.

✓ Invest idle cash in a money market fund or other suitable short-term investment vehicle.

✓ Establish an investment policy and strategy for the trust based on:

- How much income will be required to cover trust expenses and meet the income requirements of trust beneficiaries.

- The short, intermediate and long-term cash needs to cover anticipated principal distributions.

- The income tax brackets of the trust and the beneficiaries who receive income from the trust.

- The known or estimated termination date of the trust.

✓ Diversify the portfolio by:

- Types of securities (i.e., stocks, bonds, cash, real estate, mortgages, etc.)

- Characteristics (i.e., income, growth, size of company, etc.)

- Industry (i.e., durable goods, utilities, transportation, technology, finance, etc.)

- Companies within industries.

- Bond maturities.

✓ Establish specific dates (not less than once a year) to review the portfolio. The review should cover:

- Any changes with regard to the needs of the beneficiaries, such as a requirement for more income or a principal distribution, which will necessitate an adjustment to the portfolio.

- The need to switch to taxable or non-taxable bonds based on changes in interest rates and/or the tax brackets of beneficiaries.

- A review of the investment policies to determine if they continue to be appropriate to the objectives of the trust or need to be modified.

- A review of the investment advisor's performance, fees and adherence to the terms of the contract.

CHAPTER 12

Managing Real Estate Assets

KEY POINTS

- Maintaining adequate insurance coverage on real estate is an important trustee responsibility.

- Environmental contamination can put the trust at risk and requires special attention by the trustee.

- A trustee must be proactive in making repairs and improvements to real estate assets in order to preserve and protect the property.

There are two reasons why real property will be kept in a trust after the death of the settlor. The first reason is that the surviving spouse may continue to occupy the family residence, or the weekend cottage or some other property is being maintained for use by the settlor's children. In the second situation, the settlor made investments in real estate and, as part of his or her estate plan, transferred the property into a revocable living trust. The terms of the trust and the type and nature of the real estate will determine how the property is managed. The trustee's management of the residence is relatively simple; the surviving spouse occupies the home and usually assumes responsibility for routine maintenance. Investment real estate, on the other hand, can require a considerable commitment of time especially if multiple commercial properties are owned by the trust.

Regardless of what type of real estate is owned, the trustee must see to it that it is properly managed. Some basic responsibilities include reviewing and making sure that the properties have adequate insurance coverage, addressing any environmental concerns, and maintaining the properties by paying property taxes and making repairs.

Insurance

An important task is to review the insurance on the property and be sure that the coverage is sufficient to protect the property and the trust. The policy should name the trustee as an additional insured and provide for replacement of the property at its current market value should a loss occur. It should also have adequate liability coverage in the event of a lawsuit that results from an accident on the property. It may be necessary to obtain a current appraisal in order to evaluate whether or not the coverage is adequate. Extended coverage for broader protection from wind, explosions, civil disturbances, aircraft and other causes should be considered. The coverage should also include worker's compensation and rent insurance, in addition to fire, liability and casualty protection. Depending on the type of property, the trustee may also want to obtain coverage for environmental cleanup in case contamination is discovered in the future. A trustee would be wise to seek the advice of an insurance agent who specializes in this area of risk management.

Environmental Issues

When environmentally contaminated property becomes an asset of a trust the trustee may be responsible for the cleanup. A trustee can be held liable under the Comprehensive Environmental Response, Compensation and Liability Act of 1980 (CERCLA) and the Superfund Amendment and Reauthorization Act of 1985 (SARA) for any contamination that is discovered while the property is owned by the trust. In 1996, congress changed the extent to which fiduciaries were held liable under CERCLA for environmental damages on property held in trust. Until the new law was enacted, trustees could have been held personally liable for clean-up costs associated with environmental damage if the assets of the trust could not cover those costs. However, the new law limits the liability for the cleanup to the value of the assets in the trust and does not hold the trustee responsible for any excess costs if the following conditions are met:

- **The trustee cannot be both the trustee and the beneficiary of the trust.**

- **The trustee cannot receive benefits from the trust that exceed customary or reasonable compensation.**

- **The trustee cannot have caused or contributed to the contamination.**

- **The trust cannot be organized for the primary purpose of, or engaged in, a trade or business for profit.**

- **There must be a bona fide trustee and not one who acquires ownership or control with the objective of avoiding liability.**

Even if liability is limited to trust assets, managing contaminated trust property may be more than a trustee wants to take on. Unintentionally, a trustee might cause or contribute to the contamination of the property potentially exposing him or her to personal liability. Performing some due diligence before accepting the trusteeship is prudent. Corporate fiduciaries do an extensive evaluation before accepting a trustee appointment where property is contaminated or where there is a possibility of contamination. An individual trustee would be wise to do the same. The following checklist can be used as a guide for a preliminary evaluation of the property or to review an environmental inspection report:

- **Identify potential problem properties. These include such things as industrial and manufacturing sites, agricultural land, properties containing asbestos materials, and sites where electric transformers or large** capacitors have been stored. A partial list of additional problem properties would include service stations, dry cleaners, junk yards, plating companies, air conditioning companies, laundromats, and so forth;

- make inspections of all sites where there might be problems. See the Audubon Society Field Checklist below for inspection parameters. It is also a good idea to evaluate adjacent properties which might have contaminated the trust property;

- evaluate the types of activities in which tenants are engaged. Businesses that handle certain types of hazardous materials may be required by state law to prepare a business plan consisting of emergency plans and procedures, inventory of hazardous materials, and a training program for employees. Fiduciaries should also be wary of seemingly innocuous tenants such as jewelry stores that use highly toxic chemicals in the manufacturing process;

- examine the chain of title for prior owners who might have used toxic materials;

- if hazardous materials are being used, examine company records to determine whether the tenant is properly storing, disposing and transporting those materials. It is also advisable to examine regulatory agency files. The EPA and local agencies maintain records of companies which request permits to use hazardous materials and those involved in cleanups;

- obtain an environmental audit. The EPA states that an environmental audit should be designed to "verify compliance with environmental requirements; evaluate the effectiveness of environmental management systems already in place; or assess risks from regulated and unregulated materials and practices;"

- obtain indemnification from the current operator, tenant or subsequent purchaser;

- check existing insurance policies to determine if they provide environmental coverage;

- consider sale, distribution or abandonment. Unfortunately, it is not likely that any of these three alternatives will protect a fiduciary who knows, or has reason to know, of the existence of hazardous materials on the property.

FIELD CHECKLIST FOR INITIAL DETERMINATION OF POSSIBLE PRESENCE OF HAZARDOUS WASTE ON PROPERTY TO BE ACQUIRED BY NAS (NATIONAL AUDUBON SOCIETY)

I. On-Site Conditions

A. Present or past industrial use of property.

B. Proximity to industrial facilities likely to generate wastes.

C. Road access (to facilitate dumping).

D. Presence of barrels, drums, fragments, paint cans, etc.

E. Presence of other debris from past or present waste dumping.

F. Presence of oil ponds or other liquids or oil slicks on puddles.

G. Presence of stressed vegetation (different coloration, stinted growth, bare spots, etc.).

H. Examine both sides of all roads and paths (for their full lengths) for signs of waste disposal.

I. Presence of mounding or unusual soil disturbances.

J. Presence of surface or underground storage tanks.

K. Presence of asbestos insulation in buildings or utility installations.

L. Automobile parking, truck storage, railroad storage or other possible sources of spilled oil or gasoline.

M.   Is ground water in proximity of property potable?

II. Other Investigations

A. From owner, neighbors or "old-timers," obtain history of the use of the property.

B. Check title history for industrial ownership.

C. Check regional office of U.S. Environmental Protection Agency, state and local environmental agencies and local health departments for record of problems and complaints.

D. Talk to local police to see if there have been problems or complaints.

E. Obtain aerial photograph from local tax assessor, U.S. geological survey or local flying club.

F. Talk to local planning and/or zoning officials regarding current and projected plans for the area.

Seeking professional assistance from an environmental specialist is a good idea. A professional evaluation will help to assess what will be necessary to properly manage the property. Some trusts allow a problem property to be segregated by the trustee into its own separate trust so that it does not contaminate other trust assets and subject them to cleanup liabilities. The following is an example of such a provision:

"The Trustee shall have the power to set aside as a separate trust, to be held and administered upon the same terms as those gov-

erning the remaining trust property, any interests in property, for any reason, including but not limited to a concern that such property could cause potential liability under any federal, state, or local environmental law."

Regardless of how the trust is structured, the trustee needs to perform a thorough evaluation of environmentally plagued property in order to properly manage it.

Maintaining the Property

Maintaining real property falls in the category of preserving and protecting trust assets. It includes seeing to it that all applicable property taxes and assessments are paid when due. If the property is a residence that is occupied by the surviving spouse, an exemption or other allowance that will result in a lower tax may be available. The trustee should make the proper request or application to take advantage of the property tax reduction. The trustee should also file an appeal to the tax authorities if the trustee feels that the property tax is too high relative to its value.

Previously mentioned, maintenance also includes adequate insurance and making sure that the premiums are paid when due. The trustee can be held personally liable if a claim for damages to the property is rejected because the premiums had not been paid on time. A tickler system should be established to cover these and any other payments that have a critical due date. Failure to receive a bill from the insurance company or taxing authority may not be a defensible position for not making the payment on time.

Repairs are always necessary to maintain the property. Conduct an initial inspection to identify anything that needs repair. If the repairs are large enough, say over $500, the trustee should solicit bids for the work. The repair work needs to be clearly described to the contractor and any limitations on the scope of the work outlined and agreed to—in writing. The trustee should also inspect the completed work and, if unsatisfactory, see that corrections are made. Major improvements such as a new roof, additions, construction of a new building or other permanent types of improvements are investments in the property. The decision to expend such funds should be based on the cost of the improvement and expected returns in terms of additional rent or potential appreciation in the value of the property. In considering expenditures for these purposes, the trustee needs to consider how they will affect the interests of the beneficiaries. Ordinary repairs are charged against the income of the trust and reduce the amount payable to the income beneficiaries. Major improvements are paid from principal, which affect the interests of the remaindermen.

Managing a Residence

The trust document will usually contain language to maintain the family residence for the benefit of the decedent's surviving spouse. The trust will typically own a fractional interest in the residence, usually one-half, with the surviving spouse owning the other half. A well-drafted trust will have a specific provision that makes it clear that the surviving spouse has use of the residence during his or her lifetime:

> *"Upon the settlor's death, if the settlor's spouse survives, the settlor requests, but does not direct, that the settlor's spouse be allowed the full, free, and undisturbed occupancy of the primary residence of the settlor and such spouse as that residence was prior to the settlor's death."*

Some trusts make no reference at all to the use of the residence by the surviving spouse. However, as long as the surviving spouse is a beneficiary of the trust, the trustee usually has the authority to allow the spouse to use the property. Unless otherwise directed by the terms of the trust, expenses for maintenance of the residence should be shared equally between the spouse and the decedent's trust, assuming each owns a one half interest. If the surviving spouse is entitled to receive income and/or principal from the trust, the trustee could pay all of the maintenance expenses. The trustee will have very little day-to-day management responsibilities since the surviving spouse is occupying the residence and is usually handling the routine maintenance. The trustee's primary duty is to preserve the property for those who will ultimately inherit it. This means assuring that timely repairs are made, taxes are paid and proper insurance coverage is maintained.

Frequently asked is whether or not the surviving spouse can sell the property if half of it is owned by the decedent settlor's trust. The answer is yes, since the surviving spouse owns the other half and the surviving spouse is given use and possession of the property. The trustee, of course, has a responsibility to the other trust beneficiaries and should not agree to a sale if the terms of the sale are clearly a "bad deal" for the surviving spouse and the decedent's trust.

Managing Investment Property

Real estate assets will either be improved or unimproved property. If the property is vacant land, the trustee has a duty to make the property productive unless the trust directs otherwise. The trustee can sell the land and invest the proceeds, lease it or operate it to produce income. If there is only one beneficiary and he or she is entitled to the income from the trust, the trustee can make the property available for the beneficiary's use and would not necessarily be obligated to make the property income producing. If the land is in a rural or depressed area selling the land may be the only alternative.

Improved property could be a single-family dwelling that is leased, a small apartment building, large condominium or commercial or industrial investment. If the property is subject to a long-term lease, the trustee may only need to collect the rent and see to it that the lessee abides by the terms of the lease. The management of larger properties will take considerably more time and effort. This usually necessitates hiring a property manager to handle the day-to-day management of the property. The selection process should be thorough, ending with the trustee assured that the agent will be responsive and produce the best results for the trust. The key to effective management and control of large properties through an agent is to have a sound management agreement between the trustee and the agent. In detail, the contract should outline the rights, duties, responsibilities and obligations of both the trustee and agent. The agent is usually responsible for collecting the rents, making repairs within the limits set by the trustee and maintaining accounting records including individual tenant files. The trustee should make sure that the net rental income is remitted to the trustee on a timely basis so it can be paid out to the income beneficiaries or invested. The agent's accounting records should be reviewed periodically for accuracy and, if necessary, audited annually.

Managing Out-of-State Property

Managing real estate that is located in another state requires special attention. Unless the trustee travels frequently to the state in which the property is located, he or she will have difficulty responsibly managing the property. A well-drafted trust will address this problem and specifically authorize the trustee to appoint a special trustee to be responsible for managing the property:

> "If at any time any trust property is situated in a jurisdiction in which any trustee is unable or unwilling to act, to appoint in an instrument signed by the trustee a person or corporation to act as special trustee with respect to that property in that jurisdiction, and such special trustee and every successor trustee so appointed shall have all the title, powers, and discretion with respect to the property that is given to the special trustee by the trustee. The net income from the property in the other jurisdiction and any net proceeds of its sale shall be paid over to the trustee;"

If the trust document does not permit delegation of the responsibility to a special trustee, consideration should be given to petitioning the court for reformation of the trust or seek the courts authority to appoint a special trustee. Absent either of these options, the trustee should at least hire an agent in the state in which the property is located to manage the property. As with any other agent hired by the trustee the trustee is responsible to closely supervise and review the actions of the agent.

Real Estate Management Checklist

✓ Evaluate all properties for environmental hazards and take steps to prevent contamination to the property. Refer to the checklists in this section.

✓ Have an insurance agent review the policies on the property and obtain adequate coverage.

✓ Establish ticklers to pay insurance premiums and property taxes.

✓ Conduct an inspection of the property periodically and make needed repairs.

✓ Evaluate unimproved property and implement a plan to make it productive.

✓ Hire a property manager, if necessary, and monitor his activities.

✓ Hire a special trustee to manage out-of-state property.

CHAPTER 13

Managing Business Interests

KEY POINTS

- Unless specifically authorized under the terms of the trust, local law or court order, a trustee cannot retain a closely held business interest in a trust.

- In selling a closely held business interest, the sales price must be fair and reasonable. A professional appraiser should be retained for this purpose.

- If a closely held business is to be retained, a thorough evaluation must first be made in order to support this decision.

- If an "S" corporation is owned by the trust, it must qualify under the terms of the trust to retain its status.

As the population ages, the small businesses upon which the family wealth has been built will pass through trusts or be managed by trustees. The responsibility for managing a decedent's closely held business in his trust has some unique characteristics. A closely held business interest may have been held by the settlor's revocable living trust prior to death as part of the estate plan or may have been owned by the decedent individually and became an asset of the trust through a pour-over Will. The business interest can be a sole proprietorship, general partnership, limited partnership, subchapter "S" corporation, "C" corporation or limited liability company (LLC.) Each form has its own distinguishing characteristics. Generally, the proprietorship, partnership, sub-chapter "S" corporation and limited liability company are pass-through entities. That is, the income is taxed directly to the holder of the interest. The "C" corporation is taxed differently. The "C" corporation pays a tax on its earnings. As earnings are paid out to the stockholders in the form of dividends, the stockholders again pay income tax on the dividends they receive. This "double taxation" of income is what distinguishes the "C" corporation from the other forms of business ownership.

Selling the Business

Unless the trust document, local law or a court order authorizes or directs the trustee to retain the business interest, the trustee has a duty to dispose of it and invest the proceeds in investments suitable for the trust. Continuing the business for any purpose other than its sale may not be considered prudent under some state statutes. Selling a closely held business takes time; a trustee must keep the business going to facilitate orderly liquidation. The business must be managed to preserve its value as a going concern and to avoid defaulting on any loans that the business has. Contracts need to be performed in order to maintain the value of the business and avoid litigation. When a decision is made to sell the business, the trustee may discover that there is a very limited market or no market at all.

Prior to death, the settlor may have entered into a buy-sell agreement, which would make the sale of the business relatively easy. A buy-sell agreement is an agreement between an individual owner and the other owners of the business that provides for the purchase of a decedent owner's interest in the business. The agreement usually establishes the purchase price and often allows for periodic price changes as the value of the business changes. The trustee under a buy-sell agreement has no choice but to sell the business in accordance with the terms of the agreement. Often life insurance is used to provide funds for the purchase. Some buy-sell agreements only give the buyer a first right of refusal. If the right is not exercised, the trustee must take on the responsibility of selling the business.

The trustee has a duty to use reasonable care, skill and prudence in selling the business. If challenged, the trustee must be able to demonstrate that the price for which the business was sold was fair and reasonable. Selling a business interest is not like selling a publicly traded stock whose value is easily ascertained. There is no index or reference book that can give the trustee a value or sales price. Valuing a closely held business is complex. To establish a value, a professional appraiser needs to be retained. Competent appraisers use a variety of methods to arrive at a value, such as comparing the business with similar enterprises. Other techniques include evaluating the capitalization of income, book value versus market value, common stock of the company, liquidation value versus the going concern value, historical rates of return, price earnings ratio and factual or intrinsic value versus market value.

The valuation of a business for estate tax purposes, which may consider minority interest and lack of marketability discounts, is not necessarily the same value that should be used to establish a sales price. The trustee should hire a specialist for this purpose and develop a marketing plan for selling the business. It is also a good idea to hire someone to negotiate the terms and sell the business. As part of the selling process the trustee should identify potential buyers, such as the decedent's business partners, family members who may want to own the decedent's interest in the business, owners of similar businesses, competitors and customers of the business.

If the closely held business is a corporation and is a major estate asset, the trustee may want to take advantage of Section 303 of the Internal Revenue Code to pay taxes and expenses. Section 303 allows the trustee to redeem shares of the company stock without the proceeds being treated as a taxable dividend. When certain conditions are met, the redemption is considered a stock sale and the proceeds will be treated as long-term capital gains. This is a good way to get cash out of the business with favored tax treatment, if there is a desire to keep control of the business by limiting the number of shares that must be redeemed to provide cash for the payment of estate taxes, funeral costs and administration expenses. To qualify for a Section 303 redemption, the value of the stock must represent more than thirty-five (35%) percent of the decedent's adjusted gross estate and only those shares that are needed to cover the expenses can be redeemed.

Managing the Business

The rationale for retaining and managing a closely held business interest should be restricted to a limited number of scenarios.

Retention is appropriate if:

- **The trust document specifically directs the trustee to retain the business interest without any liability to the trustee.**

- **The trust will terminate in a relatively short period of time and the beneficiaries have indicated a desire to retain the business.**

- **The business interest is profitable, fits within the overall strategy of the trust's investment portfolio and its retention does not represent an unreasonable risk.**

As mentioned, if the trustee is to retain a closely held business interest, the trust document or local law must authorize it. A typical trust provision might read as follows:

"To conduct business in partnership or in a joint venture with other persons, partnership or corporations; to continue and operate any business, ranch or farm transferred to the trust by the settlor, whether during the settlor's lifetime or by Will, and to do any and all things deemed appropriate by the trustee, including the incorporation of the business, ranch or farm and the investment of additional capital, for such time as the trustee shall deem advisable, without liability for any loss resulting

*from the continuance or operation of the business, ranch or
farm, except for the trustee's own negligence, and to close out,
liquidate or sell the business, ranch or farm at such time and
upon such terms as the trustee deems advisable."*

Unless the trust document specifically directs the trustee to
retain the business, a decision to keep it should only be made after
a thorough evaluation. The following are some of the issues that
need to be considered before a decision is made:

- **Are the current managers capable of carrying on the
  business?**

- **Will the ages of the managers and other owners have
  an effect on continuing the business?**

- **Does the trust have a controlling or minority interest?**

- **Is the return on investment reasonable?**

- **Do past and projected future earnings of the company make it a worthwhile investment?**

- **Will the returns meet the needs of current beneficiaries and provide value for the remaindermen?**

- **Are there any current or potential business liability
  issues? If so, are they manageable?**

- **Will the business interest represent a concentration
  in the portfolio?**

If the closely held business is a limited partnership interest, the
trustee has no authority or control over the activities of the enterprise. Also, liability is limited to the amount invested in the partnership. The success or failure of the business is in the hands of
the general partner. However, the trustee should review the activities of the general partner to assure that decisions to withhold or
distribute cash flow coincide with the business of the partnership.
The trustee must assess the general partner's ability and the viabil-

ity of the business in deciding whether or not to retain the limited partnership interest. If a trust holds a general partnership interest, the trustee will control management of the business. A general partner has unlimited liability and has a duty to manage the partnership in the best interests of the limited partners. The trustee also has a duty to manage the partnership in the best interest of the beneficiaries. These obligations should be consistent with each other and not create a conflict of interest. A trustee should consider converting the general partnership interest to a Limited Liability Corporation (LLC) or "S" Corporation to limit the trust's liability.

If the closely held business interest is a corporation ("S" Corporation or "C" Corporation) the trustee needs to determine whether the trust holds a controlling or minority interest. Control does not necessarily mean owning more than fifty percent of the outstanding shares of the company's stock. Depending on who the other shareholders are, such as shareholders who are the beneficiaries of the trust, a smaller holding could give the trustee effective control over the business. The trustee needs to assess whether or not to serve as an officer or director of the company. This decision should be based on the need to maintain control over the business and have access to information versus the potential liability in being actively involved in day-to-day operations. If the trustee decides to serve as a director or officer, he or she should not receive any fees or other compensation from the company. The trustee should also be sure that the company maintains adequate officers' and directors' liability insurance. If the trustee chooses not to serve as an officer or director he or she should attend all stockholders meetings to facilitate informed decisions when voting on issues that affect the company.

At the very least, the trustee needs to continually monitor the activities of the business. This should include the frequent review of the company's financial reports. The trustee should regularly evaluate the company's profit and loss statements, balance sheet, sales reports and other pertinent financial data. In addition, the trustee should review the minutes of the meetings of the board of directors and any committee meetings that are pertinent to the operation of the business. Periodic on-site inspections should also be made to observe the general operation of the business, working conditions and condition of the plant and equipment.

Sub-Chapter "S" Corporations

The sub-chapter "S" corporate ("S" corporation) form avoids the "double taxation" associated with the "C" corporation. There is no corporate income tax. Instead, the income is "passed through" to the stockholder and is only taxed once. This is an important income tax benefit that the trustee needs to preserve. After the death of the settlor, when a trust owns "S" corporation stock, it must meet certain requirements in order to maintain its status. Whether the stock is held in the marital or credit shelter trust, the terms of the trust must provide that:

1) **There be only one income beneficiary;**

2) **Principal distributions can only be made to the income beneficiary;**

3) **The income beneficiary's interest must terminate on the beneficiary's death or the termination of the trust, whichever is earlier;**

4) **If the trust terminates during the life of the income beneficiary, the principal must be distributed to the beneficiary; and**

5) **The trust income must be required to be distributed to the beneficiary or actually distributed to the beneficiary.**

The marital trust will usually meet these qualifications. However, the credit shelter trust may not. If the business will be kept and it is a growth asset, it should be put in the credit shelter trust. If the credit shelter trust, or any other type of trust, does not qualify, the IRS says that the "S" corporation status will not be terminated if:

1) **The situation resulting in disqualification was inadvertent;**

2) **Corrective steps are taken within a reasonable period of time; and**

3) **The "S" corporation and each shareholder agree to retain the "S" corporation election status.**

The trustee may have to amend the trust to bring it into compliance if, by the terms of the trust, the trustee is given the authority to do so. If the trust does not allow the trustee to amend the trust, consideration should be given to petitioning the court for reformation of the trust to avoid losing the "S" corporation status.

Managing Business Interests Checklist

✓ **Arrange for the sale of closely held business interests unless directed to do otherwise under the terms of the trust, local law or by court order.**

✓ **Obtain valuations from qualified business appraisers.**

✓ **Is there a buy-sell agreement?**

✓ **Does the stock qualify for redemption under Section 303 of the Internal Revenue Code for the payment of taxes and expenses?**

✓ **Does the trust authorize retention of the business?**

✓ **Evaluate rationale for retention.**

✓ **If trust owns the majority interest, get appointed as a director and/or officer of the enterprise.**

✓ **If the business is an "S" corporation, take the necessary steps to retain its status.**

CHAPTER 14

Making Discretionary Distributions to Beneficiaries

KEY POINTS

- Under the terms of a continuing trust, a trustee will likely be required to exercise discretion in distributing income and/or principal to the beneficiaries.

- In making discretionary distributions, a trustee must interpret the dispositive provisions of the trust, understand the creator's intent, evaluate the needs of the beneficiary, and exercise reasonable judgement.

- Accurate records of each discretionary distribution should be maintained for the life of the trust.

When Discretion Needs to be Exercised

Deciding when and under what circumstances the income and principal will be distributed to the trust's beneficiaries is one of the fundamental responsibilities of a trustee. Many trusts are designed specifically to have the trustee assume the role of a parent, grandparent or other person who was concerned with, or had responsibility for, protecting and maintaining the financial well-being of the beneficiary(ies). In assuming this responsibility, trustees are usually given very broad authority and the courts generally will not interfere with the trustee's exercise of this discretion unless the trustee has been dishonest, arbitrary, capricious, acted in bad faith, made a mistake or was extraordinarily imprudent or unreasonable. Needless to say, this responsibility must be performed with great care and diligence and it is important for the trustee to understand the basic principles of discretionary decision-making.

The instructions in a trust can be very specific, can require the trustee to exercise discretion, or both. Specific payment directives are fairly straightforward. For example, if the trust directs that a beneficiary is to receive $500 per month for life, the trustee merely pays the beneficiary this amount. Exercising discretion, on the other hand, requires the trustee to make subjective judgements in distributing income and principal to the trust beneficiaries. It is important that a trustee clearly distinguish between discretionary and non-discretionary provisions.

The use of the word *"shall"* in a trust document indicates that the trustee is *required* to take an action or make an income or principal distribution. The use of the word *"may"* implies that the trustee must *exercise discretion* in disbursing funds or taking an action. It is helpful to distinguish between the common types of dispositive provisions in a trust where these terms have relevance. For income tax purposes, the Internal Revenue Service classifies trusts into two general categories that distinguish discretionary from non-discretionary trusts. One is called a *simple* trust the other a *complex* trust:

Simple Trust

A simple trust requires all of its income to be distributed to the income beneficiary(ies). There is no provision for the payment of principal or the terms of the trust specifically prohibit principal payments. The following is an example of dispositive language under a simple trust:

*"From the date of the settlor's death until the termination of this trust, the trustee **shall** pay to the beneficiary all of the net income of the trust."*

Some trust documents will simply not include a provision for the distribution of principal. Others will specifically prohibit principal distributions.

Complex Trust

Complex trusts give the trustee discretion with regard to the payment of income, principal or both. A trust may require income to be paid out, but gives the trustee discretion to distribute principal. Such a provision may read as follows:

> *"From the date of the settlor's death until the termination of this trust, the trustee shall pay to or for the benefit of the beneficiaries herein named all of the net income of the trust. The trustee shall also pay to or for the benefit of the beneficiaries such portions of the principal for their health, education, maintenance and support, **as the trustee shall determine in the trustee's sole discretion.** Discretionary payments **may** be made to the beneficiaries in such amount, for such purposes, at such time and in such manner as the trustee shall determine in the trustee's uncontrolled discretion, with or without considering other resources available to them and without being required to keep the payments equal or proportionate."*

Another category of complex trust gives the trustee discretionary authority to distribute both income and principal. The language used in this type of trust might read as follows:

> *"After the settlor's death the trustee may, at any time, and from time to time, pay to or apply for the benefit of any one, all, or none of the beneficiaries, so much of the income and so much of the principal of the trust as the trustee, in its sole discretion, shall deem advisable for the health, education, maintenance and support of such beneficiary, or beneficiaries. In making any distributions, the trustee shall have discretion to take into consideration all other funds available to such beneficiary, or beneficiaries, for such purposes."*

These discretionary powers are referred to as express powers because they are written instructions to the trustee. If the trust document does not contain a specific written directive the trustee must look to state law for express authority, if any. If neither the trust document nor local law give the trustee express discretionary authority, the trustee can assume that he or she has the implied power to exercise discretion based on the general terms, purposes and intent of the trust. In this latter case it is a good idea for the trustee to get court approval and obtain the consent of all of the beneficiaries.

Distribution Guidelines

There is an inherent conflict between the current and remainder beneficiaries of a trust. Current beneficiaries want the trustee to maximize distributions to them during the period they are eligible to receive benefits. Also, if there is more than one current beneficiary, there will be competition among them for the resources of the trust. The trustee, unless otherwise directed in the trust, does not have to make equal distributions among the beneficiaries. The remaindermen, on the other hand, want to maximize their inheritance and therefore hope that the trustee does not make frequent and/or large principal distributions from the trust. In managing these conflicting viewpoints, the trustee is duty bound to be impartial. In making discretionary distributions, a trustee must evaluate the needs and particular circumstances of each beneficiary when deciding who gets what and how much. In most trusts, the current beneficiaries will usually be given preference over remaindermen. However, the trustee also has a duty to protect the principal of the trust for the remaindermen to the extent that it is not used for the current beneficiaries. To assure that distributions are used for the intended purpose, payments should be distributed directly to the payee (i.e., university, landlord, doctor, etc.) rather than to the beneficiary. If payments are made to a beneficiary, receipts should be obtained, again, to prove that the payment was used for the purpose for which the distribution was made.

Making discretionary payments from a trust is not an exact science. It is a process that includes following the terms of the trust, ascertaining the needs of the beneficiaries, using good judgment and exercising prudence. The place to start, obviously, is to read the provisions of the trust. In addition to defining who the beneficiaries are and their interest in the trust, many trusts will express the settlor's intent. The settlor's intent, whether expressed or implied, is what ultimately determines how a trustee is to exercise discretion. Some trust documents will express the settlor's desire to benefit current beneficiaries first and that the interests of remaindermen are secondary to that purpose. This tells the trustee that the trust is to be managed primarily for the current beneficiaries. The settlor may also express that the needs of the surviving spouse shall have preference over the needs of other current beneficiaries such as children and grandchildren.

There are common words and phrases that are used in a trust document to describe the purposes for which discretionary distributions are to be made. These words are usually defined under local law and generally have the following meaning:

Health: Routine medical services, mental health care, hospitalization, medications, medical devices and supplies, long-term nursing care, substance-abuse program services, rehabilitation, ancillary health care services, x-ray and laboratory services, premiums for health insurance, ambulance services and outpatient aftercare services.

Education: Includes pre-school, primary and secondary education and education at an accredited public or private college or university. Graduate level education, professional, technical or vocational school is generally not included unless specifically provided by the terms of the trust. Education expenses include tuition, books, room and board, incidental expenses, clothing, travel expenses to and from school, supplies, student fees, tutors and other expenses in connection with the education program.

Maintenance and support: Includes normal living expenses such as housing, clothing, food, insurance premiums, medical care and may include the expenses of dependants. The level of support is usually dependent upon the standard of living enjoyed by the beneficiary during the settlor's lifetime and the financial resources of the trust.

Welfare: Having to do with those things in life that have a relationship to one's physical well-being and comfort and which are dependent upon the individual's financial resources. This term generally means providing for basic living requirements.

Emergency: Having to do with a sudden or unexpected occurrence where the beneficiary's financial resources are insufficient to deal with the matter and require that prompt action be taken.

Standard of living: This is the style in which a beneficiary lived immediately prior to the death of the settlor, including the type of home that the beneficiary lived in, the type of automobile driven, the number of employees hired for domestic and other tasks, the amount of travel enjoyed, club memberships, etc.

If the settlor's intent (and the document so directs) is to maintain the standard of living of the beneficiary, other financial resources that are available to the beneficiary need not be considered. On the other hand, if the trust document directs that distributions are to be based on need, then the trustee must consider the beneficiaries' other financial resources in determining whether or not a need exists. As with any other trust provision, if there is any doubt as to the meaning of a particular directive or stipulation, the trustee should obtain an interpretation from the attorney who drafted the trust. The trust attorney will also have knowledge as to the settlor's intent.

Protective Provisions

Most trusts contain a clause that is designed to protect current beneficiaries and the interests of remaindermen. The so-called *spendthrift provision* is a common trust concept and is sometimes provided for under local law. It prevents a current beneficiary from encumbering, in any way, his interest in the trust. For example, a beneficiary's creditors cannot make a claim against the trust for amounts owed, although the trustee could distribute funds to the beneficiary to pay off debts if a distribution under the circumstances was appropriate. A typical spendthrift provision might read as follows:

"No beneficiary shall have any right to anticipate, transfer, or encumber any part of any interest in the trust estate, nor shall any part of the beneficiary's interest be liable for that beneficiary's debts or obligations (including alimony) or be subject to attachment, garnishment, execution, creditor's bill, or other legal or equitable process, provided that this Article shall neither prevent any beneficiary from exercising any power of appointment granted in this agreement or limit a marital deduction otherwise available to the settlor's estate."

Another protective provision is a clause that directs the trustee not to make distributions to a beneficiary that would disqualify that beneficiary from receiving government assistance. This provision is intended to allow efficient use of the trust assets for all beneficiaries by requiring a beneficiary to first take advantage of any financial assistance that may be available through government programs before requesting funds from the trust. This type of protective provision is fairly specific and straightforward:

"In the event that any beneficiary of any trust established hereunder is entitled to Medicare, Medicaid, or other governmental assistance (or would be if the existence of such trust were ignored) because of physical or mental infirmity (including but

not limited to, being a patient in a long-term health-related facility), then the trustee shall not, in such circumstances, make any discretionary distributions of principal or income to or for the benefit of such beneficiary, other than for the purpose of providing for such expenses incurred by the beneficiary which are not otherwise covered by such government assistance."

In some states, a beneficiary may not qualify for public assistance regardless of this language. The trustee should seek guidance from the trust's attorney if the question is raised.

The Discretionary Distribution Process

In evaluating a beneficiary's request for a distribution from income or principal, the trustee should follow a systematic process. This will facilitate the trustee's duty of impartiality and establish a consistent method for making discretionary distributions. The process should include a thorough evaluation of all the facts and circumstances surrounding the beneficiary's request. The first step is to have the beneficiary submit his or her request in writing. The request should include all of the pertinent information to support the request and assist the trustee in making a decision. A format similar to the one outlined below can assist both the beneficiary and the trustee with this part of the process:

Dear: _____ (Name of trustee) _____

The following information is furnished in support of my request for a discretionary distribution from the _____ (Name of trust) _____ :

Birth date:

Dependents: (Give full details of ages, relationship to you, etc.)

Nature and amount of request: (Give full details, dates, amounts, bill, etc.)

The following assets are owned by me (Indicate if ownership is in your own name, joint with spouse, or others):

	Approx Value	Income Generated	Mortgage
Home			
Other Real Estate			
Stocks and Bonds			
Bank Accounts			
Other Assets	_____	_____	_____
TOTALS			

Income generated from other sources, i.e., employment, etc.:

Description	Amount

Expenses:

_____

TOTAL

Other facts regarding either the reason for this request or my income and property, which I believe, will help you in considering my request:

I hereby certify the above statements to be true, correct and complete to the best of my knowledge and belief.

_____   _____
(signature)   (date)

_____   _____
(name of beneficiary)   (phone no.)

If the beneficiary's income has to be considered as part of the decision, the trustee should also obtain copies of the beneficiary's tax returns for the last three years.

Before a distribution is made, the trustee must thoroughly evaluate the request. The review should take into consideration the following:

- **What is the purpose of the request?**

- **Is the purpose authorized under the terms of the trust?**

- **Has the beneficiary clearly outlined how the funds will be used?**

- **Is the amount requested too large relative to the size of the trust?** If the amount will significantly impact the ability of the trust to carryout its purpose and meet future needs, a smaller distribution or other alternative—such as making a loan to the beneficiary—should be considered. If the trust has many years left before it terminates, principal distributions should be kept to a reasonable level.

- **Will the distribution accomplish the purpose and intent of the trust?**

- **Are there liquid funds available to cover the amount(s) needed?** If not, a plan to raise the needed funds must be developed and implemented.

- **How will the distribution impact the other beneficiaries?**

- **Will the payment result in a taxable distribution, subject to a generation-skipping tax?** If so, additional funds may need to be distributed to cover the tax. To determine the total amount of the distribution (including the tax) divide the amount of the request by one minus the generation-skipping tax rate.

Example:

Amount of request: $10,000

Tax rate: 55%

$$\frac{\$10{,}000}{(1-.55)} = \$22{,}222.22 \text{ (Amount needed)}$$

Documentation

Maintaining complete and thorough records is important to the discretionary distribution process and trust administration in general. If asked to defend a particular discretionary decision many years after it was made, a trustee will be hard pressed to remember the facts and circumstances of the distribution when records are incomplete or not kept at all. Requests should always be in writing. It should contain sufficient information to allow the trustee to make an informed and rational decision and serve as an accurate record of the transaction. These records should be maintained for the entire term of the trust. A format similar to the following can be used to document each discretionary distribution:

DISCRETIONARY DISTRIBUTIONS

Date:
Distribution requested by:
Age:
Purpose of distribution: (Attach letter of request)
Amount requested:
Previous discretionary distributions to this beneficiary during this trust year: $_____ (Income) $_____ (Principal)
$_____ Total
Purpose: Previous discretionary distributions to this beneficiary since inception.
$_____(Income) $_____(Principal)
$_____ Total
Income payments currently distributable to this beneficiary from the trust.
$_____
Source of funds from the trust:
Reasons for denial/approval of this request:
Date distribution was made:
Amount: $_____

Loans

As an alternative to an income or principal distribution, the trustee can facilitate the beneficiary's request by making a loan. A loan should be considered if an outright distribution would materially affect the trust's ability to meet the future needs of all beneficiaries. The loan would provide funds to meet the beneficiary's current need and be returned to the trust for use at some future date. In some circumstances, loans can also be made where the purpose of the request does not exactly fit the provisions of the trust. A loan is considered an investment made by the trustee and the interest rate and terms of the loan should be similar to what is available in the marketplace at the time the loan is made. Contact a financial institution for current rates and terms. In addition, the trustee should obtain a life insurance policy on the life of the beneficiary borrower for the amount of the loan. The trust should be the owner and beneficiary of the policy. This is to protect the trust in the event the beneficiary dies before the loan is paid off. The premiums should be paid by the trust.

Discretionary Distributions Checklist

✓ Read the dispositive provisions of the trust and, if necessary, obtain an interpretation from the trust's attorney.

✓ Determine which provisions require the trustee to make distributions and which call for the trustee to exercise discretion.

✓ In considering a request for a discretionary distribution, obtain in writing, the following information from the beneficiary:

   1) Purpose of the request.

   2) Amount.

   3) List of assets.

   4) Sources and amount of income.

   5) Other facts and information in support of the request.

✓ Evaluate the request thoroughly, taking into consideration:

   1) Whether or not the distribution is authorized under the terms of the trust.

   2) Whether or not a need exists.

   3) The amount of the request relative to the size of the trust. Will the distribution materially affect the ability of the trust to meet the future needs of the beneficiaries?

   4) Are sufficient funds available to cover the distribution?

✓ Make distributions directly to the payee (i.e., university, landlord, doctor, etc.) or obtain receipts.

✓ Consider a loan as an alternative to making a distribution.

CHAPTER 15

Maintaining Accounting Records

KEY POINTS

- A trustee is responsible for maintaining accurate accounting records and providing periodic reports to the beneficiaries.

- Trust accounting is unique in that it requires the trustee to separate receipts and disbursements into income and principal categories.

- The Uniform Principal and Income Act describes the rules and general principles of trust accounting.

- A qualified accountant or other professional who is familiar with trust accounting rules should be retained, at least initially, to establish accounting records for the trust.

Beneficiaries under a trust have the right to be kept reasonably informed at all times regarding the administration of the trust and the trustee has a duty to so inform them. Trustees also have an obligation to provide beneficiaries with information relevant to a beneficiary's interest in the trust as it relates to the trusts' assets, liabilities, receipts and disbursements. Trust accounting reports should reflect the actions taken by the trustee and other activities relating to the administration of the trust during the reporting period. Trust documents will usually contain language giving the trustee responsibility for maintaining proper accounting records and dealing with accounting decisions. Such a provision might read as follows:

"To determine all matters of trust accounting in accordance with generally accepted principles of trust accounting as established by controlling law or customary practices..."

Even without specific language, under the general law of trusts and local statutes a trustee is responsible for this function. Describing the various transactions that occur during the administration of the trust in a manner that provides beneficiaries with a clear picture of trust activities takes careful thought and application. Transactions should be described in plain language and the accountings should contain enough information concerning the administration of the trust to fully explain the trust's activities. Trust accountings are normally maintained on a cash basis and should include:

1) **a listing of all property owned by the trust, with a description of each asset;**

2) **income on hand at the beginning of the accounting period;**

3) **income received during the accounting period, the date it was received, and a description of its source;**

4) **income disbursed during the accounting period, the date of payment, to whom payment was made, and for what purpose;**

5) **income on hand at the end of the accounting period;**

6) **additions to principal during the accounting period, the dates received and a description of the source;**

7) **assets that were sold or charged off during the accounting period;**

8) **investments made during the accounting period, a description of the investment, the date of acquisition, and cost of purchase;**

9) **principal disbursements made during the accounting period, the date of the payment, to whom payment was made, and for what purpose;**

10) **the trust principal cash and trust assets on hand at the end of the accounting period.**

Trust accounting has some unique characteristics compared to the accounting records and reports associated with a corporation, partnership, or proprietorship. Receipts and disbursements in a trust are classified as either income or principal. This is the one characteristic that distinguishes fiduciary accounting from any other type of recordkeeping. A trust has two classes of beneficiaries—the current beneficiaries and the remaindermen. The current beneficiaries are entitled to all or a portion of the income and principal during the term of the trust. Or, one group of current beneficiaries may only be entitled to the income while another group is limited to principal distributions. The remaindermen are the beneficiaries who inherit the trust assets when the trust terminates. The classification of receipts and disbursements between income and principal will have a direct impact on what each class of beneficiaries receives from the trust. The trustee has a duty to be impartial when allocating receipts and disbursements between income and principal, taking into account the interests of current beneficiaries and remaindermen.

Uniform Principal and Income Acts

A trustee is required to follow the terms of the trust in allocating receipts and disbursements between income and principal. For example, the trust document may direct the trustee to credit capital gains distributions from mutual funds to income. These distributions would normally be allocated to principal but, because the trust directs otherwise, the allocation must follow the terms of the trust. Absent specific directions under the terms of a trust regarding how a particular accounting transaction is to be handled, the Uniform Principal and Income Act (the 1931 Act, the revised 1962 Act or the revised 1997 Act), which most states have adopted in one form or another, should be referred to for guidance. The Acts are default laws. That is, they will apply in the absence of contrary provisions in the trust document. The Acts cover 80% to 90% of all trust transactions and are referenced by accountants and other trust professionals for the majority of trust accounting questions. It should be pointed out that, unlike other entities such as corporations and partnerships, trust accounting rules will differ from state to state and the directives under trust documents will not always be consistent. The following states have enacted one of the Uniform Acts:

STATES THAT HAVE ADOPTED THE 1931 ACT

Alabama	Pennsylvania	Virginia
Colorado	Tennessee	West Virginia
Oklahoma	Vermont	

STATES THAT HAVE ADOPTED THE 1962 ACT

Alaska	Kentucky	Ohio
Arizona	Maryland	Oregon
Arkansas	Michigan	South Carolina
California	Minnesota	South Dakota
Connecticut	Mississippi	Texas
Florida	Montana	Utah
Georgia	Nebraska	Washington
Hawaii	Nevada	Wisconsin
Idaho	New Jersey	Wyoming
Illinois	New York	
Indiana	North Carolina	
Kansas	North Dakota	

The Uniform Principal and Income Acts have some common trust accounting definitions:

Income receipts—Income consists of earnings from the use or investment of principal. It includes dividends, interest, rents and other receipts received as a return on principal or the corpus of the trust.

Principal receipts—Principal is the trust property itself and is accounted for separately from income. It includes the proceeds received from the sale of any trust assets, stock dividends, insurance proceeds, royalties from depletable resources, allowances for depreciation, principal payments received on a loan and other receipts that will eventually be distributed to the remaindermen.

Income charges—All expenses incurred in connection with the administration, management or preservation of the trust property are income charges.

Principal charges—Costs of investing and reinvesting principal, principal payments on debts and obligations of the trust, trustee fees attributable to principal as provided by law or the terms of the trust, expenses incurred in taking or defending any action to protect the trust property, extraordinary expenses in making capital improvements to principal assets and taxes on capital gains or other receipts allocated to principal are all principal charges.

The Revised Uniform Principal and Income Act (1962) classifies the more common types of transactions that occur in a trust between income and principal:

Income receipts	Principal receipts
• dividends	• sales proceeds
• interest	• stock dividends
• rents	• insurance proceeds
• receipts from business and farming operations	• royalties
	• depreciation
	• principal payments on notes

Income charges	Principal charges
• taxes on income	• principal payments on notes
• insurance premiums	• capital improvements
• interest on notes	• taxes on capital gains
• ordinary repairs	• expenses for sale of trust
• ½ of trustee fees	property
	• trustee fees not charged
	to income

Depreciation

In theory, if an asset such as a building is depreciating in value, the remainder beneficiaries will receive a smaller inheritance. If the building was rented or leased, the income beneficiaries would receive the benefit from the asset, through distributions of income, at the expense of the remaindermen. To preserve the value of the building for the remaindermen, some trust documents require that the trustee transfer from income to principal a reasonable amount for depreciation. The amount should be based on the useful life of the depreciating asset and does not need to be held as a separate fund. The 1962 Revised Uniform Principal and Income Act mandates the depreciation charge against income. The 1997 Revised Uniform Principal and Income Act eliminates this mandatory requirement, but allows the trustee to make the charge in the trustee's discretion. This is a judgement call that will depend on what impact a depreciation charge will have on the income beneficiaries. The 1931 Uniform Principal and Income Act does not have a provision for depreciation. Again, the trustee needs to determine what is required under the trust document and/or local law.

Unproductive Property

The Uniform Principal and Income Act provides that an income beneficiary is entitled to delayed income from the proceeds of the sale of property that did not produce sufficient income prior to its sale. Most Acts define under-productive property as property that has not produced an average net income of at least one-percent (1%) annually. The delayed income is defined as the difference between the net proceeds from the sale and the amount which, had it been invested at simple interest of four percent (4%) per year while the property was under-productive, would have produced the net proceeds. The delayed income amount is classified as income and the balance is principal. The 1997 (new) Act eliminates this rule. However, most states have not as yet adopted the 1997 Act.

The National Conference of Commissioners on Uniform State Laws has approved a new (1997) Uniform Principal and Income Act. The primary purpose of this latest version is to make the Act consistent with the principles embodied in the Uniform Prudent Investor Act, which many states have adopted. The 1997 Act is written to facilitate a trustee who adopts modern portfolio theory techniques in investing trust assets under the Uniform Prudent Investor Act by allowing the trustee to transfer principal to income. The 1997 Revised Uniform Principal and Income Act also makes some changes to the 1962 Act including establishing separate rules for deferred compensation, elimination of the mandatory provision for depreciation and elimination of the unproductive property rule. Most states will eventually adopt the new Act and trustees need to ascertain which rules apply in their jurisdiction.

Trust Accountings

Trust accounting should provide useful information to the beneficiaries and other interested persons regarding the transactions that take place during the accounting period. Beneficiaries should be able to clearly understand the transactions that affect their interests in the trust. There is no one accounting format that is used for all trusts. States that require accountings to be filed with the court may prescribe a specific format. However, all trust accountings should incorporate the basic principles of accounting and the separation of income from principal. The following is an example of a trust accounting:

ACCOUNT SUMMARY

Income (cash):

Beginning balance	$ 10,000
Receipts	7,868
Disbursements	-1,713
Distributions to beneficiaries	-15,900
Ending balance	$ 255

Principal (cash):

Beginning balance	$ 1,500
Receipts	21,700
Disbursements	-12,675
Distributions to beneficiaries	-10,500
Ending balance	$ 25

Principal (assets):

Beginning value	$ 853,065
Unrealized gains (losses)	82,460
Ending value	$ 935,525

Balance on hand   **$ 935,805**

RECEIPTS AND DISBURSEMENTS OF INCOME

Date	Description	
1/1	**Beginning balance**	**$ 10,000**
	Interest – money market a/c	458
2/1	Dividend – IBM	195
	Interest – money market a/c	460
2/10	Property taxes – Star Manor	-538
2/12	Dividend – America Online	318
2/15	Interest – U.S. Treasury Note,	
	5 ½%, due 7/15	1,375
	Trustee's fee	-1,175
3/1	Dividend – AT&T	550
	Interest – money market a/c	462
3/15	Interest – American Bank CD	2,250
3/30	3 mos. Rent, Apt 107, Star Manor	1,800
	Distributions to beneficiaries:	
	John Porter	-5,300
	Sally Smith	-5,300
	Fred Porter	-5,300
	Ending balance	**$ 255**

RECEIPTS AND DISBURSEMENTS
OF PRINCIPAL

Date	Description		
1/1	Beginning balance	$	1,500
1/15	Sold 100 shs. IBM		11,200
	Deposit money market a/c		-11,500
2/15	Trustee's fee		-1,175
3/15	Withdraw money market a/c		10,500
	Distribution to beneficiary		
	Fred Porter		-10,500
3/30	**Ending balance**	**$**	**25**

	TRUST ASSETS		
Shares /		**Cost or**	**Market**
Face Value	**Description**	**Carry Value**	**Value**
	Star Manor		
	Apartment 107		
	105 Chestnut Ave.	$ 125,000	$ 225,000
$100,000	Money Market A/C	100,000	100,000
$150,000	American Bank—CD	150,000	150,000
$ 50,000	U.S. Treasury Note,	49,000	48,525
	5 ½%, due 7/15		
1,500 shs.	IBM	136,000	168,000
3,000 shs.	America Online	75,000	159,000
2,500 shs.	AT&T	90,000	85,000
		$ 725,000	**$ 935,525**

Again, the trustee's objective should be to provide the beneficiaries with a clear picture of the trustee's management of the trust. At least initially, a trustee would be well advised to seek assistance from a qualified CPA or other professional who is familiar with trust accounting rules to set up and maintain the accounting records for the trust.

Terminating Trusts

When a trust terminates at the death of the settlor, accounting for the administration during the period from the settlor's date of death through the final distribution of the trust assets is similar to accounting for a probate estate. A trustee must account for property (other than cash) that is specifically and separately bequeathed to a beneficiary from other trust property. All income attributable to the specific bequest property must be accounted for separately and all expenses attributable to the bequest must be deducted from that income. The property's income includes all income accrued prior to, and after the settlor's death. This income, less expenses, follows the property and is distributable to the beneficiary.

Terminating Income Interests

Under the 1931 and 1962 Uniform Principal and Income Acts an income beneficiary or his or her estate is entitled to income (other than dividends) accrued but not received at the time his or her income interest ended. For example, if a beneficiary's income interest ends on June 30, as a result of that beneficiary's death, and a six month interest check on a bond is received on July 15, the beneficiary's estate is entitled to the interest earned from the last interest payment through June 30. However, some trust documents eliminate this right to accrued income by providing that:

"Upon the death of any income beneficiary the interest and estate of such beneficiary in all income of the trust estate then undistributed shall terminate, regardless of when the same shall have accrued, and all such income shall be paid and distributed as though it had accrued immediately after the death of such beneficiary."

This provision makes accounting for the income a lot simpler. The new 1997 Revised Uniform Principal and Income Act also eliminates the accrual requirement from the 1931 and 1962 Acts.

Making the wrong accounting decision can be costly, as errors typically are not discovered during the period of administration. Accounting errors are usually identified at the time the trust terminates, which can be many years after the error was made. For example, a remainder beneficiary may learn that an expense was charged against principal sometime during the term of the trust when it should have been charged to income. As a result, the remainder beneficiary received less than he or she would have received had the error not occurred. Also, it may be difficult, if not impossible, to collect the amount of the erroneous charge from the income beneficiaries, who should have incurred the expense in the first place. Statutory interest or lost opportunity costs could be assessed against the trustee to reimburse the trust and make the remainder beneficiary whole.

A qualified accountant is the logical advisor to assist the trustee in addressing fiduciary accounting issues and maintaining accounting records for the trust. At the very least, a trustee should seek professional help in the initial stages of establishing the accounting records. Again, in dealing with accounting matters, the trustee and his or her accountant should first refer to the trust document regarding an accounting question, and then to the Uniform Principal and Income Act, for guidance.

Trust Accounting Checklist

✓ Review the provisions in the trust that pertain to trust accounting matters.

✓ Does the trust require a transfer from income to principal for depreciation?

✓ Review the Uniform Principal and Income Act under local law.

✓ Describe accounting transactions so the beneficiaries can easily understand them.

✓ Retain a qualified accountant to establish the accounting records for the trust and, if necessary, to maintain them.

✓ Establish a tickler to provide regular accounting reports (at least annually) to all beneficiaries.

CHAPTER 16

Fiduciary Income Taxes and Other Filing Requirements

KEY POINTS

- If a personal representative has not been appointed, the trustee will be responsible for filing the estate tax return and any other returns due after the decedent's death.

- In a continuing trust, a trustee is required to file a federal fiduciary income tax return and may also be required to file a state fiduciary income tax return for every year the trust is in existence.

- In order to properly manage the trust, a trustee should understand some of the basic rules of trust taxation.

- Fiduciary income tax returns are complex and a CPA who specializes in this area of taxation should be hired to prepare the returns.

Trustees are required to file income tax returns for the trusts they manage and may also have the responsibility to file other returns. Generally, the personal representative is responsible for filing the decedent's final income tax returns, the federal estate tax return, and fiduciary income tax returns during the period of estate administration. However, if there is no probate and there-fore no reason to have a personal representative appointed by the court, "any person in actual or constructive possession of any property of the decedent" (IRC Sec. 2203) is responsible for filing the returns. The trustee of the decedent's trust is typically in charge of the decedent's property and therefore has this responsibility. Others who may be "inadvertent executors" and have this responsibility include surviving joint tenants, the decedent's heirs and any individual who has possession of the decedent's property.

In administering a trust, the trustee must make sure that the taxes are paid before other expenses. The Internal Revenue Service holds a trustee personally liable for any federal taxes due if the trustee prior to satisfying any tax obligations makes other payments. However, the trustee is not liable if debts, such as the decedent's funeral expenses and administration costs, have priority over federal taxes under local law. Also, there is no liability if the trustee paid the decedent's debts and was not aware that any federal taxes were due.

Decedent's Final Income Tax Returns

If a personal representative has not been appointed, the trustee has the responsibility for filing the final income tax returns for the decedent. The trustee should consult with the surviving spouse regarding income tax and other planning issues. The surviving spouse and trustee have the option of filing a joint final return. Refer to *Chapter 7 Administering the Estate–Tax Returns* for a list of things to consider.

The decision to file joint or separate returns involves important tax planning considerations. Unless a trustee has sufficient experience in income tax planing, he or she should seek advice from a competent tax professional.

The trustee should file Form 5495, *Request for Discharge from Personal Liability Under Internal Revenue Code Section 6905*. Within nine months after receipt of the request, the IRS will notify the trustee that the tax liability has been satisfied and the trustee will be discharged from personal liability for any future deficiencies. If the IRS has not notified the trustee, he or she will be discharged at the end of the nine-month period.

Federal Estate Tax Return

The trustee should coordinate filing of the Federal estate tax return, Form 706, with the personal representative. A number of issues require the trustee's input, such as deciding whether medical and administration expenses will be taken on the estate tax return or fiduciary income tax returns, allocating the generation-skipping tax exemption, making the QTIP election, deciding on whether or not to use the alternate valuation, disclaimers and other elections. Remember, if a personal representative has not been appointed, the trustee will have the responsibility for filing this return and making the elections. It is important that the trustee (or personal representative) obtain an early determination of the estate tax and release from liability to protect him or herself. See *Chapter 7 Administering the Estate—Tax Returns and Tax Elections and Other Postmortem Planning Issues* for more details involving the filing of the estate tax return.

Fiduciary Income Tax Returns

For federal income taxes, irrevocable trusts are treated as separate taxable entities and require the trustee to file a fiduciary income tax return each year. Many states also require that a state fiduciary income tax return be filed.

There are special rules under the Internal Revenue Code that apply to the taxation of trusts. These rules are very complex. A trustee should not attempt to file the trust return(s) without the assistance of a CPA who is experienced in this area of taxation.

It is important that the trustee understand the basics of trust taxation to assist him or her in the administration of the trust. A basic understanding of how trusts are taxed will also aid in reviewing the tax return(s) if prepared by a CPA.

TAXABILITY OF TRUST INCOME

Generally, the trust receives a deduction for income distributions that are made from the trust to beneficiaries and the beneficiaries are required to report the income distributions on their individual income tax returns. Any taxable income that is not distributed to beneficiaries is taxed to the trust.

The trustee is required to file a Federal Fiduciary Income Tax Return (Form 1041) if:

1) **the trust has any taxable income;**

2) **the trust's gross income is $600 or more; or**

3) **any beneficiary is a non-resident alien.**

Every trust that is required to file Form 1041 must have a tax identification number, which is an Employer Identification Number (EIN). The EIN can be obtained from the IRS by completing Form SS-4, Application for Employer Identification Number and either mailing it or faxing it to them. It also can be obtained by telephone with a requirement that the form be mailed or faxed within 24 hours after the call. Information concerning the income and expenses of the trust are reported on Form 1041. The income reportable by the beneficiaries is shown on Schedule K-1, which is part of Form 1041. The Schedule K-1 form must show the income taxable to the beneficiary along with the beneficiary's name, address and Social Security Number. A copy of Schedule K-1 must be provided to each beneficiary who receives income from the trust.

Grantor Trusts

A grantor trust is one in which the grantor (settlor) is still living and retains sufficient control over the trust that he or she is considered the owner of the trust. Sufficient control means that the grantor has retained a reversionary interest (i.e., right to receive all of the trust property at some point) in the trust, the power over the beneficial enjoyment of the trust, administrative powers in the trust, the power to revoke the trust and the right to receive the trust's income. A common example of a grantor trust is a Revocable Living Trust.

A grantor trust is not considered a separate taxable entity. All income, deductions and credits are reported on the grantor's (settlor's) individual income tax returns. Generally, the Fiduciary Income Tax return, Form 1041, is required to be filed for a grantor trust if the settlor is not the trustee or co-trustee. Income and deductions, etc., are not reported on the return. Instead a detailed statement outlining the income, deductions and credits that are taxable to the grantor is attached to the return. However, the Fiduciary Income Tax Return, Form 1041, is not required to be filed for a grantor trust if the grantor is the trustee or co-trustee, as in the case of a self-trusteed revocable living trust. In this case the trust income, deductions and credits are reported directly on the grantor's Individual Income Tax Return, Form 1040. The grantor must furnish all payors of income with his or her social security number and the payors will report the income just as if it had been paid directly to the grantor.

If the grantor is not the trustee or co-trustee of the grantor trust, a trustee has two alternative ways of reporting:

1) **The trustee can provide the name and social security number** *of the grantor,* **along with the address of the trust, to all of the payors of income during the taxable year. If this option is used, the trustee is not required to file a Form 1041 return with the Internal Revenue Service.**

2) **The trustee can provide the name, address and tax identification number** *of the trust* **to all payors of income. The trustee must then file with the Internal Revenue Service appropriate 1099 forms that report each type of income, show the trust as the payor and show the grantor as the payee.**

If the trustee uses either of these alternatives, he or she must furnish to the grantor a statement that reflects all income, deductions and credits attributable to the grantor along with any other information necessary for computing the grantor's taxable income. As a practical matter, it is easier to file the Form 1041 return.

Distributable Net Income (DNI)

Trust income is taxed where it ends up. A trust can either be a conduit, passing all of its income out to beneficiaries, or retain some or all of the income, as is the case in a discretionary trust. Taxation of income that is distributed to a beneficiary is based on a concept called Distributable Net Income (DNI), a principle that is unique to the taxation of estates and trusts.

DNI is basically the *taxable income* of the trust (i.e., taxable income less deductible expenses). DNI determines the amount that is taxable to a beneficiary and how much of a distribution deduction is allowed on the trust's fiduciary income tax return (Form 1041). Deductible expenses may include charges against principal. DNI does not include the personal exemption deduction or capital gains and losses allocated to principal. However, it does include tax exempt interest. DNI is not trust accounting income. Trust accounting income is the income received by the trust, less all expenses paid from the income account. Trust accounting income is usually what is distributed to beneficiaries. DNI can differ from trust accounting income because deductible expenses, which are part of DNI, may be charged against principal and therefore would not reduce the trust accounting income distributed to beneficiaries.

Example:

	Income	Principal
Dividends	$4,000	
Interest	$6,000	
Trustee Fees	(500)	(500)
	$9,500	**$ (500)**

Trust Accounting Income:

Income	$10,000
Expenses	(500)
Distribution To Beneficiaries	**$ 9,500**

Distributable Net Income (DNI):

Income	$10,000
Deductions	(1,000)
DNI	**$ 9,000**

In the above example, the beneficiary reports taxable income of $9,000 (DNI) instead of the actual income he or she received from the trust (i.e., trust accounting income.) On the tax return(s) for the trust, the trustee deducts the amount of DNI distributed to beneficiaries. Generally, what taxable income remains after the DNI deduction is taxed to the trust.

Simple Trusts

A trust is classified as either a simple trust or a complex trust for federal income tax purposes. A simple trust, by its terms, requires all of its income to be distributed during the taxable year. It does not provide for charitable distributions and does not distribute any principal during the tax year of the trust. Instead of a personal exemption, a simple trust is allowed a deduction of $300. A beneficiary of a simple trust must include DNI in his or her gross income even if the income was not actually distributed during the year. A trust may be a simple trust in one year and a complex trust in a year in which the trust makes a distribution of principal to a beneficiary. The trustee is required to file a Fiduciary Income Tax Return, Form 1041, for this type of trust.

Complex Trusts

A trust that is not a simple trust in any one year is a complex trust. A complex trust provides for discretionary distributions of income, can make distributions to a charity or is a simple trust that distributes principal during the taxable year of the trust. Filing a Fiduciary Income Tax Return, Form 1041, is also required for this type of trust and is allowed a deduction of $100. The deduction for distributions to beneficiaries cannot exceed DNI and any tax-exempt income must be subtracted from the deduction. In a complex trust, allocation of DNI to beneficiaries is based on a "Tier System". This system is to assure that a beneficiary who receives mandatory distributions under the trust receives the maximum amount of DNI before allocating the balance, if any, to other beneficiaries. The system has two tiers:

TIER ONE DISTRIBUTIONS—Distributions of income that are required by the terms of a trust to be made to a beneficiary.

TIER TWO DISTRIBUTIONS—Distributions of either income or principal that are in the discretion of the trustee.

Complex trusts can make discretionary distributions from income, principal or both. Discretionary distributions are Tier Two Distributions and will carry out taxable income to the beneficiary only to the extent that DNI has not been allocated to Tier One Distributions. For example, if all of the DNI has been allocated to Tier One Distributions, any beneficiary receiving a Tier Two Distribution will not be taxed on that distribution. If Tier One distributions do not exceed DNI, the beneficiaries who receive Tier Two distributions will be taxed proportionately on the remaining DNI. These are very complex computations and the only reason they are mentioned here is to alert the trustee to the fact that distributions of principal may not necessarily be exempt from income tax. Trustees should consult a CPA before making a principal distribution that is intended to be tax-free.

As mentioned in *Chapter 7 Administering the Estate—Tax Returns,* the tax paid by an estate or trust is higher than for an individual because the taxable income threshold for the maximum rate is lower. For example income retained in a trust that exceeds $8,650 is taxed at the maximum federal rate of 39.6% (year 2000 rates.) For an individual, the maximum rate of 39.6% does not apply until the individual's taxable income exceeds $288,350 (year 2000 rates.) This should not, by itself, be a reason for the trustee to distribute all of the trust's income to beneficiaries who may be in lower tax brackets. The trustee's first duty is to follow the terms of the trust and carry out its purpose. If the trust is expected to pay at least $1,000 in tax on any income retained in the trust, the trustee must make estimated tax payments during the year.

65-Day Rule

A trustee of a complex trust may elect to treat distributions paid within 65 days after the close of a trust tax year (i.e., 12/31) as having been made on the last day of that tax year. This gives a trustee some flexibility as to when a beneficiary is taxed on trust income. It also gives the trustee time to compute distributions that will carry out DNI in a complex trust and possibly allocate the distribution to a year in which it does not. Once it is made, the election is irrevocable and cannot be in excess of the greater of trust accounting income or DNI for the tax year. The 65-day rule does not apply to simple trusts since all of its income is taxable to the beneficiaries in the year it is required to be distributed, regardless of whether it is actually distributed or retained in the trust.

Generation-Skipping Tax

As mentioned in *Chapter 7 Administering the Estate–Tax Returns,* a trustee may be required to report generation-skipping transfers from a trust and pay any taxes that are due. Again, transfers subject to the tax fall into three general categories:

DIRECT SKIP—a transfer, subject to federal gift or estate tax, of a property interest directly to a skip person.

TAXABLE DISTRIBUTIONS—any distribution from a trust to a skip person.

TAXABLE TERMINATION—termination of an interest in a trust which results in a distribution to a skip person.

A skip person is one who is two or more generations below the transferor (i.e., settlor/decedent). This is typically the settlor's grandchild. If the parent of a skip person predeceased the settlor, that person moves up a generation and is not considered a skip person. For example, John's daughter, Mary, has two children. Mary dies before her father, John. Distributions to Mary's two children would not be generation-skipping transfers.

If a personal representative has not been appointed, a trustee is required to file a United States Gift (and Generation-Skipping Transfer) Tax Return, Form 709, to report a pre-death direct skip transfer that the decedent made but did not report prior to his or her death. A trustee may also be required to report on the Federal Estate Tax Return, Form 706, any generation-skipping transfers that occur at the decedent's death by bequest under the decedent's Will or trust. Distributions from a trust to a skip person during the term of the trust, and at the termination of the trust, must be reported on Form 709, United States Gift (and Generation-Skipping Transfer) Tax Return.

	Who files the return	Who pays the tax
Direct Skip	Transferor	Transferor
Taxable Distribution	Trustee	Beneficiary (Transferee)
Taxable Termination	Trustee	Trustee

Retirement Plans Payable to the Trust

The rules regarding the taxability of retirement plans (i.e., IRA, pension plan, profit sharing plan, 401(k), etc.) payable to trusts are complex. In general, there are two sets of rules that apply to these distributions. One set applies when the decedent dies before the *required beginning date.* The required beginning date is April 1 of the year following attainment of age 70½. In general, if a decedent dies prior to the required beginning date, all of the plan benefits must be distributed by the end of the fifth year following the death. The distributions do not have to be even, as long as the entire amount in the plan is distributed before the end of the five-year period. This is referred to as the *five year rule.* If the decedent had named a non-spouse *designated beneficiary* under the retirement plan, including a qualified trust, the designated beneficiary can elect to have the distributions paid over the life expectancy of the designated beneficiary. This is called the *life expectancy method.*

The second set of rules applies when the decedent dies after the required beginning date. If a decedent named a designated beneficiary, including a qualified trust, under his or her retirement plan, the distributions must continue to be made over the balance of the joint life expectancy of the decedent and the designated beneficiary.

If a qualified trust is the designated beneficiary, life expectancy is based on the age of the oldest beneficiary of the trust.

A trust will qualify as a designated beneficiary for the purpose of these taxability options if:

1) **The trust is valid under state law.**

2) **The beneficiaries are identifiable under the trust document.**

3) **The trust is irrevocable or, by its terms, will become irrevocable upon the death of the participant.**

4) **Certain documentation is provided to "the plan administrator."**

5) **All beneficiaries of the trust are individuals.**

6) **No person has the power to change the beneficiary after the participant's death.**

Under rule 4 above, the trustee is responsible for fulfilling the documentation requirement. The trustee is required to provide the plan administrator with either of the following:

1) **A final list of all of the beneficiaries of the trust (including contingent and remaindermen beneficiaries) with a description of the conditions on their entitlement, as of the date of death. Certify that, to the best of the trustee's knowledge, this list is correct and complete and that the trust is valid under state law. Certify that the trust is irrevocable as of the decedent's death and the beneficiaries are identifiable. The trustee must also agree to provide a copy of the trust document to the plan administrator upon demand.**

2) **Provide the plan administrator with a copy of the actual trust document.**

The trustee must provide documentation to the plan administrator within nine months after the date of death. If rules 1 through 6 are not complied with in the case of a decedent who dies before the required beginning date, all of the benefits must be distributed to the trust within five years (five-year rule) of the decedent's death. The life-expectancy method will not be available. If the rules are not complied with in the case of a decedent who dies after the required beginning date, the distributions will be based on the decedent's life expectancy only and not on the joint life of the decedent and the oldest beneficiary of the trust. If the decedent's spouse is the primary beneficiary of the trust, the more favorable rules that apply to spouse-beneficiaries may be available. Complying with the rules will give the trustee the option of maximizing the deferral of the tax.

Again, these rules are complex and the trustee should seek guidance from a qualified professional.

Trustee's Checklist for Filing Tax Returns

✓ Make a list of the returns that need to be filed and their due dates.

✓ Apply for a federal identification number for the estate tax return and *each trust* that is required to file fiduciary income tax returns.

✓ If a personal representative has not been appointed, prepare and file the Federal Estate Tax Return, Form 706, if the decedent's gross estate is close to or exceeds the exemption equivalent amount.

✓ File a request for an early determination of the federal estate tax and release from personal liability.

✓ Coordinate the filing of the decedent's final individual income tax return(s) with the surviving spouse. File Form 5495, Request for Discharge from Personal Liability Under IRC Section 6905.

✓ Utilize the 65-day rule to plan for and manage the taxation of distributions to beneficiaries.

✓ File Form 709 for any distributions that are made to skip persons that are the result of a taxable distribution and/or taxable termination.

✓ Hire a qualified CPA to prepare and file the estate tax, fiduciary income tax and generation-skipping tax returns.

✓ Get advice from a tax professional when handling distributions from qualified retirement plans.

CHAPTER 17

Termination of the Trust and Final Distribution of the Assets

KEY POINTS

- A trust's termination is usually triggered by an event such as the death of a surviving spouse, or other beneficiary, or upon a beneficiary's attainment of a certain age.

- A trustee is required to wind up the affairs of the trust and distribute the assets to the remainder beneficiaries within a reasonable time.

- The termination process may differ from trust to trust depending on the type of trust and the language contained in the document.

As a general rule, a continuing trust must terminate at some point in time unless it is a charitable trust, in which case, it can continue in perpetuity. Most states have a *rule against perpetuities* which says that a trust cannot extend beyond a period measured by "lives in being plus twenty-one years." This period begins at the settlor's date of death, or when the trust becomes irrevocable, and extends for the lifetime of the youngest beneficiary, who is alive at the point the trust became irrevocable, plus twenty-one years after the death of that beneficiary. As a matter of "public policy", the rule against perpetuities is designed to assure that the property placed in trust eventually passes from one generation to another and back into the public domain. A few states, such as

Alaska, Delaware and South Dakota, do not have a rule against perpetuities. Common events that trigger a trust's termination include the death of a surviving spouse, the death of a beneficiary or a beneficiary's attainment of a certain age. Another condition that may terminate a trust is if the market value of the trust assets falls below a specified dollar amount or level where it is no longer economical to maintain the trust. This amount is usually specified in the trust.

Upon termination, a trustee is required to wind up the affairs of the trust within a reasonable period. A trustee will not be relieved of his or her responsibilities until the assets have been distributed or the trustee has been formally discharged by the court. During the termination process, the trustee is required to protect the trust property, pay final expenses and distribute the assets to the remaindermen. A trustee will be held accountable for any unreasonable delay.

Closing Procedures

The steps for closing a continuing trust are similar to those for a trust that terminates upon the death of the settlor. The principal exception is that there is no requirement to file a federal estate tax return. The following are some of the steps that need to be taken:

1) **Identify who the remainder beneficiaries are. Considerable time may have lapsed since the settlor's death and some beneficiaries may not have outlived the termination of the trust. The dispositive provisions of the trust must be carefully reviewed to determine proper succession, i.e., per stirpes, per capita, per capita at each generation, etc. (see *Chapter 7 Administering the Estate—Distributing Assets*)**

2) **Notify the beneficiaries that the trust has terminated and describe the specific provisions that relate to their inheritance. Also, outline the steps that will be taken and an approximate time frame for closing the trust.**

3) If termination is due to death, obtain a certified copy of the death certificate. If termination was due to attainment of an age, obtain a birth certificate.

4) Obtain reissue instructions from all beneficiaries, including how assets are to be titled, current address, social security number and name and address of a local bank through which delivery can be made if assets cannot be delivered personally.

5) Value all securities, real estate and other assets that will be distributed to the beneficiaries.

6) Prepare a distribution schedule that includes the tax cost basis for each asset. (See *Chapter 7 Administering the Estate–Distributing Assets,* for an example of a distribution schedule.)

7) Check the trust document for language regarding the accrual of income. If the document is silent and local law does not otherwise preclude the requirement to accrue income, accrue all undistributed income from the last income distribution to the beneficiary to the date of termination and pay this amount to the beneficiary or his/her estate.

8) Have the attorney for the trust prepare new real property deeds.

9) Arrange for the preparation and filing of the final fiduciary income tax return(s). Reserve sufficient funds to cover the preparation fee and any taxes that may be due.

10) Re-register all securities in accordance with the beneficiary's instructions and the distribution schedule.

11) Prepare the final accounting for the period from the termination date of the trust through and including

all transactions prior to making final distribution of the assets to the beneficiaries. Deliver the accounting to the beneficiaries and file with the court, if required.

12) **Obtain an approval of the final accounting, receipt for the assets delivered and a release of liability from all beneficiaries. (See example of form of approval receipt and release in *Chapter 7 Administering the Estate–Distributing Assets.*)**

13) **Prepare a *supplemental final accounting* from the end date of the final accounting through and including the final distribution of the cash balance. Provide this to the beneficiaries and file with the court, if required.**

As a general rule, the trustee's responsibilities with respect to the administration of the trust terminate upon final distribution of the assets to the remaindermen. If the termination of the trust is subject to a court proceeding, the court will provide the trustee with a formal discharge of the trustee's duties. Getting the beneficiaries to approve the accounts may be a way to avoid a court proceeding and reduce termination costs by eliminating the need for the court to appoint a master to audit the accounts of the trustee.

Marital Trusts

As discussed earlier, in order to qualify for the marital deduction, an *estate trust* and a *power of appointment trust* must meet certain requirements. In the case of an estate trust, upon the death of the surviving spouse, all of the accrued income and principal must be paid to the surviving spouse's estate. The trustee needs to contact the personal representative of the surviving spouse's estate and obtain instructions for delivery of the trust assets to the estate. If the marital trust is a power of appointment trust, the trust must give the surviving spouse a testamentary power of appointment.

A general testamentary power of appointment clause usually gives the trustee fairly specific directions as to how the assets are to be distributed if the surviving spouse exercises the power of appointment. The following is an example of such a provision:

"Upon termination, the trust estate then remaining, including the accrued but undistributed income and particularly the income for the period between the last income distribution date and the death of the settlor's spouse, shall be paid to or held for the benefit of such person or persons, or corporation or corporations, or the estate of the settlor's spouse, in such amounts and proportions and for such estates and interests, and outright or upon such terms, trusts, conditions, and limitations as the settlor's spouse shall appoint by Will by specific reference to this power of appointment."

The trustee must obviously obtain a copy of the surviving spouse's Will in order to determine who the remainder beneficiaries of the trust are. If the surviving spouse does not exercise all, or a portion of, the power of appointment, the marital trust will usually say that the assets not appointed shall be added to the credit shelter trust (i.e., by-pass trust, family trust, residuary trust, "B" trust, etc.).

Since all marital trusts are subject to federal estate tax in the surviving spouse's estate, the trustee should coordinate the valuation of the marital trust assets with the surviving spouse's personal representative. The trust may also provide that it pay its proportionate share of the estate tax, due on the marital trust assets, to the personal representative.

Distribute In Cash Or In Kind?

Most trust documents give a trustee the power to make final distribution of the trust assets in cash or in kind, (i.e., distribution of the assets themselves):

"To make distribution in kind, in money, or partly in each, without requiring pro rata distribution of specific assets at fair

market value as determined by the trustee on the effective date distribution."

If similar language is not contained in the trust, many states give the trustee this authority under local law. The reason for this is that it is not always possible to split some assets among several beneficiaries. For example, a $5,000 corporate bond could not be split evenly among six beneficiaries because the minimum denomination for a bond is $1,000. With the authority to distribute cash, the trustee can sell the bond and split the cash proceeds six ways. As an alternative, the bond, or other asset, could be given to one beneficiary and another asset given to the other beneficiaries. Any differences in the value of these assets can be equalized with cash. However, the trustee should first obtain the consent of the beneficiaries. Another issue has to do with creating a taxable transaction. If a beneficiary is entitled to receive a dollar, or pecuniary, amount under the trust and the trustee satisfies the bequest by making a distribution in kind, the trust will be treated as having sold the property to the beneficiary and will realize a capital gain, or loss. Pecuniary bequests should be satisfied with cash assets to avoid this problem. Assets should be sold only if directed by the terms of the trust, the sale is absolutely necessary to protect the value of an asset, all beneficiaries direct that an asset be sold, or an asset cannot be split among multiple beneficiaries. If there is only one remainder beneficiary, the trustee must distribute in kind. The Restatement (Second) of Trusts section 345, provides that:

> *"If upon termination of the trust there is a single beneficiary who is entitled to the trust property, it is the duty of the trustee to convey the property to him, rather than to sell it and to pay him the proceeds, unless it is otherwise provided by the terms of the trust."*

If sale of the assets is contemplated, the trustee should seek the approval of the beneficiary first. In a 1992 case, a bank was surcharged by the court for not getting the approval of the beneficiary before liquidating the trust assets.

Distributing the Property

Once the assets have been re-registered, delivery of the assets should be made in person for those beneficiaries who live close to the trustee. Where personal delivery of the assets is not possible, the name and address of a bank through which distribution can be made should be obtained from the beneficiary. The idea is to have a responsible entity deliver the assets and obtain the proper signature on the receipt from the beneficiary. If a beneficiary is a protected person (i.e., minor or someone who is disabled), his share needs to be distributed to the beneficiary's legal representative. If the legal representative is unknown, the trustee must see to it that the share is protected for the benefit of that beneficiary. A well-drafted trust document will give the trustee guidance in this regard. Even if not specifically included in the trust document, the following outlines some of the options with respect to the disposition of *protected property* (i.e., property distributable to a protected person):

> *"The trustee may distribute any protected property to or for the benefit of such beneficiary [1] directly to the beneficiary, [2] on behalf of the beneficiary for the beneficiary's exclusive benefit, [3] to any account in a bank or savings institution either in the name of such beneficiary or in a form reserving title, management, and custody of such account in a suitable person for the use of such beneficiary, [4] to an individual or corporation as custodian for a minor under the Uniform Transfers to Minors Act or Uniform Gifts to Minors Act or for an adult under a Uniform Custodial Trust Act, [5] in any form of annuity, [6] in all other ways provided by laws dealing with gifts or distributions to or for minors or persons under disability, and [7] to any suitable person with whom the beneficiary resides or who has the care or control of the beneficiary, without obligation to see to the further application of such distribution, and the receipt for distributions by any such persons shall fully discharge the trustee."*

Depending on the nature of the trust (i.e., difficult assets, difficult beneficiaries, existing or pending litigation), if the beneficiaries of the trust refuse to give the trustee a release and discharge, the trustee should consider seeking court approval of its accounts to protect himself or herself from future claims.

Termination/Distribution Checklist

✓ Follow the termination steps outlined in this section.

✓ Review the trust to determine if income must be accrued and paid to the beneficiary or to his/her estate.

✓ Is the marital trust an estate or power of appointment trust?

✓ If the trust gives a power of appointment to a spouse or other beneficiary, has the power been exercised?

✓ Does the trust provide that it pay its proportionate share of estate taxes?

✓ Can distribution be made in cash or kind?

✓ Prepare a distribution schedule and discuss with beneficiaries before finalizing.

✓ If assets cannot be distributed personally, distribute the beneficiary's share through his or her bank.

✓ Deliver an accounting and the assets to each beneficiary and obtain a Receipt and Release.

✓ Submit the final accounts and receipts to the court, if required or if the beneficiaries are not willing to approve the accounts and give the trustee a release.

CHAPTER 18

Managing Other Types of Irrevocable Trusts

KEY POINTS

- The standards of conduct and principles of trust administration discussed in this chapter apply to all types of irrevocable trusts.

- There are administration requirements that are unique to certain types of irrevocable trusts.

- Some irrevocable trusts are considered abusive by the Internal Revenue Service and individuals should avoid serving as trustee of these types of trusts.

The discussion, thus far, has centered primarily on the management of the marital and credit shelter type trusts. The same duties, responsibilities and principles of trust administration also apply to other types of irrevocable trusts. The more common types of irrevocable living trusts (i.e., irrevocable trusts that are created while the settlor or grantor is living) have been described in *Chapter 1 Serving as a Personal Representative and/or Trustee–Irrevocable Trusts*. Some types of irrevocable trusts have unique administration requirements. These requirements are primarily tax related and will either be described under the terms of the trust or under the Internal Revenue Code.

Children's Gift Trusts

These are trusts established by a parent to make gifts to a child and qualify for the annual gift tax exclusion. The trustee controls when and under what circumstances the child receives the funds. Children's gift trusts, which are described under sections 2503(b) and 2503(c) of the Internal Revenue Code, have the following unique administration characteristics:

- **The trust must terminate when the child reaches age twenty-one and the trustee must distribute all of the income and principal to the child at that time.**

- **In a 2503(c) type of trust, distributions can be made in the discretion of the trustee. However, in the 2503(b) type of trust, income must be distributed to the beneficiary.**

- **Distributions from the trust are taxed at the parent's marginal tax rate until the child attains the age of fourteen (14). This is referred to as the "kiddie tax". After the child reaches age fourteen the tax is paid at the child's individual income tax rate.**

Irrevocable Life Insurance Trust

The purpose of an Irrevocable Life Insurance Trust is to remove the ownership of life insurance from the settlor and avoid taxation of the face amount of the policy at the settlor's death. When the trust is created the settlor will either transfer an existing insurance policy to the trust or have the trustee purchase a new policy(ies) on the settlor's life. The settlor usually deposits funds to the trust periodically to cover the payment of premiums and any administration costs. In administering this type of trust the trustee needs to be aware of certain requirements:

- If an insurance policy is transferred or added to the trust, the settlor must survive three years in order to avoid having the proceeds taxed in the settlor's estate. If the settlor dies within three years, the trustee must so notify the settlor's personal representative and provide the personal representative with Form 712, which is provided by the insurance company and reports the amount of the insurance and interest paid on the policy.

- As deposits are made to the trust to cover premiums and administration costs, the trustee must notify the beneficiaries that they have the right to withdraw those funds. This right lapses after a period of time stated in the trust document. This *"crummey power"* is required to qualify the deposit for the annual gift tax exclusion. Failure of the trustee to give proper notice will subject the deposits to gift taxes.

- The trustee should periodically review the policies with an insurance agent to assure that they are performing as expected and that the insurance company is viable. If a problem exists, the trustee is required to take appropriate action to safeguard the interests of the beneficiaries.

- Often the irrevocable life insurance trust is established to provide cash to pay estate taxes. To the extent that this cash is used directly to pay the estate tax, that amount will be included in the decedent's taxable estate. A well-drafted trust will allow the trustee to purchase assets from the estate to provide the needed cash, thereby avoiding this problem. The trustee needs to coordinate the purchase of assets with the personal representative.

GRITs, GRATs and GRUTs

The grantor-retained income trust (GRIT), grantor-retained annuity trust (GRAT) and grantor retained unitrust (GRUT) serve primarily to shelter future appreciation of the property transferred to the trust from federal estate tax. As previously mentioned, the advantages of these devices have been significantly curtailed by Congress in recent years. However, they still have application in some circumstances and many of these trusts that were established in earlier years still exist. A trustee's responsibilities in managing these types of trust include:

- In the case of a GRIT, paying the net income of the trust to the grantor. In the case of a GRAT, computing the fixed annuity and paying that amount to the grantor each year. In the case of a GRUT, determining the amount of the payout each year, based on the percentage stated in the trust document and the fair market value of the trust assets at the beginning of each tax year.

- For GRATs and GRUTs, managing the trust's portfolio to efficiently produce the returns necessary to meet the stated payout requirement in the trust document.

- If the grantor dies before the end of the stated term of the trust, the trust assets will be taxed in the grantor's estate and the trustee must value the assets as of the grantor's date of death for federal estate tax purposes.

- If the grantor survives the term of the trust, the trust must be terminated and the assets distributed to the named remainder beneficiaries.

Charitable Remainder Trusts

Charitable remainder trusts are one of the last tax-advantaged trust arrangements that have remained virtually untouched by Congress. For those individuals who have a charitable intent, the charitable remainder trust offers significant advantages including an income tax deduction based on the amount transferred to the trust, an estate tax deduction, avoidance of capital gains taxes if the property in the trust is sold and the retention of an income stream for life. There are several types of charitable remainder trusts. The most common are the charitable remainder annuity trust (CRAT) and the charitable remainder unitrust (CRUT). The CRAT pays a fixed annuity to the grantor and/or the grantor's spouse or other beneficiary for life. The CRUT pays an amount based on a stated percentage of the trust assets to the grantor and/or the grantor's spouse or other beneficiary for life. Charitable remainder trusts are subject to many rules that the trustee must follow in order to maintain the trust's tax advantaged status. Some of the administrative duties that apply to a charitable remainder trust include:

- **In the case of a CRAT, computing the fixed annuity and paying that amount to the grantor each year. For a CRUT, determining the amount of the payout each year, based on the percentage stated in the trust document and the fair market value of the trust assets at the beginning of each tax year.**

- **Managing the investments efficiently to meet the payout requirement of the trust. If the trust allows the use of principal to supplement income, and the payout percentage is high, a *total return* strategy should be used to manage the portfolio. With a high payout percentage such as 9% or 10%, the portfolio should be weighted toward equities (i.e., stocks) in order to achieve the return needed to meet the payout requirement.**

- Some trusts provide that only the net income can be distributed. These trusts are referred to as net income trusts or NIMCRUTS. If the payout requirement is 9% and the current income (i.e., dividends, interest, rents, etc.) is only 4%, that is all that can be paid out. These types of trusts usually have a "make up" provision that will require the trustee to maintain records of the years in which there is a shortfall. If the net income in future years exceeds the stated percentage payout, the trustee can pay the excess to make up for the shortfalls in prior years.

- The trustee shall not engage in any act of self-dealing, as defined in Section 4941(d) of the Internal Revenue Service Code (Code).

- The trustee shall not make any taxable expenditure as defined in Section 4945(d) of the Code.

- The trustee shall not make any investments that jeopardize the charitable purpose of the trust, within the meaning of Section 4943 of the Code.

- The trustee is prohibited from incurring unrelated business taxable income within the meaning of Section 512 of the Code.

- The trustee is prohibited from incurring debt-financed income within the meaning of Section 514 of the Code.

Other Trusts

Other types of irrevocable trusts are established for a variety of purposes. Again, the important thing to remember is that the standards of conduct and principles of trust administration discussed in this book apply to all irrevocable trusts. It is important that the trustee understand the basic purpose and intent of these trusts in order to manage them properly:

- **Qualified Personal Residence Trust (QPRT)**—A QPRT is a trust that holds the grantor's residence for a specified period of years while allowing the grantor to retain the right to use the property. If the grantor dies before the term ends, the property will be included in the grantor's estate. However, if the grantor survives the term, it will be excluded from the grantor's estate because title will have passed at that point, typically to the settlor's children. The trust can provide for the payment of fair rent to allow the grantor to continue to live in the house beyond the term of the trust. The trust document must prohibit the trustee from selling or transferring the property to the grantor or the grantor's spouse.

- **Special Needs Trust**—A special needs trust is designed to put funds aside for a beneficiary without those funds disqualifying the beneficiary from receiving public assistance. The trust provides that the trustee is to use his or her discretion in making distributions to the beneficiary and only to supplement the funds available through public assistance.

- **Wealth Replacement Trust**—A wealth replacement trust is nothing more than a separate Irrevocable Life Insurance Trust (ILIT) whose purpose is to replace the inheritance that was lost as a result of property transferred to a Charitable Remainder Trust (i.e., CRAT, CRUT, NIMCRUT). A life insurance policy equal to the value of the property transferred to the Charitable Remainder Trust is purchased in the Wealth Replacement Trust. It is subject to the same rules that apply to any other ILIT and is managed accordingly.

- **Spendthrift Trust**—Although most family or credit shelter trusts contain a spendthrift provision, a separate irrevocable trust is sometimes created specifically to protect a particular beneficiary from his creditors and divorce. The Spendthrift Trust precludes the beneficiary from having access to principal, either by prohibiting principal distributions or giving the trustee sole discretion to make payments from principal. This restriction prevents the creditors of the beneficiary from reaching the trust assets. The trustee must evaluate every principal distribution and be assured that the funds are being used for the purpose for which they were disbursed.

- **Charitable Lead Trust (CLT)**—A Charitable Lead Trust pays a specific dollar amount or fixed percentage of the value of the trust to a charity each year for a specified term. At the end of the term, the trust property is either distributed to or retained in trust for the benefit of non-charitable beneficiaries (i.e., children, grandchildren, etc.) The purpose of the CLT is to remove the income from the grantor, having the same effect as a charitable income tax deduction, and also to make a gift to the remainder beneficiaries.

As is the case with almost any arrangement that attempts to avoid taxes and creditor claims, some will stay within the spirit of the law and others will try to push the limits. The Internal Revenue Service has given notice that they consider the following trust arrangements abusive:

- **The Business Trust**—The owner of a business transfers the business to a trust in exchange for units or certificates of beneficial interest. The business trust makes payments to the trust unit holders or to other trusts created by the owner that purport to reduce the taxable income of the business trust to the point where little or no tax is due from the business trust. Most states do not recognize business trusts.

- **Equipment or Service Trust**—An equipment trust is formed to hold equipment that is rented or leased to the business trust, often at inflated rates. The service trust is formed to provide services to the business trust, often for inflated fees.

- **Family Residence Trust**—The owner (grantor) of the family residence transfers the residence, including its furnishings, to a trust, which is leased back to the grantor. The trustee takes depreciation and other expenses to reduce or eliminate the taxable income from lease rent. The trust claims the exchange results in a stepped-up basis for the property and the owner reports no gain.

- **Charitable Trust**—The owner transfers assets to a purported charitable trust and claims either that the payments to the trust are deductible or that payments made by the trust are deductible charitable contributions. However, in fact, the payments are principally for the personal educational, living, or recreational expenses of the owner or the owner's family.

- **Final Trust**—In some multi-trust arrangements, the U.S. owner of one or more abusive trusts establishes a trust that holds trust units of the owner's other trusts and is the final distributee of the income. A final trust often is formed in a foreign country that will impose little or no tax on the trust.

For obvious reasons, it would be prudent for an individual not to serve as a trustee for these types of trusts. The IRS has advised that taxpayers and/or the promoters of these trust arrangements may be subject to civil and/or criminal penalties.

Irrevocable Trust Administration Checklist

✓ Set up and administer the trust in accordance with the rules and standards of conduct that apply to all irrevocable trusts.

✓ Read the trust document and identify any special provisions that apply to the administration of the trust.

✓ Identify, by consulting with the attorney for the trust or other qualified professional, any special legal requirements that apply to the administration of the trust.

✓ Develop an investment strategy that meets the specific current payout requirements of the trust and protects the interests of remaindermen.

CHAPTER 19

Trustee's Fees

KEY POINTS

- All trustees are entitled to receive reasonable compensation for their services.

- Most trust documents will contain a provision that covers the trustee's compensation. In the absence of a provision in the trust, local law usually speaks to what trustees can charge for their services.

- If the trustee's fee is not specifically stated in the trust document or local statutes, reasonable compensation should be based on the size of the trust, responsibilities assumed, and level of difficulty and time required to manage the trust.

Although many individual trustees, for one reason or another, do not charge a fee for their services, all trustees are entitled to receive reasonable compensation for the services they perform and the responsibilities they assume. Being a trustee requires a considerable time commitment and, as discussed in previous chapters, may expose one to personal liability. As in any other job, a trustee should rightfully receive remuneration for services performed and the courts have always recognized a trustee's right to just compensation. There may be a practical reason to charge a trustee's fee. If the trust is a terminating trust, and the trustee is also the sole remainder beneficiary, taking a fee may be a good way to minimize taxes. Trustee's fees are deductible by the trust for tax purposes and if the tax rate on taxable trust income is higher than the income tax bracket of the trustee/beneficiary, taking trustee fees has the effect of having these funds taxed at a lower rate.

In determining trustee compensation, the trustee must first look to the trust document. If the document does not contain a trustee compensation provision, the trustee must then refer to local statutes.

Provisions in the Trust Document

Some trust documents contain a specific fee schedule for the trustee's compensation. The fee can be a percentage of income, principal or both. In some cases, the trustee's fee is a flat fee and in others, an hourly rate. Some trust documents provide that the trustees' fees will be what is allowed under local statutes. Most modern trust documents do not prescribe a specific fee schedule, but make reference to "reasonable compensation." The following is a typical compensation clause:

> *"The trustee shall be entitled to reasonable compensation for its services. Such compensation shall be commensurate with the services actually performed. The trustee shall also be entitled to reimbursement for expenses necessarily incurred in the administration of the trust estate."*

This language puts the burden of determining compensation on the trustee. In deciding what to charge, a trustee should look to local law and what is traditionally charged for trustee services in the community. Like any other trust issue, the trustee can ultimately seek the court's approval of his or her fees. An alternative would be to negotiate a fee directly with the beneficiaries of the trust.

Statutory Fees

Most states have laws that prescribe the compensation a trustee is entitled to charge. Some have rates for corporate trustees and separate schedules for individual trustees. In some jurisdictions, the fees are based on a percentage of the principal value of the trust. In others, the fee is based on a percentage of income; some allow both principal and income charges. The theory behind having both an income and a principal fee is that it provides an incentive for the trustee to increase both income and principal, thereby benefiting the income beneficiaries and remaindermen. It also allows both income beneficiaries and remaindermen to share the cost of administration. Other states do not prescribe a formula, but instead require that the trustee's fees be reasonable. The court ultimately makes the determination as to what is reasonable and what is not. If the trust document makes specific reference to the statutes, of course that is what the trustee is entitled to charge. If the trust document does not contain any reference to trustee compensation, the trustee can usually charge what is provided under local law. (See *Appendix I*)

Extraordinary Fees

Most statutory and traditional (i.e., banks, trust companies and other professional fiduciaries) fee schedules are designed to compensate the trustee for administration services normally performed in a trust. They are not intended to cover extraordinary services. Extraordinary services include:

- **managing a closely-held business;**

- **gathering information for and managing litigation involving the trust;**

- **managing, selling or leasing real estate;**

- **serving as an officer or director of a company whose stock is owned by the trust;**

- **filing the decedent's final income tax returns;**

- **filing fiduciary income tax returns for the trust; and**

- **filing the estate tax return.**

These are generally outside the scope of services that a trustee is normally expected to perform. Charges for these and similar services should be made separately.

What is "Reasonable?"

Reasonable compensation largely has been determined by tradition and the courts. The case law on the subject has taken several factors into consideration, which are good guidelines for trustees in determining what to charge:

Size of the trust—Trustee's fees should bear some relationship to the size of the trust. The fees should not impose such an economic cost to the trust as to prevent achieving its purpose or put an unreasonable financial burden on the beneficiaries. As a guide, the trustee should compare his or her fee, as a percentage of the value of the trust, with the percentage fee charged by professional fiduciaries and investment managers. For example, if a trustee receives $5,000 a year for managing a trust worth $500,000, this represents a fee of 1% (i.e., $5,000 ÷ $500,000.) This percentage is roughly what investment managers charge.

Responsibilities assumed—In accepting the duties and responsibilities for a trust, the trustee can be held personally liable for any loss that may occur as a result of his or her actions. The larger the trust, the greater the potential liability. Part of the trustee's fees should take into consideration the trustee's willingness to take on these responsibilities and assume the associated risks.

Problems and difficulties in managing the trust—Not all trusts are the same. Some are more difficult to manage than others. For example, a trust that owns several businesses or commercial real estate interests, some of which are involved in litigation, will be far more difficult to manage than a simple trust invested in mutual funds and bank deposits. Trusts that have a greater degree of difficulty should entitle the trustee to above-average compensation.

Time and service required—The time that it takes to manage the trust and serve its beneficiaries is a key factor. Challenges to a trustee's fees will often be based on how much time it would take someone else to manage the same trust and what those charges would be. Keeping time records is a good idea, not only to defend against a beneficiary complaint, but also as a basis for adjusting the trustee's compensation, where appropriate.

Other considerations—Other circumstances also need to be considered. A trustee may possess a special skill, such as tax planning, and bring this expertise to bear on the management of the trust. This special service may result in tax savings for the trust that, without the expertise of the trustee, might not be realized. In this case, the trustee should be entitled to higher compensation. A trustee should also receive additional fees for unusual accomplishments such as the sale of a closely held business or the successful completion of a real estate development deal.

After considering the above factors, a comparison of what is being charged in the community by other trustees and what is allowed under local law should be made in determining what is reasonable. A particular jurisdiction will have a range of fees that are customarily charged by banks, trust companies and in some cases individuals who serve as trustees. This information is readily available through banks and trust companies, estate-planning attorneys, CPAs and other financial professionals. This data should form the basis upon which an individual trustee's charges are made. Statutory fees or even the fees charged by banks and trust companies may be too low for a given trust. In this case the trustee should consider negotiating the fee directly with the beneficiaries of the trust. If the fees are charged against income and the current beneficiaries agree to the fee, there should not be a problem. However, the current beneficiaries cannot bind the remaindermen and if some, or all, of the negotiated fees are charged to principal, questions regarding the appropriateness of the fees could be raised by the remaindermen at the termination of the trust.

Many statutory fees provide a division of charges between income and principal. Typically, if local law allows both an income and principal fee, the income fee is charged against income and the principal fee is charged against the principal of the trust. In the case of a trustee's fee based solely on the value of the principal, half of the fee should be charged to income and the other half to principal. This is the most equitable way to handle the charges and is consistent with the way the courts have ruled on this issue where a split has been disputed.

Where an individual is named both the personal representative and the trustee, the question that is often raised is whether or not the fiduciary is entitled to personal representative and trustee fees on the same property. While there are exceptions among the various states, the general rule is that a separate fee is paid to a personal representative for receiving and paying over to the trustee the assets of the estate. The trustee is entitled to a fee on those same assets for taking possession of and managing them in the trust. So the answer is yes.

Co-Trustees

The compensation of co-trustees is dictated by the terms of the trust document. Again, if there is no provision, the trustees must look to local law. Every state is different. In some states, each trustee is entitled to the full allowable trustee fees. In others only one fee is chargeable to the trust and the co-trustees must share that fee as they agree between themselves. If there is no agreement, the court must decide how the fees are to be split. In the case of a bank or trust company serving as a co-trustee, the institution will normally insist on being paid the full fee. However, in some cases they will negotiate a fee split with the individual co-trustee. Fee-splitting arrangements should always be in writing.

Trustee Compensation Checklist

✓ Review the trust document or local law to determine what fees are permitted.

✓ Determine if any extraordinary services will be required and include appropriate charges for these services.

✓ If the trustee is authorized to receive "reasonable compensation", consider having all beneficiaries agree to the fee.

✓ If compensation is based on a percentage of trust assets, charge one half of the fee to income and the other half to principal.

✓ Commit to writing any agreement to split fees with a co-trustee.

GETTING
HELP

CHAPTER 20

Where to Get Help

> **KEY POINTS**
>
> - Most personal representatives and trustees will need professional help with the administration of the estate or trust.
>
> - Hiring professional agents is a legitimate expense of administration.
>
> - Many professionals specialize in providing services to personal representatives and trustees.

Personal representatives and trustees face many difficult and time-consuming tasks while administering an estate or trust. Only the foolhardy will attempt to deal with the more complex issues without professional help. Individual fiduciaries are responsible for their actions and in some situations may be held personally liable for not hiring professionals when they lack the necessary expertise to properly perform the task. When and where to get help will, of course, depend on the particular issue that needs to be addressed. If the matter is one of legal interpretation or consequence, an attorney who specializes in that area of law should be consulted. If the question is procedural or authoritative in nature, such as whether or not the personal representative or trustee can hire agents to assist in the administration of the estate or trust, the answer can usually be found in the Will or trust or by referencing local statutes. Most modern Will and trust documents authorize hiring agents. The reason is obvious. It is highly unlikely that an individual personal representative or trustee will possess the skills and expertise necessary to handle the administration of the estate or trust.

Some individuals may feel that the reason they were selected was to save money. They may also think that they would betray this intent by hiring agents and incurring the "additional" expense. Just the opposite is true. While minimizing expenses is always an objective, the testator or settlor also expects the individual to perform the job correctly to protect the interests of his or her beneficiaries. The expectation is that the individual will use the resources of the estate or trust to carryout this objective. The laws are also written with this in mind. Hiring consultants to assist and advise the personal representative or trustee is proper and an appropriate administration expense chargeable to income. In fact, some statutes make specific reference to the charging of agents' fees to the estate or trust.

Accountants

Accountants should be used for their expertise in the fields of accounting and taxation. Because of the high level of accounting and tax expertise required, only Certified Public Accountants (CPAs) should be retained. A CPA can provide assistance with tax returns, tax elections, trust accounting reports, court accountings, inventories, business valuations and addressing a variety of tax, fiduciary accounting and planning issues. In addition, a CPA can assist the personal representative or trustee develop and analyze budgets, audit business and commercial real estate interests and resolve management problems that may exist with a closely held business. However, accountants should not necessarily be the final answer to a particular tax or accounting question. Accountants are prohibited from engaging in the unauthorized practice of law. A tax attorney should be retained if a particular tax or accounting question requires a legal opinion with regard to interpretation or application of the tax law. Most accountants will refer a client to an attorney when this situation occurs. Accountants can also be relied upon to make objective recommendations. CPAs do not receive compensation for recommending a particular investment or insurance product or referring a client to another professional. Accountants work closely with other professionals in a community and are a good source for referrals to investment advisors, insurance agents, attorneys and other professionals.

Attorneys

An attorney is usually required when a personal representative or trustee interacts with the courts. This is typically the case in a formal probate proceeding. Attorneys can give advice on a broad range of legal and non-legal matters. These include guidance with regard to probate proceedings, interpretation of contracts and other legal documents, guidance on the effects of local law on the administration of estates and trusts, dealing with creditor rights issues, interpreting the legal rights of heirs and other issues that require interpretation and application of the law. The attorney who prepared the Will or trust is the logical choice to represent the estate or trust in court. He or she should be familiar with the decedent's estate plan, family and financial affairs. However, the attorney who prepared the original Will and/or trust may not have an interest in representing the estate or trust or may not have sufficient experience in the area of administration. The personal representative or trustee is responsible for hiring the attorney and it is therefore important to retain someone who will devote the time and who has experience with estate and trust administration. The fiduciary should also make sure that expensive attorney time is not used for tasks that can be accomplished at a lower cost by someone else.

Banks and Trust Companies

Banks and trust companies are in the business of providing fiduciary services including serving as a personal representative and trustee or acting as an agent to assist the fiduciary with administration. Banks and trust companies bill themselves as "one-stop" shops because typically, they have all of the facilities to administer estates and trusts in house. Using a bank or trust company to serve as a personal representative or trustee can be expensive, particularly for smaller accounts. However, if the bank or trust company provides services as an agent of the personal representative or trustee, the cost might be lower depending on the particular services that are needed.

One of the advantages of using a bank or trust company is that they do not get sick or go on vacation and therefore provide continuity in the administration of the estate or trust. Individuals are human and must devote time to their own business and family affairs. Banks and trust companies can be useful in mitigating conflicts between the personal representative or trustee and other family members. For example, if the individual personal representative or trustee is also a beneficiary, he or she could be viewed by other family members as not being totally objective with regard to the management decisions that are made. Banks and trust companies are usually not well equipped to manage a closely held family business. This type of asset can be better handled by a family member or other individual who is familiar with the business. If the estate or trust is complex, using a corporate fiduciary may be a way of reducing liability exposure. Banks and trust companies are also covered by insurance for any errors they make.

Stockbrokers

Most stockbrokerage firms provide individual portfolio management services, in addition to their retail brokerage activities (i.e., recommending stocks and bonds for purchase or sale). The large brokerage firms now own one or more trust companies through which fiduciary services are also offered. However, they are new at this business and the services may be limited and only available in the state where the trust company is located. Some firms deliver limited fiduciary services through their brokerage offices, using the account executive (i.e., broker) as a liaison between the trustee client and the trust officer who works out of the nearest trust company office. Brokerage firms are capable of managing a trust's securities portfolio, but are not usually equipped to handle the management of other assets such as real estate. Management of the portfolio is either handled by portfolio managers within the firm or outside money managers hired by the company. Management fees can run anywhere between 1% to 3% of the portfolio's value.

Investment Advisors

Independent investment advisors can also be hired to manage the trust's securities portfolio. The difference between a stockbroker and an independent investment advisor is that a stockbroker is in the business of recommending the sale and purchase of individual securities and mutual funds to his or her client and investment advisors manage portfolios. The broker receives compensation from the commissions that are charged on the securities trades that are made. An investment advisor is usually paid a fee for managing the portfolio. The fee is based on the value of the portfolio and not on the securities that are bought and sold. Fees vary depending on the size of the account or whether the assets are invested in mutual funds, individual securities or a combination of the two. The fees, generally, are 1% of the portfolio's value and may be lower for larger accounts. It is important that the advisor understand the terms of the trust, its objectives, the needs of the income beneficiaries, and the applicable rules under the Uniform Prudent Investor Act. Most independent investment advisors do not provide other fiduciary services.

Financial Planners

A financial planner's primary function is to assist individuals develop and implement a comprehensive personal financial plan.

Financial planning includes budgeting and cash flow analyses, long-term savings, retirement planning, investments, tax planning, estate planning and risk (insurance) management. Financial planners can assist a personal representative or trustee with any of these component needs if the planner has experience in dealing with these issues in a fiduciary context. Financial planners usually have an orientation toward investments and insurance since they may be compensated through the use of these products. A financial planner may also have a strong background in estate planning and can be helpful to a personal representative or trustee in making decisions that affect a beneficiary's estate plan. Some planners emphasize tax planning and may have expertise in fiduciary taxation.

Insurance Agents

An insurance agent should be consulted when evaluating the insurance coverage for estate and trust assets. Agents should be engaged to investigate the physical condition of estate or trust property and recommend any changes necessary to reduce hazards and protect fiduciary assets. The coverage should include protection from fire, theft, loss of use, liability and other risk exposures. If additional coverage is needed, the personal representative or trustee should be advised as to the most economical way to obtain the needed coverage. The fiduciary should use the insurance agent who handled the decedent's policies prior to death. However, the personal representative or trustee can use any agent or firm as long as it does not create a conflict of interest.

Realtors

A real estate agent should be retained if the estate or trust holds real estate that needs to be sold. Hiring an agent that has expertise in the area in which the property is located is the prudent choice. The realtor should also specialize in the particular type of property (i.e., residential, commercial or industrial) that is being sold. Before making a selection, the personal representative or trustee should discuss the sale with three different realtors and list the property with the realtor that has the highest level of experience and success in marketing the particular type of property that is being sold. Some real estate firms can also provide property management services for income-producing residential and commercial properties, including marketing and advertising, collection of rents, physical care of the premises, procuring supplies and equipment, making repairs, hiring employees and maintaining accounting records. Although a realtor may be familiar with the principles of valuing real estate, most do not provide formal appraisal services. However, they are a good source for referrals. Most are very familiar with the quality and price ranges of experienced appraisers and can recommend one that is best suited to the particular property that needs to be valued.

WHO CAN ASSIST YOU

Administration Issues	Accountant	Attorney	Bank/ Trust Co.	Stockbroker /Investment Advisor	Financial Planner	Insurance Agent	Realtor
Interpreting Will / Trust Provisions		X	X	X			
Fiduciary Accounting	X		X		X		
Federal Estate Tax Return, Form 706		X	Some	X			
Fiduciary Income Tax Returns		X	Some	X		Some	
Funding the Marital/ Credit Shelter Trusts	X	X	X		Some		
Discretionary Distributions			X	X		Some	
Investment Management			X	X	X		
Insurance Evaluation						X	
Real Estate Mgt.			X				X
Management of a Closely Held Business	X	X	Some	Some	Some		
Tax Elections & Planning	X	X	Some		X	Some	
Representation Before Tax Authorities	X	X			Some		
Developing Budgets & Cash Flow Forecasts	X		X	X	X		
Lease Renegotiations		X					X
Legal Questions & Litigation Issues		X					
Court Representation		X					
Sale of Real Estate							X
Valuation of Securities	X		X	X	X	Some	
Valuation of Real Estate						Some	
Questions Regarding Permitted Transactions Under the Will, Trust or Local Law	Some	X	X				

WHO CAN ASSIST YOU, Cont.

Administration Issues	Accountant	Attorney	Bank/ Trust Co.	Stockbroker /Investment Advisor	Financial Planner	Insurance Agent	Realtor
Business Valuations		X	Some			Some	
Custody of Securities			X	X			
Buying and Selling Securities			X	X	X	X	
Rights of Creditors		X					
Impact of Community Property Laws		X	X	X		Some	
Planning for Special Use Valuation		X	X	X		Some	
Options for Settling Employee Benefits and Life Insurance Claims	X	X	X		X	X	
Surviving Spouse's Elective Rights			X	X			
Disclaimers Some		X	X	X		Some	
Sale of Business Interests		X	X	X	X		
Planning for Extension of Time to Pay Estate Taxes	X	X	X		X		

CHAPTER 21

How to Select Advisors

KEY POINTS

- **Selecting an agent should be based on the task that needs to be performed or the expertise required to deal with a particular fiduciary issue.**

- **Doing your homework and asking the right questions will reduce the possibility of hiring the wrong person.**

- **Once an agent is hired, the personal representative or trustee must oversee and supervise the agent's activities.**

Who Do You Hire?

Who should you hire as an agent? Can he or she be trusted? Does he or she have the necessary skills and expertise? Will you pay too much? The number and variety of financial experts out there is mind-boggling. Anyone can call himself or herself a financial planner or advisor, and there are many to choose from including CPAs, CFAs, CLUs, ChFcs, CTFAs and many, many others. To add to the confusion, there is no one agency that regulates all financial advisors or uniform standards that apply to all groups. Fees that financial advisors charge vary widely and some will not accept a client whose assets fall below a minimum dollar amount. Deciding on who to hire can be a perplexing experience, but it does not have to be.

Doing your homework and asking some basic questions will greatly improve your chances of hiring the right person. Some basic questions to ask when selecting an advisor include:

- **What relevant education and/or credentials does the advisor have in his or her field?**

- **Do the credentials require continuing education to maintain the designation? If so how many hours are required?**

- **What professional organizations does the advisor belong to and how active is he or she in those organizations?**

- **How long has the advisor been practicing?**

- **Ask the advisor for references. Talk to other professionals and the advisor's clients.**

- **Ask your banker about the advisor's reputation.**

- **Discuss your selection with friends, relatives, etc., who have some knowledge about the advisor's business or a related field.**

- **Are you compatible with the advisor's personality and business philosophy?**

- **Check with the appropriate government regulatory agency as to whether any complaints have been registered against the advisor.**

- **Ask for a list of other professionals with whom the advisor maintains a close working relationship.**

- **Ask the advisor if he or she will be working directly with you or will an associate be providing the services.**

- **Find out how the advisor will be compensated. Will you be advised before extraordinary services are performed and before charges for these services are made?**

- **Ask the advisor how much insurance he or she carries to cover errors and omissions.**

- **Discuss the procedures and methods that the advisor will use in assisting you.**

"You seem to know something about law. I like that in an attorney."

The selection should be based on the particular service that is needed and additional information pertaining to the advisor's particular area of expertise should be obtained before the final selection is made:

Accountant

- **Is the individual a certified public accountant (CPA)?**

- **Is the CPA licensed to practice in the state in which the estate or trust is located?**

- Does the CPA have experience in handling fiduciary matters (i.e., preparation of estate tax returns, fiduciary income tax returns, fiduciary accountings, etc.)?

- What percentage of the CPA's practice is devoted to fiduciary services?

- Is the CPA a member of the American Institute of Certified Public Accountants (AICPA), which subjects its members to a code of professional ethics?

- Will other individuals within the firm be performing any of the work? If so, what is their level of experience and will they be closely supervised by the CPA?

- What will be the charges for the work performed?

Attorney

- How long has the attorney practiced in his or her given field?

- What percentage of his or her time is spent handling the type of estate or trust matter that the fiduciary needs assistance with?

- Is the attorney amenable to consulting with the fiduciary's other advisors such as the CPA, banker, insurance agent, etc.?

- Is there a charge for an initial consultation?

- What is the attorney's hourly rate?

- Will the attorney consult with you when the charges are likely to exceed the initial estimate and before you are billed for the services?

- Will providing the needed services affect the attorney's malpractice insurance coverage? In other words, are the services excluded under the policy?

- Will others who are compensated at a lower rate perform clerical services and will the fees reflect that lower rate?

Bank or Trust Company

- How large is the operation? What is the value of assets under administration and management?

- How long has the institution been in the fiduciary services business?

- What are the charges? Is there a minimum? Obtain fee schedules.

- What is the size and structure of the investment department?

- What investment style is used to manage fiduciary portfolios?

- What is their investment performance record? Obtain 1, 3, 5, and 10-year results.

- Obtain a sample of accounting reports. What is the quality? How frequently are reports provided?

- What is the rate of personnel turnover?

- What is the average experience (number of years) of investment officers, trust officers, management personnel and others who are directly involved in handling fiduciary accounts?

- What credentials are trust and investment officers required to hold?

- Who (i.e., trust officer, committee, manager, etc.)

will make the decisions concerning the services that will be provided?

- Obtain annual reports, booklets and other materials describing the institution and the services provided.

- Interview trust officers and supervisory personnel.

- Obtain the name and title of the manager of the trust department.

- How much of the operation is outsourced to other companies and what affect will that have on the services provided?

Financial Planner

- What credentials (i.e., CFP, ChFc, CPA, etc.) and licenses does the planner hold.

- What experience does the planner have in advising clients on fiduciary matters?

- How long has the planner been in business?

- How is the planner compensated—fee for service or commissions for selling products?

- What kind of investment track record does the planner have?

- Who are the other professionals that the planner works with and what is their level of experience?

- What percentage of the planner's practice is devoted to assisting personal representatives and trustees?

- How familiar is the planner with the rules and regulations that affect personal representatives and trustees?

- How many estate and trustee clients does the planner have?

Stockbroker

- Is the brokerage firm familiar with the Uniform Prudent Investor Act?

- Will an advisor hired by the brokerage firm manage the portfolio?

- What is the manager's performance record? Obtain 1, 3, 5, and 10-year performance numbers.

- How many fiduciary accounts does the brokerage firm handle?

- What is the investment philosophy and strategy of the firm?

- What is the rate of personnel turnover?

- Is diversification to reduce risk part of the brokerage firm's style?

- How often will the broker contact the personal representative or trustee to review the portfolio and investment results?

- Can the agency agreement be terminated at any time? If so is there an exit or termination charge?

- Interview the manager who will handle the account to ascertain whether or not the manager's personality is compatible with yours.

Investment Advisor

- What credentials and licenses does the advisor hold?

- Is the advisor familiar with the Uniform Prudent Investor Act?

- Is the advisor a "registered representative?"

- What is the manager's performance record? Obtain 1, 3, 5, and 10-year performance numbers.

- How many fiduciary accounts does the advisor handle?

- How long has the advisor been managing estate and trust accounts?

- How many years of experience does the advisor have?

- Is diversification to reduce risk part of the advisor's style?

- What was the biggest investment mistake the advisor made and what steps have been taken to prevent repetition?

- How often will the advisor contact the personal representative or trustee to review the portfolio and investment results?

- Will you be compatible with the advisor?

Insurance Agent

- What credentials and licenses does the agent hold?

- How long has the agent been in business?

- Is the agent a broker that uses insurance products from various companies or does he or she sell one company's products only?

- What type of insurance does the agent specialize in?

- Will the insurance agent service the policy(ies) after it is sold?

- How often will the agent review the coverage?

- Will the agent keep the personal representative or trustee current with the estate's or trust's loss exposures and informed about changes in insurance laws, forms and rates?

- Has the agent handled insurance cases for estates and trusts before?

- How many estate and trust clients does the agent serve?

- What is the reputation of the insurance companies the agent represents? How are they rated by Best, Standard and Poors, Duff and Phelps and other rating services?

Realtor or Property Manager

- What credentials and licenses does the agent hold?

- How long has the realtor or property manager been in business?

- Is the prospective agent familiar with the area in which the property is located?

- Is the prospective agent licensed to perform the services required?

- Does the property manager have experienced personnel to handle collections, repairs, supplies, insurance, accounting, etc.?

- How many properties does the agent handle at any one time?

- **What are the charges?**

- **What is the frequency of accounting reports? Are they audited?**

- **If a sale is involved, how will the property be marketed?**

- **Can the sales contract be canceled after six months if the property has not been sold?**

- **How frequently will rental income be disbursed?**

- **Before rental income is paid out, will the funds be invested in a money market account?**

- **What threshold disbursement amount will require the authority of the personal representative or trustee before the agent makes payment?**

In carrying out the responsibilities imposed on a personal representative or trustee, as set forth in the governing document and/or local law, a fiduciary must select advisors wisely. While technical competence is important, so too is the advisor's business philosophy regarding the management of the estate or trust. The advisor's attitudes should be agreeable and compatible with those of the individual fiduciary. The needed services should be clearly explained to the agent and outlined in a written agreement signed by both the agent and the fiduciary. Professional advisors should not be used for routine work and good records should be kept of the services provided. The records can be used as a reference in the event a question arises regarding the services that were performed. Remember that the personal representative or trustee is expected to exercise care, skill, and caution in managing the estate or trust. To carry out this responsibility, the fiduciary must exercise a reasonable degree of prudence in selecting the agent. Once an agent has been hired, the fiduciary must employ oversight and supervision of the agent's activities to assure that the services contracted for are delivered satisfactorily and that the integrity and interests of the beneficiaries are preserved.

APPENDIX I

State-by-State Summary of Statutory Provisions

The information contained in this appendix may not be accurate as the laws in a particular state may have changed or the author may have misinterpreted existing statutes. This information should only be used as a general reference and the author assumes no responsibility for anyone relying on it as a literal translation of state laws.

State	Type of Probate Proceeding	Transfer by Affidavit	Compensation of Personal Representative	Annual Compensation for Trustee
Alabama	Formal	none	Reasonable	Approved and allowed by probate court.
Alaska	Small Estates, Informal, Formal, Supervised	Yes, if value of decedent's estate is less than $15,000	Reasonable	Reasonable
Arizona	Small Estates, Informal, Formal, Supervised	Yes, for personal property if personal property, less liens and encumbrances, does not exceed $30,000	Reasonable	Reasonable
Arkansas	Formal	none	Personal property: 10% of 1st $1,000, 5% of next $4,000, 3% on the balance. Real property: Reasonable, subject to court approval	In accordance with the terms of the trust
California	Formal, over $100,000	Yes, if value of real and personal property does not exceed $100,000.	4% on the first $15,00, 3% on the next $85,000, 2% on the next $900,000, 1% on the next 9,000,000, .5% on the next $15,000,000, and over $25,000,000 - reasonable as determined by the court	Reasonable

State	Type of Probate Proceeding	Transfer by Affidavit	Compensation of Personal Representative	Annual Compensation for Trustee
Colorado	Small Estates, Informal, Formal	Yes, if the fair market value of the property does not exceed $27,000.	Reasonable	Reasonable
Delaware	Formal	None	As allowed by rule of the County of Chancery.	Reasonable in accordance with the document creating the trust.
District of Columbia	Abbreviated, Standard, Small Estates	None	Reasonable	Reasonable
Florida	Formal	Yes, for exempt personal property, personal property exempt from the claims of creditors, and non-exempt personal property the value of which does not exceed the sum of funeral expenses and necessary medical expenses of the last 60 days of illness	3% on the first $1 million of value, 2.5% above $1 million to $5 million, 2.7% above $5 million to $10 million, and 1.5% on all amounts over $10 million.	Reasonable
Georgia	Formal	None	As specified in will or agreement signed by all beneficiaries. Otherwise 2.5% on moneys received by personal representative and 2.5% on moneys paid out, 10% on amount of interest made, 3% on value of in-kind property distributed and 10% of annual income on land	Same as for personal representative plus .5% on the value of trust assets annually
Hawaii	Small Estates, Informal, Formal	Yes, if gross value of the decedent's personal property does not exceed $100,000	Reasonable	7% on first $5,000 of income rec'd., 5% on all income over $5,000, .5% on the value of trust assets each year, 1% of value at inception, 1% of value at termination, 2.5% on cash principal received after inception, 2.5% on final payment of cash principal

State	Type of Probate Proceeding	Transfer by Affidavit	Compensation of Personal Representative	Annual Compensation for Trustee
Idaho	Small Estates, Informal, Formal, Supervised	Yes, if the value of the entire estate subject to probate, less liens and encumbrances, does not exceed $25,000	Reasonable	Reasonable
Illinois	Independent Administration, Summary Administration (petition to the court for distribution if gross value of estate does not exceed $50,000), Supervised Administration	Yes, if gross value of estate does not exceed $50,000	Reasonable	Reasonable
Indiana	Unsupervised, Formal	Yes, if gross probate estate, less liens and encumbrances, does not exceed $25,000	Reasonable	Reasonable
Iowa	Formal	Yes, if gross value of decedent's personal property does not exceed $10,000	6% on 1st $1,000, 4% between $1,000 and $5,000, 2% over $5,000	Reasonable
Kansas	Informal , Supervised, Simplified	None	As provided under the will or for services that are just and proper	For services that are just and proper
Kentucky	Formal	None	5% of the value of the personal estate plus 5% of the income collected	6% of income; 3/10 of 1% on value of trust assets
Louisiana	Small Estates (Gross value of $50,000 or less), Formal	Yes, under small estates procedure	2 1/2 % of the amount of the inventory	Reasonable
Maine	Small Estates, Formal, Informal	Yes, if the value of the entire estate, less liens and encumbrances, does not exceed $10,000	Reasonable	Reasonable

State	Type of Probate Proceeding	Transfer by Affidavit	Compensation of Personal Representative	Annual Compensation for Trustee
Maryland	Small Estates, Formal	None	On the value of property subject to administration: 9% on the first $20,000, $1,800 plus 3.6% on the excess over $20,000	6% on all income from real estate and mortgages, 6 1/2 % on the first $10,000 of all other income, 5% on the next $10,000, 4% on the next $10,000, 3% on the rest; 4/10 of 1% on the first $250,000 of value, 1/4 of 1% on the next $250,000, 3/20 of 1% on the next $500,000, and 1/10 of 1% upon any excess
Massachusetts	Small Estates, Formal	None	As allowed by the court	As allowed by the court
Michigan	Small Estates, Formal	None	Reasonable	Reasonable
Minnesota	Formal, Informal	Yes, if the value of the entire estate, less liens and encumbrances, does not exceed $20,000	Reasonable	Reasonable
Mississippi	Formal	None	Sum not to exceed 10% on the whole estate administered	Reasonable
Missouri	Small Estates, Supervised (formal), Independent (informal)	None	On the value of all personal property and the proceeds of real property sold: 5% on the 1st $5,000, 4% on the next $20,000, 3% on the next $75,000, 2¾% on the next $300,000, 2½% on the next $600,000, 2% on all over $1,000,000	No reference (presumed reasonable)
Montana	Small Estates, Formal, Informal	Yes, if the value of the entire estate, less liens and encumbrances, does not exceed $7,500	Reasonable	Reasonable

State	Type of Probate Proceeding	Transfer by Affidavit	Compensation of Personal Representative	Annual Compensation for Trustee
Nebraska	Small Estates, Formal, Informal	Yes, if value of entire estate, less liens and encumbrances, does not exceed $25,000	No reference (presumed reasonable)	Reasonable
Nevada	Small Estates, Formal	Yes, if gross value of the decedent's property in the state does not exceed $20,000 and does not include real property	Upon the whole amount of the estate: 4% on the 1st $15,000, 3% on the next $85,000, 2% on all above $100,000	Reasonable
New Hampshire	Small Estates, Formal	None	No reference (presumed reasonable)	Reasonable
New Jersey	Small Estates, Formal	Yes, by spouse, if total value of assets of an intestate will not exceed $10,000. If intestate assets will not exceed $5,000 and intestate does leave a surviving spouse, one heir, with the consent of other heirs, can transfer the property	6% on all income received. 5% on value of corpus up to $200,000, 3 1/2 % over $200,000 up to $1,000,000, 2% over $1,000,000	6% on all income received. $5.00 per thousand of corpus on 1st $400,000, $3.00 per thousand in excess of $400,000
New Mexico	Informal, Formal	Yes, if total value of the estate, less liens and encumbrances, does not exceed $30,000	Reasonable	Reasonable
New York	Small Estates, Formal	None	For receiving and paying out all sums of money, 5% on 1st $100,000, 4% on next $200,000, 3% on next $700,000, 2½% on next $4,000,000, 2% on all over $5,000,000	1% on paying out principal (charged to principal). Annual commissions: $10.50 per $1,000 on the 1st $400,000 of principal, $4.50 per $1,000 on the next $600,000, $3.00 per $1,000 on all over $1,000,000 (1/3 charged to income, 2/3 charged to principal)

State	Type of Probate Proceeding	Transfer by Affidavit	Compensation of Personal Representative	Annual Compensation for Trustee
North Carolina	Summary Administration, Formal	Yes, if the value of all personal property, less liens and encumbrances, does not exceed $10,000	Determined by the clerk of the court upon the filing of a petition	5% on 1st $5,000 of income, 4% on next $7,500 of income, 3% on next $12,500 of income, 2 1/2% on next $25,000 of income, 2% on all over $50,000. 4/10 of 1% on 1st $25,000 of principal, 3/10 of 1% on next $25,000, 2/10 of 1% on next $50,000, 1/10 of 1% on next $100,000, 1/20 of 1% on all over $200,000
North Dakota	Small Estates, Informal, Formal	Yes, if the value of the entire estate, less liens and encumbrances, does not exceed $15,000	Reasonable	Reasonable
Ohio	Formal	None	Upon all personal property, including income, 4% on 1st $100,000, 3% on next $300,000, 2% on all over $400,000. Also 1% on the value of unsold real estate	No reference. Presumed reasonable
Oklahoma	Small Estates, Formal	None	5% on 1st $1,000, 4% on next $5,000, 2 1/2% on all over $6,000	Reasonable
Oregon	Small Estates, Formal	None	7% on 1st $1,000, 4% on next $9,000, 3% on next $40,000, 2% on all over $50,000	Reasonable
Pennsylvania	Small Estates, Formal	None	Reasonable	Reasonable
Rhode Island	Small Estates, Formal	None	Reasonable	Reasonable

State	Type of Probate Proceeding	Transfer by Affidavit	Compensation of Personal Representative	Annual Compensation for Trustee
South Carolina	Small Estates, Informal, Formal	Yes, if the value of the entire probate estate, less liens and encumbrances, does not exceed $10,000	5% on the value of all personal property and the sales proceeds of real property (minimum is $50 regardless of value). 5% of the income earned by the estate	Reasonable
South Dakota	Informal, Formal	None	Reasonable	Reasonable
Tennessee	Small Estates, Formal	None	Reasonable	Reasonable
Texas	Small Estates, Temporary Administration, Independent Administration, Administration of Community property	Yes, if the value of the entire assets of the estate, not including homestead and exempt property, does not exceed $50,000.	5% on all cash received and on all cash paid out, except for paying out to heirs and legatees. The aggregate of the fees shall not exceed 5% of the gross fair market value of the estate	Reasonable
Utah	Small Estates, Informal, Formal	Yes, if the value of the entire estate subject to administration, less liens and encumbrances, does not exceed $25,000	Reasonable	Reasonable
Vermont	Small Estates, Formal	None	$4.00 per day	$4.00 per day
Virginia	Small Estates, Formal	Yes, if value of the entire tangible personal property subject to probate does not exceed $10,000	Reasonable	Reasonable

State	Type of Probate Proceeding	Transfer by Affidavit	Compensation of Personal Representative	Annual Compensation for Trustee
Washington	Small Estates, Formal	Yes, if the value of the decedent's entire probate estate, not including the surviving spouse's community property interest in any assets which are subject to probate, less liens and encumbrances, does not exceed $60,000	Reasonable	Reasonable
West Virginia	Formal	None	Reasonable	Reasonable
Wisconsin	Small Estates, Informal, Formal	Yes, if solely owned property does not exceed $10,000	2% on inventory value, less any mortgages or liens	No reference. Presumed reasonable
Wyoming	Formal	Yes, if the value of the entire estate, less liens and encumbrances, does not exceed $70,000	10% on the 1st $1,000, 5% on the next $4,000, 3% on the next $15,000, 2% on all amounts over $20,000	No reference. Presumed reasonable

APPENDIX II

ESTATE ADMINISTRATION CHECKLIST

Estate Administration Checklist

Estate of_____

Date of Death _____

Beneficiaries:

Name	Relationship
_____	_____
_____	_____
_____	_____
_____	_____
_____	_____

Date of Will _____

Date of trust _____

	Estimated Completion or Due Date	**Date Completed**
Obtain original Will	_____	_____
Obtain copy of trust	_____	_____
Arrange funeral	_____	_____
Select attorney	_____	_____
Arrange for:		
Special administration	_____	_____
Family allowance	_____	_____
Elective share	_____	_____
File notice to creditors	_____	_____

	Estimated Completion or Due Date	Date Completed
Gather information:		
Obtain names, addresses & phone numbers of relatives	_____	_____
Obtain birthdates for all minors	_____	_____
Obtain birthdates of individuals whose inheritance is contingent on attainment of a certain age	_____	_____
Obtain names and addresses of witnesses to Will	_____	_____
Prepare inventory of probate assets	_____	_____
Prepare inventory of non probate assets	_____	_____
Obtain list of insurance policies	_____	_____
Prepare list of known debts	_____	_____
Obtain copy of deeds, leases, contracts, etc.	_____	_____
Obtain copy of pension, profit sharing, IRA and other employee benefit plan documents	_____	_____
Obtain copy of income, gift or other tax returns filed by the decedent	_____	_____
Retain advisors:		
Accountant	_____	_____

	Estimated Completion or Due Date	Date Completed
Investment advisor	_____	_____
Realtor	_____	_____
Insurance agent	_____	_____
Trust Company, Bank	_____	_____
Other _____	_____	_____

Review Will and trust with family _____ _____

Assemble and protect assets:

Secure residence _____ _____

Safeguard personal items _____ _____

Store automobile _____ _____

Change mailing address _____ _____

Re-register bank and other accounts _____ _____

Insure real estate and other property _____ _____

Evaluate securities and other financial assets _____ _____

Arrange for the management of the decedent's business _____ _____

Estimate cash requirements _____ _____

Raise needed cash _____ _____

Pay claims _____ _____

	Estimated Completion or Due Date	Date Completed
File tax returns:		
Decedent's final income tax returns	_____	_____
Fiduciary income tax returns	_____	_____
Federal estate tax return	_____	_____
State inheritance tax return	_____	_____
Exercise tax elections	_____	_____
Prepare accountings:		
Annual	_____	_____
Final	_____	_____
Pay administration expenses:		
Attorneys fees	_____	_____
Personal representative fees	_____	_____
Appraiser fees	_____	_____
Advisor fees	_____	_____
Debts	_____	_____
Taxes	_____	_____
Other	_____	_____
Obtain early determination of the federal estate tax	_____	_____
Final distribution of assets	_____	_____
Obtain receipts and release from beneficiaries	_____	_____
Obtain discharge from court	_____	_____

APPENDIX III

TRUST ADMINISTRATION CHECKLIST

Name of trust: _____

Date of trust: _____

Current beneficiaries:

Name	Address	Phone No.
_____	_____	_____
_____	_____	_____
_____	_____	_____
_____	_____	_____
_____	_____	_____
_____	_____	_____

Remaindermen:

Name

_____

_____

_____

_____

_____

Terminating or Continuing Trust? _____

(If terminating trust, refer to Estate Administration Checklist)

Probate: Yes _____ No _____

Personal Representative:

    Name: _____

    Address: _____

    Phone No:_____

    Fax No: _____

	Estimated Completion or Due Date	Date Completed
Obtain pertinent documents:		
Trust document and all amendments	_____	_____
Copy of Will	_____	_____
Deeds	_____	_____
Leases	_____	_____
Insurance policies	_____	_____
Contracts	_____	_____
Death certificate	_____	_____
Copy of pension, profit sharing, IRA plan documents	_____	_____
Copy of income & gift tax returns	_____	_____
Other	_____	_____
Gather information:		
Names, addresses, phone numbers, dates of birth and tax brackets of all current beneficiaries	_____	_____
List of remaindermen	_____	_____
List of trust assets	_____	_____
Obtain bank and brokerage account statements	_____	_____
Trust accounting reports, if any	_____	_____

	Estimated Completion or Due Date	Date Completed
Family tree	_____	_____
Copy of federal estate tax return (From 706)	_____	_____

Initial Set-up Steps:

Prepare inventory	_____	_____
List debts and encumbrances	_____	_____
Obtain an appraisal/ valuation of alltrust property as of settlor's date of death or inception date of trust	_____	_____
Take possession/control of all trust assets	_____	_____
Apply for Employer Identification Number (EIN)	_____	_____
Re-register all bank, brokerage accounts and other assets into the name of the trustee	_____	_____
Collect life insurance proceeds	_____	_____
Collect employee benefits payable to trusts	_____	_____
Notify all payors to mail future payments to trustee	_____	_____
If specific bequest is income-producing Property, separate into segregated account	_____	_____

	Estimated Completion or Due Date	Date Completed
Review terms of the trust with beneficiaries	_____	_____
Accrue income to date of death, if applicable	_____	_____
Retain advisors: Attorney	_____	_____
Accountant	_____	_____
Investment advisor	_____	_____
Realtor	_____	_____
Insurance agent	_____	_____
Trust Company, bank	_____	_____
Other	_____	_____

Initial Administration Steps:

Determine income needs of the beneficiaries	_____	_____
Exercise tax elections	_____	_____
File final tax returns (i.e., estate and decedent's final return)	_____	_____
Obtain final determination of estate tax	_____	_____
Perform initial review of trust investments	_____	_____
Estimate initial cash requirements (i.e., estate taxes, specific bequests, debts, final expenses, etc.)	_____	_____

	Estimated Completion or Due Date	Date Completed
Raise needed cash	_____	_____
Fund marital, credit shelter and generation-skipping trusts, if applicable	_____	_____
Distribute/pay specific bequests	_____	_____
Review the terms of the trust and clarify provisions that are ambiguous or misleading	_____	_____
Review the Uniform Principal and Income Act	_____	_____
Review the Prudent Investor Act	_____	_____
Develop an investment policy and strategy	_____	_____
Obtain fee-sharing agreement from co-trustee (s)	_____	_____

On-going administration:

Principal distributions? Yes _____ No _____
Income distributions:
    Discretionary? _____
    Non-discretionary? _____

Frequency of investment reviews:
    Quarterly _____
    Semi-annual _____
    Annual _____

Frequency of accounting reports:
    Monthly _____
    Quarterly _____
    Annual _____
Event that triggers termination of the trust: _____
Termination date of trust: _____

GLOSSARY

Accumulated Income: A portion of the income in a trust that is retained for future payment to a beneficiary or a another future use.

Adjudication: The finding and decision of a court regarding disputed matters.

Adjusted Gross Estate (AGE): The aggregate of a decedent's property (gross estate) less allowable funeral expenses, administration expenses, debts, taxes and losses.

Affidavit: A specific statement that is sworn before a notary public.

Alternate Valuation Date: A date six months from the decedent's date of death that is used for valuing estate assets as an alternative to using the date of death value for determining the federal estate tax.

Ancillary Administration: Subordinate or auxiliary and in addition to the principal settlement or administration of an estate or trust. Usually outside the jurisdiction of the state in which the principal estate or trust is being managed.

Annuity: A series of payments at regular intervals for a number of years or over a lifetime.

Appraisal: The valuation of property.

Appreciation: The increase in value of property.

Assignment: The legal conveyance of the title to property from one person or entity (i.e., estate, trust, etc.) to another person or entity.

Basis: The purchase cost of an asset, less depreciation on depreciable property.

Beneficiary: An individual or organization that receives a benefit from a trust, estate, life insurance policy, pension plan or other contract or agreement which designates who is to receive the property upon death.

Bequest: A gift of property under a Will.

Bond: An obligation, usually of a corporation, government or municipality, whereby the entity agrees to pay interest and repay the amount borrowed upon certain conditions.

Book Value: The value at which a corporation or other entity carries its assets on financial statements.

Broker: A representative of a company who handles sales of the products and services sold by that company, such as a stockbroker, insurance broker, real estate broker, etc.

Capital Gain: The difference between what was paid for an asset (income tax basis) and what it is sold for.

Cash Value: The amount of cash that is available upon the surrender of an insurance policy.

Charitable Lead Trust: A trust arrangement that requires a stream of payments to a charitable beneficiary for a specified period, with the remainder distributable to non-charitable beneficiaries.

Charitable Remainder Trust: A trust whose income is paid to an individual over time, usually the lifetime of the beneficiary, with the remainder paid to a charitable organization.

Claim: The application for the amount due from a decedent's estate and the amount due under an insurance policy.

Codicil: A formal amendment to a Will.

Common Law: The legal system in existence in English-speaking countries. A term that refers to its general principles as contrasted with specific statutes.

Community Property: Property acquired during marriage in which a husband and wife have an undivided one-half interest by virtue of their marriage.

Conservator: A person or corporate fiduciary that is appointed by a court to care for the property of a protected person (i.e., minor or incompetent).

Construction: A court procedure that seeks interpretation of a Will or trust.

Contingent Remainder: A future interest in property, usually through a trust, that is dependent on a stated condition, such as the death of a present beneficiary.

Corporate Fiduciary: A bank or trust company that is authorized to perform fiduciary services in its capacity as personal representative, trustee or guardian.

Corpus: The principal or capital of an estate or trust.

Credit Shelter Trust: A trust that is funded with the Unified Credit Exemption Equivalent amount. The purpose of the trust is to avoid taxation of this amount and any appreciation upon the death of the surviving spouse.

Crummey Power: A provision in a trust that allows a beneficiary to have direct access to deposits made to an irrevocable trust, which allows the deposits to qualify for the annual gift tax exclusion.

Current Yield: The annual income from an investment divided by its current market value.

Custody Account: An account that has as its purpose the holding, safeguarding and accounting of the property that is deposited to it.

Decedent: A deceased person.

Descendant: An individual who is descended in direct line from another.

Deed of Trust: A document conveying property to a trustee. Usually, but not necessarily, real property.

Depreciation: The decrease in value of property.

Devise: A bequest of real property by a Will.

Devisee: A person who receives real property by Will.

Direct Skip: An outright transfer of property to a skip person during one's lifetime or at death.

Disclaimer: Intentionally refusing to accept property for the purpose of avoiding estate, gift and generation-skipping transfer taxes.

Discretionary Trust: A trust whose provisions give the trustee the authority to pay income or principal to or for the benefit of the beneficiary(ies) as the trustee sees fit.

Distributable Net Income (DNI): The amounts paid, credited or required to be distributed from an estate or trust that is includable in the beneficiary's gross income for tax purposes.

Dividend: A distribution of cash or stock by a corporation to its shareholders.

Diversification: The process of investing a trust portfolio in different types of securities and industries and among other asset classes for the purpose of spreading risk.

Document: Anything that is printed or written that serves as proof of something, such as a will, trust, deed, etc.

Domicile: An individual's permanent home or residence. Not necessarily where he or she lives.

Donee: A person or entity that receives a gift.

Donor: A person who makes a gift. Also, a person who creates a trust and transfers property to it.

Election: Making the choice between an alternative right, such as tax and funding elections for an estate or trust.

Elective Share: A statutory right given to a surviving spouse to elect to receive a specified amount of the deceased spouse's estate instead of what has been provided under his or her Will.

Equities: A reference to the stock holdings in an investment portfolio.

Estate: The property of a decedent.

Estate Tax: A tax imposed on the value of property upon the death of the owner.

Exculpatory Provision: A clause in a Will or trust that relieves the fiduciary from liability.

Executor: An individual (male), bank or trust company appointed by a court to settle a decedent's estate. Also referred to as a personal representative.

Executrix: A female individual appointed to settle a decedent's estate.

Exemption Equivalent: The amount whose gift or estate tax is equal to the Unified Credit and which can be given away during lifetime and at death without any transfer tax.

Face Amount: The amount stated on an insurance policy that will be paid upon the death of the person whose life is insured.

Fair Market Value: The price at which property would change hands between a willing buyer and a willing seller.

Fiduciary: A person, bank or trust company that holds property for the benefit of someone else, such as a personal representative of an estate, a guardian for a protected person or a trustee of a trust.

Fiduciary Accounting: Financial records that reflect the value of assets and all transactions that affect the administration of an estate or trust and the interests of the beneficiaries.

Fiduciary Accounting Income (FAI): The amount of net income (i.e., income less expenses charged against income) that is distributable to beneficiaries as distinguished from income that is taxable to the beneficiaries.

Flower Bonds: Certain issues of U.S. Treasury bonds that are purchased at a discount and are redeemable at their par value to pay the federal estate tax.

Future Interest: The right to possession or use of property that has been postponed until some future event.

Generation-Skipping Tax: A tax imposed on transfers of property to persons at least two generations below the transferor.

Gift Tax: A tax imposed on transfers of property by gift during one's lifetime.

Gift Tax Exclusion: The amount that is not subject to a gift tax. Tax-free gifts up to $10,000 can be made per each individual annually. Husband and wife can give up to $20,000 gift tax-free.

Governing Document: The Will, trust or other document that controls the activities of the personal representative, guardian or trustee.

Grantee: The person who is given property or granted property rights by means of a trust or other document.

Grantor: The person who transfers property or property rights to another person. Also referred to as one who creates a trust.

Grantor Trust: A trust that is considered owned by its creator, the grantor, under the Internal Revenue Code, which subjects the grantor to taxation of all of the trust's income and capital gains.

Gross Estate: The fair market value of all property in which a decedent had an interest at date of death and which is required to be included in his or her estate for federal estate tax purposes.

Guardian Ad Litem: A person, bank or trust company appointed by a court to represent a minor or incompetent person with regard to a court proceeding.

Heir At Law: A person legally entitled to receive the property of a decedent who died without leaving a valid Will.

Holographic Will: A Will written entirely in a person's own handwriting.

Identifying Number: A number required by the Internal Revenue Service for identifying taxpayers. For individuals (not deceased persons) this number is their social security number. For other taxpayers, such as estates and trusts, that number is an Employer Identification Number (EIN).

Incapacity: The condition of a person who is incapable of managing his or her affairs due to physical or mental impairment.

Incidence Of Ownership: Having sufficient rights in an insurance policy which makes the proceeds subject to estate tax.

Income: The earnings from property in an estate or trust, such as dividends, interest, rents, etc., as distinguished from the principal or corpus.

Income Beneficiary: A beneficiary who is entitled to receive the income from a trust.

Individual Retirement Account (IRA): An account, set up by an individual, that allows deductible contributions and tax deferral on earnings until funds are withdrawn.

Inheritance Tax: A tax imposed by some states on the right to receive property at death as distinguished from the federal estate tax, which is a tax imposed on the value of one's property at death.

In Kind: Distribution of the property itself (i.e., stocks, bonds, real estate, etc.) as contrasted to a distribution of cash.

Instrument: A formal or legal document.

Insured: The person whose life an insurance policy covers.

Intangible Property: Property such as stocks, bonds or notes that represent an ownership interest.

Inter Vivos: Transactions conducted while someone is living, such as an inter vivos gift and the creation of an inter vivos trust.

Intestate: Dying without leaving a valid Will.

Inventory: List of assets in an estate or trust that describes the property and their values.

Irrevocable Trust: A trust that, by its terms, cannot be revoked.

Issue: All descendants from a common ancestor (i.e., children, grandchildren, etc.).

Joint Tenancy (with rights of survivorship): The holding of property between two or more persons. Upon the death of one tenant, the surviving tenant(s) will become the owner(s) of the property by operation of law.

Judicial Accounting: An estate or trust accounting that is required to be submitted to a court for review.

Jurisdiction: The place or area of authority to hear and determine legal matters by a court.

Keogh Plan: A type of retirement plan for self-employed individuals.

Legacy: A gift made by Will.

Legal Title: Title to property that is enforceable by the courts.

Legatee: A person who receives a bequest under a Will.

Letters of Administration: A document issued by a court giving authority to an administrator the court appoints to settle an estate.

Letters Testamentary: A document issued by a court appointing a personal representative who has been nominated under a will and giving that person the authority to settle the estate.

Lien: An encumbrance on property to secure a monetary obligation.

Life Estate: The right to use or enjoy the income from property for someone's lifetime.

Life Insurance Trust: An irrevocable trust that owns life insurance. The proceeds from the policy(ies) that are paid to the trust are not subject to estate taxes.

Lineal Descendant: A person in the direct line of descent, such as a child or grandchild.

Living Trust: A trust that is established during the creator's lifetime.

Living Will: A document that states the wishes of a person regarding the removal of life support procedures in the event of a terminal illness.

Lump-Sum Distribution: Distribution in one payment as opposed to equal installments. Special tax treatment applies to distributions of this type from a retirement plan.

Marital Deduction: A gift and estate tax deduction for property passing to a spouse.

Marital Trust: A separate trust created under a revocable living trust at the settlor's death that qualifies for the marital deduction.

Minor: A person that is under legal age.

Municipal Bond: A bond issued by a public authority, such as a county, city or state, the interest from which is exempt from federal income tax.

Net Income: The gross income received by an estate or trust less the expenses that are chargeable against the income.

Non Compos Mentis: Not being of sound mind.

Non-Skip Person: Any person who is not a skip person (see Skip Person).

Notice To Creditors: A notice published in a newspaper by a personal representative or trustee notifying the creditors of a decedent when and where to make their claims.

Nomination: The naming of a person, bank or trust company to serve as a personal representative under a Will or trustee of a trust.

Obligee: A person or entity that is owed an obligation, such as the holder of a note or bond.

Obligor: A person or entity that has an obligation to someone under a contract.

Par Value: Face value, or nominal value.

Partnership: An association of two or more people in a business enterprise that is established by a partnership agreement. Each partner has joint and several (individual) liability under this type of arrangement as contrasted with a corporation.

Pecuniary Legacy: A gift of money under a Will.

Pension Plan: An employee benefit plan that provides a stream of income for retired employees, which may or may not continue for their surviving spouse.

Per Capita: Distribution of property from an estate or trust in equal shares among all named beneficiaries, share and share alike.

Personal Property: Everything that is not real property.

Personal Representative: An individual, bank or trust company appointed by a court to settle an estate. Also called an executor.

Per Stirpes: Inheritance by right of representation in each generation. A distributee takes the share that a deceased ancestor would receive if living.

Petition: A formal request to a court for instructions, remedy or relief on a particular matter.

Pour-Over Will: A Will that names a revocable living trust as beneficiary. Its purpose is to transfer (pour over) probate assets into the trust.

Power Of Appointment: A right given to an individual to distribute property that he or she does not own. The exercise of this right is usually done through a Will.

Power Of Attorney: A written document that legally authorizes someone to act for another.

Precatory Words: Words or phrases in a Will or trust expressing a desire that something be done, but not directing that it be done.

Present Beneficiary: A beneficiary of a trust that is entitled to immediate benefits from a trust whether it be from the income of the trust, principal or both.

Principal: The property of an estate or trust as distinguished from its income. Also referred to as corpus.

Probate: The court supervised procedure to prove a decedent's last Will and testament and to settle his estate with respect to the property he owns in his own name.

Profit-Sharing Plan: An employee benefit plan the contributions to which are based on the profits of the company. The vested balance in the plan is payable to the participant upon retirement, to his or her beneficiary(ies) or to his or her estate upon death.

Protected Person: A person who, by reason of minority, incompetence or other incapacity, is under the protection of the court.

Qualified Domestic Trust (QDOT): A trust established for a non—U.S. citizen surviving spouse that qualifies for the marital deduction.

Qualified Terminable Interest Property (QTIP) Trust: A trust that qualifies for the marital deduction and also allows the deceased spouse to decide on the ultimate disposition of the trust property upon the death of the surviving spouse.

Real Property: Land, buildings and all that is permanently attached to the land as distinguished from personal property.

Remainder Interest: The interest that passes to a beneficiary upon the expiration of a period of time in which another beneficiary was entitled to the benefits from the property. In the case of a trust what remains at the termination of the trust.

Remainderman: The beneficiary that is entitled to a remainder interest.

Renunciation: When an individual, bank or trust company declines to accept the nomination to serve as personal representative or trustee.

Residue: What's left in an estate or trust after payment of all debts and expenses.

Revocable Living Trust: A trust established by a trust agreement in which the settlor (creator) retains the right to amend or revoke the trust.

Rule Against Perpetuities: A common law rule that prohibits a trust from lasting longer than a period of time that is measured by lives (i.e., beneficiaries) in being at the time the trust became irrevocable, plus twenty-one years.

Second To Die Life Insurance: An insurance policy that is based on joint lives, typically a husband and wife. The face value is payable at the death of the surviving insured individual.

Settlor: The person who creates a trust during his or her lifetime. Also referred to as the trustor, grantor and donor.

Skip Person: A person that receives property, either by outright gift or as a beneficiary, who is at least two generations below that of the transferor. This is a term defined under the Internal Revenue Code under its generation-skipping tax provisions.

Special Administrator: A person, bank or trust company appointed by a court to handle an estate until a permanent personal representative or administrator is appointed. Usually used in situations where some immediate action needs to be taken.

Special Use Valuation: A provision in the Internal Revenue Code that allows a personal representative to elect to value real property used for farming or other business use at its current use value instead of its highest and best use for estate tax purposes.

Spendthrift Provision: A provision in a trust, which prohibits a beneficiary from transferring his interest in a trust. It also prevents a beneficiary's creditor from making a claim against his interest in the trust.

Stock: A certificate evidencing ownership in a corporation.

Stock Power: A form, similar to a limited power of attorney, which is signed by the owner of stock that authorizes someone to transfer the stock.

Succession: A person becoming entitled to property under a decedent's Will or by operation of law.

Successor Trustee: A trustee that follows, and assumes the responsibilities of, a prior trustee as provided for in a trust document.

Tangible Property: Property that can be touched, such as jewelry, furniture, automobiles, etc., as distinguished from intangible property.

Taxable Estate: The adjusted gross estate less the marital deduction and/or charitable deduction.

Tenancy In Common: An undivided ownership interest in property, which upon death will pass to the decedent owner's heirs and not to the other owner(s).

Tenancy By The Entirety: Joint ownership between a husband and wife. Upon the death of one the survivor becomes the sole owner of the property by operation of law.

Testamentary Capacity: The mental capacity to make a valid Will.

Testamentary Trust: A provision under a Will that establishes a trust.

Total Return: A measure of investment performance that combines capital appreciation or depreciation and the income from the investment.

"Totten" Trust: A limited form of trust usually associated with a deposit account at a financial institution. Title is in the name of the depositor as trustee for a named beneficiary. Upon the death of the depositor the balance is paid to the beneficiary. These are also called Payable On Death (POD) accounts.

Trust: A legal arrangement where the creator of the trust, the settlor or testator in the case of a testamentary trust, transfers property to a trust and names a trustee to manage the property for the benefit of the trust's beneficiaries.

Trust Accounting: The accounting record of a trust account's activity in which income transactions are distinguished from principal transactions.

Trust Agreement: A written document outlining the terms of a trust arrangement.

Trust Company: A corporation authorized to provide fiduciary services as personal representative, administrator, trustee or guardian.

Trust Department: A department of a bank that provides fiduciary services. See Trust Company.

Trust Document: A Will, under which a trust is created, or a trust agreement.

Trustee: An individual, bank or trust company who has title to trust property and is charged with managing that property in accordance with the terms of a trust for the benefit of the trust's beneficiaries.

Trust Estate: All of the property belonging to a trust.

Trust Instrument: See Trust Document.

Trust Officer: An employee of a bank trust department or trust company who has the responsibility of supervising the administration of an estate or trust account.

Trust Property: See Trust Estate.

Trustor: A person who creates a trust. Also referred to as the settlor, donor or grantor.

Unauthorized Investment: An investment that is prohibited under the terms of a trust.

Undue Influence: The influence that someone exercises over someone else to the extent that a person does something, such as signing a Will, against his or her free will.

Unfunded Insurance Trust: A revocable living trust that has no assets. Its purpose is to receive the proceeds from life insurance policies upon the death of the settlor who is the insured. Unlike the irrevocable insurance trust, the insurance proceeds are subject to federal estate tax.

Unified Credit: A specified dollar credit amount that is applied against federal gift and estate taxes.

Unitrust: A trust, usually a charitable remainder trust, which provides a stream of income to a beneficiary, based on a percentage of the value of trust assets each year.

Variable Annuity: An annuity whose income payout fluctuates in relation to the underlying securities in the contract. Variable annuities are often used as investments. Tax on the investment's earnings is deferred until payments are made to the annuitant.

Vendee: The purchaser of an item of property.

Vendor: The seller of an item of property.

Vested Interest: A fixed interest in property whose possession and enjoyment may be postponed to a future date or event.

Vested Remainder: A fixed interest in a remainder interest. See remainder interest.

Ward: See protected person.

Wasting Trust: A trust whose assets are continually being consumed and will eventually be used up.

Widow's Allowance: A widow's right to access a specified amount of personal property, set by statute, to meet her immediate needs after her husband's death.

Will: A legal document in which a person directs the disposition of his or her property at death.

Will Contest: A legal process by which an individual attempts to prevent the probate of a Will or the disposition of the estate property in accordance with its terms.

Yield: The annualized rate of return on an investment expressed as a percentage of the amount invested.

Zero Coupon Bond: A type of bond that pays no current interest. It is purchased at a deep discount from its face value. The investment return is measured by the difference between the purchase price and the face value that the investor receives upon maturity of the bond.

INDEX

Order additional copies
for yourself, your clients and your friends.

Shipping and handling is $2.00 for the first book and $.75 for each additional book included in the same order to the same address.

Fiduciary Publishing
P.O. Box 351
Honolulu, HI 96809

Number of copies _____ X $29.95 = $_____

Shipping & Handling (see above) =   _____

Subtotal =   _____

Sales Tax @ 4.166% =   _____

TOTAL = $ _____

(make check payable to: Fiduciary Publishing)

Name _____

Company _____

Street Address _____

City _____ State _____ Zip _____

Phone (   ) _____

Fax (   ) _____

Email _____

or order from our website: www.fiduciarypublishing.com